MEMOR[...]
THE M[...]

Compiled & edited by

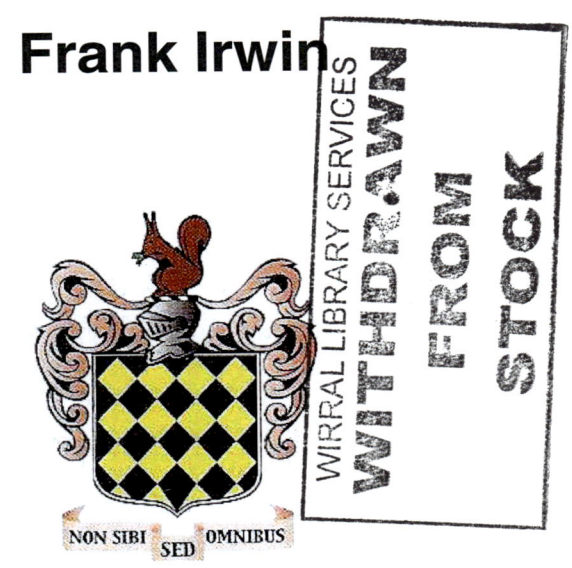

Frank Irwin

NON SIBI SED OMNIBUS

1708 - 2008

Published by

THE LIVERPOOL BLUE COAT BROTHERLY SOCIETY

MEMORIES FROM THE MID-20th CENTURY
ISBN 978-0-9557484-2-4

First published in 2007 by
The Liverpool Blue Coat Brotherly Society

Copyright © Frank Irwin 2007

Conditions of Sale:

This book is sold subject to the condition that it shall not, by way of trade or otherwise, be lent, re-sold, hired out or otherwise circulated without the publisher's prior consent in any form of binding or cover other than that in which it is published and without a similar condition including this condition being imposed on the subsequent purchaser.

All rights reserved. No part of this publication may be reproduced, stored in a retrieval system, or transmitted in any form or by any means, electronic, mechanical, photocopying, recording or otherwise, without the prior permission of the publishers.

The Liverpool Blue Coat Brotherly Society is a registered charity (No. 1072458)

www.bluecoatbrotherlysociety.webeden.co.uk

Printed and bound in the UK by Forward Press Ltd, Peterborough

MEMORIES FROM THE MID-20th CENTURY

Compiled & edited by

Frank Irwin

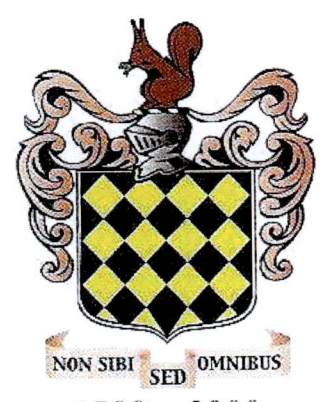

NON SIBI SED OMNIBUS

1708 - 2008

Published by

THE LIVERPOOL BLUE COAT BROTHERLY SOCIETY

ACKNOWLEDGEMENTS

Compiled by Frank Irwin, this book contains contributions from all the following, to whom the Liverpool Blue Coat Brotherly Society is extremely grateful:

Ray Livingston
Stan Livingston
Hubert Manwaring-Spencer (Formerly, Hubert Manwaring)
Dave Bolt
Eric Woodbine
Frank Hulford
Peter Clarke
Brenton Williams
David Kennedy
Kenneth Hughes
Ernie Foulder
John Howarth
William Bowden
Peter Ling
Arthur Martin
Margaret Thompson (Formerly, Margaret Bond)
Tony Salmon

Special thanks must go to Ray Livingston for the amount of support he has given, his massive contribution towards the completed article and finally for his efforts in proof-reading prior to publication.

Also thanks to my wife Barbara for her patience whilst I have been so occupied with this venture and also for her additional proof reading.

Frank Irwin

The cover picture of the Liverpool Blue Coat School was photographed and produced by Frank Irwin.

CONTENTS

Chapter 1.	The 1930s	Page 10
Chapter 2.	The 1940s	Page 32
Chapter 3.	The 1950s	Page 49
Chapter 4.	Old Blues' Memories	Page 126
Chapter 5.	General Memories	Page 175
Chapter 6.	Army Cadets & Boy Scouts	Page 181
Chapter 7.	About Teachers	Page 199
Chapter 8.	Leisure Activities	Page 210
Chapter 9.	Teachers Remember	Page 218
Chapter 10.	Afterthoughts	Page 234
Chapter 11.	Albert's visit to the school	Page 241
Chapter 12.	Vive La Difference	Page 243
Chapter 13.	Beaumaris Revisited	Page 253
Chapter 14.	Looking Back	Page 257
Chapter 15.	Illustrations	Page 262
Chapter 16.	Dr. Dickerson's Slow March	Page 300
Chapter 17.	Setting The Record Straight	Page 305
Chapter 18.	Photograph supplement	Page 306
INDEX		Page 329

THE SCHOOL'S HISTORY

The Liverpool Blue Coat School was founded in 1708 by Captain Bryan Blundell and the Reverend Robert Styth, then the rector of Liverpool. Reverend Styth took it upon himself to administer the first Blue Coat School, organising a place where poor children could learn to read and write. Bryan Blundell contributed financially and without his help, the school probably wouldn't have existed for the 300 years that it has done. The original building still stands in the town centre today, as an art gallery and shops for tourists.

When Reverend Styth died in 1713 Bryan Blundell took over as the treasurer and trustee. During this time, he noticed the poverty of the period, which was causing the children to neglect the school out of hours and so changed it into a boarding school that provided food, drink and lodgings for the younger generation. The school by then needing extending and enlarging, with constant changes, necessitating costs estimated as being between £2,000 and £3,000. The finance necessary for the school to be enlarged was once again provided thanks to Bryan Blundell; the work was finished in 1718.

Bryan Blundell died in 1756 and was succeeded by his son, who held office for just 4 years. His younger brother Jonathon then took over and held office until the turn of the century. It was only in the last 10 years of the 18th century that a uniform was introduced.

By the end of the Victorian era, it had been realised that the school buildings were inadequate and in 1899 the trustees agreed to erect a new school building in the outskirts of the city, which would cost £80,000. This amount was raised with the financial help of W.H. Shirley. Following his death in 1901, he left in his will, £38,000 towards the building of the school. Along with many other contributions, the £80,000 was eventually raised and work began on the new school in 1903 and it was completed in 1906. The Shirley Hall was named after him and it is still used as the central hub of the old school. The Blue Coat retained its role as an orphanage until the late 1940s; boys and girls in old-fashioned dress having been a familiar sight around Liverpool for many years. The school changed its status in 1948 and became a day and boarding school for boys only.

In 1984, the City Council proposed a 'cease to maintain' order for the Blue Coat. It was defeated a year later thanks to a vigorous campaign on the part of the school to win the support of the people of Liverpool. The boarding school was eventually phased out until only a few remaining boarders lived there, the rest of the students were day pupils. The school stopped accepting boarders in 1990, the same year that girls were readmitted, but to the sixth form only.

In September 2002, for the first time in more than fifty years, girls were admitted into the school alongside boys, following an entrance examination. Two splendid statuettes, different but complementary, standing to this day in the school's boardroom, clearly reveal the original inspiration of the Liverpool Blue Coat School: it was thoroughly co-educational before the word was coined.

Now that the building work has been completed, the vision of Bryan Blundell and the Reverend Robert Styth has been realised once again.

Incidentally, the school badge is the coat of arms of Bryan Blundell.

ABOUT THE BOOK

I started at the Blue Coat School in 1950, firstly walking each day, the short distance to Mosspits Lane County Primary School (Edwina Curry is one of its most famous pupils). After passing the 11+ exam, I attended the school's grammar stream until leaving in 1957.

Many years ago, as I sat with my two daughters I often used to recount tales of my life as a boarder at the school. Once I had started, it was difficult to stop as they loved the stories and demanded that I told them more. As they grew older, they often reminded me of the tales and suggested that I should write a book about those schoolboy experiences. I thought about it many times but decided that there would not be a market for such a book, and that it would have been a great deal of work purely for self indulgence. Over the years the whole idea faded and our daughters had children of their own, the memories dimmed somewhat and soon became a feature of the distant past.

Learning about the 300 years anniversary of the school gave rise to a visit to the Friends Reunited internet web site. Having sent messages to all the boys whose names appeared to be familiar to me, I received one or two replies and quite naturally we started reviving and swapping our memories. The list of names grew and now there are sixteen of us in regular communication. This number includes a former school master whose presence naturally adds interest from a teacher's perspective.

Sometime later, I suggested that as there were so many interesting stories about our school days and as they also showed just how different things were then, we should collaborate and write a book of memoirs to be sold to interested parties during 'Year 2008' with profits being donated to either the school or the Brotherly Society. All agreed and what you have before you is the result of all that collaboration. Each contributor has agreed to add his name to the story. In addition to contributing towards the final article, my role has been to co-ordinate the efforts, to edit some submissions prepare the printed works ready for publication and to obtain agreement from all parties prior to going into print. I have also indulged myself in my favourite hobby, photography, and a little bit of AutoCAD work.

This then is the result of our labours. We hope you will find the stories of interest and we feel sure that modern day pupils will be amazed, not just at our capers and antics, but also at the spartan and sometimes cruel regime under which we lived. Having said all that, we must pay tribute to the standard of education that has been achieved and maintained at the school for many years, thereby keeping the Blue Coat School at the forefront of education as Liverpool's only grammar school.

The stories and anecdotes have been written utilising the best of our long term memories. We have done our best, and if at any time in error, we apologise. My personal stories include details and photographs of my return visit to the school in 2007 after an absence of some 50 years. I hope our daughters Amanda and Julie enjoy seeing in print all the things that I recounted all those years ago and that our four grandchildren also find it of interest.

Frank Irwin (1950-1957)
Now living in Wirral

THE BLUE COAT HOSPITAL

Good Bryan Blundell safely home had brought
Rich merchandise, o'er many a stormy sea,
And now, his ship at anchor in the port,
He stood, with thankful heart, upon the quay.

The urchins playing by the river side,
Came thronging round him as he stepped ashore,
Hungry and cold, yet smiling, open eyed,
And happy, caring nought for ills in store.

And as he gazed on them, unkempt, untaught,
His loving pity shaped itself to this,
'God has been good to me, and shall I not
Do good to these poor little ones of his?'

'So with his help I will' - the project grew,
For all his soul was in it, soon there rose
A building fair, wherein the homeless knew
The joys of home, and love that held them close.

Two centuries it stood, in noblest ways
Fulfilling all its founder's pious hopes,
Then raising, for the needs of later days,
A larger home on War'tree's ancient slopes.

And Bryan Blundell, long years passed to rest,
With unforgotten fame that kings might prize,
Full many a generation since hath blessed,
From many yet to come shall blessings rise.

Written by Frank J. Leslie in about the year 1907 to be used in a pageant of celebrations marking the 700th anniversary of Liverpool's charter (incidentally, those celebrations took place on 'The Mystery' on 3rd, 5th and 6th August 1907.) Music was set by F.H. Burstall, F.R.C.O. but is now feared lost. The hymn was found c1987 by Mr. Don Redman whilst sorting through some family papers, and Harry Marsden brought it to the attention of the Brotherly Society.

CHAPTER 1
THE 1930s

SCHOOL LIFE IN THE 1930s

As we all know, the upheaval of the Second World War changed, or swept away altogether, many old institutions and ways, and of course the ancient Blue Coat School in Liverpool was not exempt from this. We also know how difficult and hard life could be for the poor during the economic slump in Great Britain that began after the Great War and lasted through the 1930s.

We who experienced the school in its post-war state feel a natural curiosity to know how life was led there in that earlier period, and until now we have had virtually only one source to turn to - Danny Ross's *A Blue Coat Boy in the 1920s*, published by Roby Press in 1996 (although it is hoped that some accounts may be found that describe how the school fared during the war, when it was removed to Beaumaris in Anglesey for the children's safety).

The writers of the present book have been fortunate in being able to turn for information to Old Blue HARRY THOMAS, whose time at the school was 1931 to 1937. Harry's description is remarkably similar to Danny's, which suggests that the school and its traditions did not change very much in those ten years, but the extra details he supplies are naturally of great interest.

Harry was brought up on nearby Fallowfield Road, so the school was a familiar local sight to him. Little did he know that he was destined to be 'in school' himself one day, but this came to pass when his father sadly died.

The pre-war school was an orphanage, so all of the pupils were boarders. In order to be eligible a pupil had to be 8 - 11 years old and be either an orphan or fatherless. He/she had also to be of the Protestant faith and resident within ten miles of Liverpool Town Hall.

Before being accepted, you had to be interviewed by the headmaster - a stressful experience for the child.

The girls were strictly segregated from the boys, and a boy found himself in serious trouble if he so much as winked or smiled at a girl, let alone tried to speak to her. Broadly speaking, the boys occupied the north side of the school and the girls the south side. The distinctive, bay-windowed room in the centre of the West Front (later to become the Old Blues' Memorial Library) was in those days a classroom used by a teacher called Miss Hipkiss. She taught the younger first-year pupils there, both girls and boys but in separate classes, of course.

The headmaster and chaplain for the whole school was the Rev. R. Bruce Wilson, and the senior teacher on the boys' side was Mr. Chynoweth (pronounced 'shin-ow-eth'). Mr. G.G. Watcyn was just one of the masters in those days, having joined the school a few years before Harry's arrival. 'Daddy' Pearson was the woodwork and metalwork master, 'Ham' Hollis the science master, Mr. Garrett the French teacher and a Scot called Mr. Ewan the art master. Miss Hackett was the wardrobe mistress.

Punishments were delivered immediately and on the spot, the master striking the culprit with his hand. The headmaster was above such matters and left all such discipline to his staff.

The school's organist, choirmaster and office clerk, 'Cock' Harling, passed away in 1931 and his replacement a few months later was Dr. F.W. Dickerson. Two temporary organists filled in during the interim. In the course of time, Dr. Dickerson composed his own slow march ('March in D') to supplant an earlier one used by the school. (More on this topic can be read in the piece that describes Albert Blundell's time at the school).

The strict separation between girls and boys extended to the dining room, the oak tables there being arranged in the following manner:

```
                              BOYS
       4                       Y         3
  [____|____|____]             X    [____|____|____]
                              BOYS
       2                              1
  [____|____|____]                  [____|____|____]  ────▶
                                                       KITCHEN
                              GIRLS

  [____|____|____]                  [____|____|____]
```

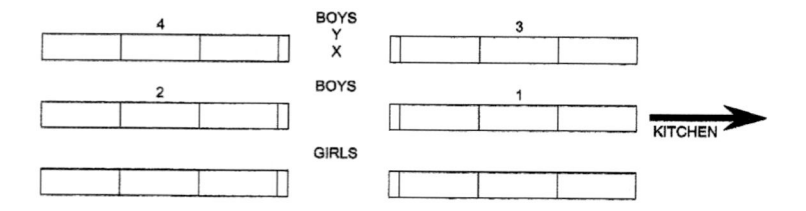

The gap was used by the servers, and each table had its own serving table at one end as shown. Both sides of the table were used and forms (i.e. backless benches) were sat on so a degree of co-operation was required when getting in or out. Across the room the girls would have had exactly the same problem.

In passing, it is interesting to compare the 1930s table arrangement with the one used in the 1950s: but this assumes that the number of tables never changed, which is not necessarily correct.

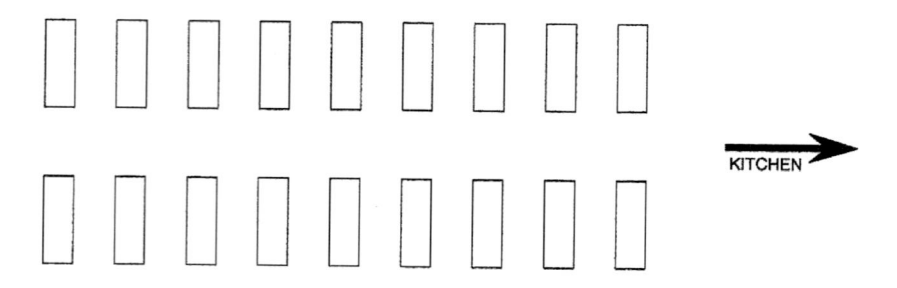

```
  ▯ ▯ ▯ ▯ ▯ ▯ ▯ ▯

                                                       ────▶
                                                       KITCHEN
  ▯ ▯ ▯ ▯ ▯ ▯ ▯
```

The children were strictly marched in and out of the dining room, and all the movements and proceedings inside were regulated by the duty master, who stood in a position marked by a 'Y' on the diagram and mainly used a gavel resting on table 4 to give commands. On one of his commands, a box was pulled out from beneath table 4's serving table and placed at position 'X' in front of the duty master, and the boy who was to say grace stood upon it. Another bang of the gavel and the grace was said. The end of the meal was also marked by a bang of the gavel, as were also the returning of thanks and some of the moves associated with the march out.

Harry once witnessed an amusing incident when a boy said the wrong grace and the master punished him by tapping him on the head with the gavel. A monitor sat at the outer end of each table and regulated and oversaw what took place on that particular table (in those days the school had monitors, not prefects). The verbal marching commands were shouted out by these monitors.

About three times per year, on set dates, the school accepted an influx of new pupils, and at those times all of the boys would be lined up and put into strict height order. Then each boy was assigned a sequential number, the smallest boy being 1, and so on up. They then received laundered clothes that bore that number, and which had previously been worn by the last holder of the number. You kept that number for a few months, until the time arrived for a fresh influx of pupils and the height assessment process was gone through again. Occasionally you were given a new shirt and underclothes. Less frequently you were given a new blazer and trousers.

Pupil numbers fell during Harry's time at the school. When he first arrived in 1931 there were about 200, but by the time he left in 1937 there were about 170-180.

To an extent, the number you were assigned also decided whereabouts in the dining hall you sat, for the smaller boys occupied tables 1 & 2 and the bigger boys tables 3 & 4. The tables were laid and later cleared up by the senior girls, who also worked in the school laundry wearing clogs.

The masters and mistresses ate their meals in the small dining room at the end of the dining room corridor, close to the kitchen, and were served there by the senior girls.

When Harry first entered the school in 1931, all the boys wore their uniform during the winter months. In the summer, the taller boys wore long trousers and the smaller boys wore shorts and a pullover.

In Harry's latter years in the school, blazers and shirts were worn for everyday wear but uniform was still used on Sundays, Prize Day and when out on parade, e.g. Trafalgar Day.

As already mentioned, conditions were difficult between the wars and the school struggled to make ends meet; the State paying 7/6d per week for an orphan and five shillings for a child that had lost its father. All of life's needs had to be provided out of this amount.

For this reason, meals in the early 1930s were shockingly meagre; just a round of bread in the case of the younger boys. In about 1935 this state of affairs improved slightly, an extra plateful of quartered bread being placed on each table (here was an opportunity for favouritism, however, for the server would place it close to you if she happened to like you). Pea soup was called 'pea-wack' by the boys.

Some may find it shocking that the younger children were treated so differently. All of the children ate together so the unfairness was obvious.

The school was supplied with bread by the local baker, John Hicks, each loaf being about eighteen inches long and squarish in shape. The boys referred to bread as 'chuck', the end crusts being known as 'toppers'. As a Sunday evening treat for the younger boys there was also a currant loaf that was cut into thick slices; this was called 'currant bango' by the boys.

Sweet courses were normally only served on Sundays or after big services in the Shirley Hall, e.g. Armistice Sunday or Old Blues Sunday. Visitors at the latter occasions would afterwards be allowed to descend the stairs to the dining room and see the boys eating their tea. A rope rail ran the length of the dining room at those times and the visitors progressed through and made their exit via the kitchens.

Personal possessions were few in those days: football boots, caseball and maybe a game. Each boy was assigned a locker - but it wasn't lockable, being fitted only with a ball-catch. The lockers occupied three walls of the playroom.

The uniform jacket was plain and unadorned save for metal buttons. The school had no badge in those days. At one time the uniform had included a flat cap, but the headmaster had had them burned *en masse* just prior to Harry's arrival.

Danny Ross came from a large family so Harry remembers one or two of his younger siblings who were at the school in his time.

If you were misbehaving and on the point of being discovered by a master, the warning word you received from a colleague was 'Douse!' No doubt this had its origin in the days of candles. Harry ascended the clock tower illicitly on several occasions; the school's ultimate 'forbidden fruit'.

No cadet force existed in those days, but the boys were regularly given military drill by Sergeant Major Porter, who was based at Wellington Road Barracks (a man who is also mentioned by Danny Ross). These skills were displayed on special occasions, most notably on Prize Day.

A firm on Dale Street (Morath Brothers) used to come and maintain the school's various mechanical clocks, including the one in the clock tower. The man who attended became known as 'Clocky', and one of the older boys would be detailed to carry his step-ladders about for him as he worked. Many of the clocks were on the girls' side of the school, of course, so the ladder-carrier found himself enjoying opportunities to talk to girls - lucky lad!

All pupils attended a service in the chapel each Sunday morning and a service in the Shirley Hall each Sunday afternoon. The latter service was attended by two of the school's trustees, who sat in special chairs facing the children and interacting at certain times during the service. The chairs used by the trustees still exist and they are in the boardroom.

Senior boys conducted the service. Chapter readers would subsequently receive a significant money gift from the trustees.

The boy who had recited his chapter on Sunday (it was done from memory) was always 'on gate' the following week, which meant that it was his duty to open the school's front doors to visitors and be available to 'go messages' for the headmaster and Dr. Dickerson about the school premises. His reward was the coppers people gave him for doing this duty; half of the total sum acquired that way being put into his 'mindings' until holiday time or an outing, such as the annual outing to Menai Bridge, and the other half going to the girl who had recited her chapter on Sunday.

All of the children were confirmed whilst at the school and it was invariably the Bishop of Warrington who did the confirming.

Harry was nine years old when he arrived at the school and he turned ten later that year, but quite a lot of the boys were as young as 8 when they started. When a boy reached 12 or thereabouts, a decision was taken about him that would affect all of his remaining time at the school; he would hope to be made a Band Boy, but if the powers that be decided that this, for whatever reason, should not be so, then he would be designated a Worker (this is what happened to Harry, the reason being that he happened to be ill with scarlet fever). Each role had its pros and cons: Band Boys had to learn music and an instrument, but on the other hand they did not have to do cleaning and polishing work around the school premises, and they had two excursions per year instead of one (more about this later). Workers did not have to learn music and master an instrument, but they had all the aforementioned drudgery jobs to face and they went on only one annual excursion.

Pupils were made to remain on the ground floor of the premises all day and were only allowed to ascend to the dormitories as bedtime approached. Bedtime for the under-14s was 7.30 p.m., whilst those over the age of 14 stayed up until 8.45 p.m.

Classes were not unduly large - about 30 boys per class, Harry thinks.

In those days no pupil possessed a radio set, not even a crystal ('cat's whisker') set, and therefore little news from the outside world filtered through.

Consequently there was no concern about the ominous rise of the Fascists in Europe as the 1930s ran their course. On the other hand, the boys were always extremely interested to hear of the latest doings of Liverpool F.C. and Everton F.C.

The school was careful to look after its pupils' teeth, eyes and hair, maintaining a fully-equipped dental surgery in a room situated at the front of the school between the chapel and the boardroom. This was used by a dentist who travelled over from his practice in Rodney Street. Various barbers attended the school from Bioletti's shop at the bottom of Church Road. Any child that needed glasses received them.

Strangely, the school not only failed to provide toothpaste but it criticised any child it caught asking a parent to procure such an item. Despite this, some children did obtain toothpaste in that way and the other children were put in the position of having to cadge some from them. The writer assumes that the good general state of the children's teeth must have been largely attributable to the lack of sugar in the school diet.

Films were only rarely seen and the place where they were shown was the Shirley Hall. They were silent, privately-made films that showed, for instance, a trustee's garden. The school had no magazine or newsletter.

As a plaque on site makes clear, the organ in the Shirley Hall was brought from the original school building in the town centre, now known as Blue Coat Chambers.

Science teacher Mr. Hollis failed to return to the school after one holiday and it emerged that he had married Miss Petite, a mistress on the girls' side. Neither of them was ever seen at the school again but the incident gave everyone a great surprise; although with hindsight it could be recalled that the pair had often held whispered conversations whilst on duty in the dining hall so the signs had been there.

Football was usually played on the home field, but also at the Lance Lane ground. Competitive cricket matches against other schools were usually played at Lance Lane. There was no 'Mystery Mile' race in those days so it must have been a post-war invention.

In the summer, in a kindly act that surprises one in the hardnosed business environment that we have now grown used to living in, the

Liverpool & North Wales Steamship Co. Ltd. took the Blue Coat pupils for a sail to Llandudno and the Menai Straits on its ship, the S.S. *St. Tudno* - the school's annual excursion. The boys would be taken on, say, Tuesday, and the girls on Thursday, leaving the company's lucrative weekend business undisturbed. At another time the Band Boys enjoyed a second excursion, so each year they enjoyed two outings instead of just one. They really 'earned their corn' on these occasions for they played their music at the start and finish of the voyage as well as at points in between, notably Llandudno and Menai Bridge. It must have made a grand impression to onlookers and provided good publicity for the steamship company.

The following diagram shows the locations of the various dormitories:

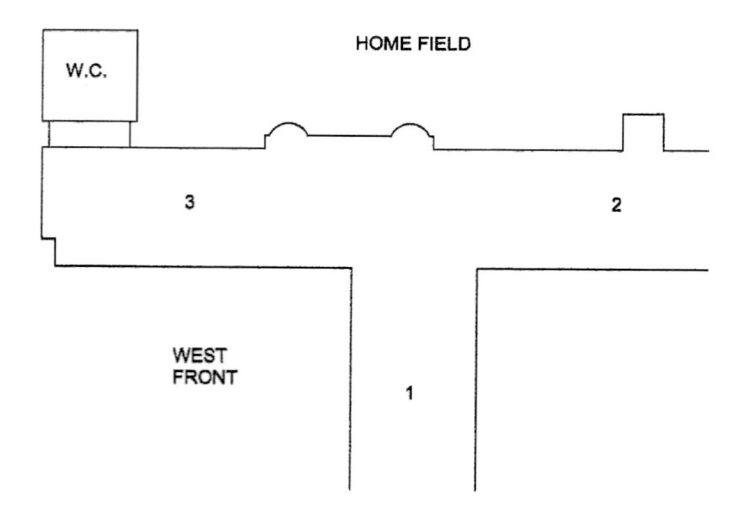

Explanation:

1 A line of five classrooms on ground floor. Blundell dormitory ('Lower 1') on first floor. Graham dormitory ('Upper 1') on second floor.

2   Cloakroom for best clothes, playroom, classroom and Band Room on ground floor. Shirley dormitory ('Lower 2') on first floor. A former 'spare' dormitory ('Upper 2') on the second floor had been converted to an art room used by both boy classes and girl classes.

3   Washroom, clothes racks/boot-polishing room on ground floor. Dormitory for over-14s on first floor ('Lower 3'). Bedwetters' dormitory on second floor ('Upper 3').

Each dormitory contained a mixture of age groups, so it was frequently the case that the younger boys were disturbed by the later arrival of the older boys.

Harry often found himself polishing his dormitory floor (Graham dormitory), a process that began a month or so before Prize Day and was carried out firstly by applying Ronuk polish by hand and secondly rubbing with the dummy; a heavy wooden block that was swung from side to side on a stick. Harry was assigned to do about half of the room and meet with his opposite number in the middle. Unfortunately, girls had to pass through that dorm when they were *en route* to the art room beyond and some of the more spitefully minded girls would deliberately scuff the soles of their shoes on Harry's completed work, spoiling it.

'Lower 1' (Blundell dormitory) was the one that was deemed most likely to be seen by visitors so there was an electric polisher available there. Consequently, the workers there had an easier time than Harry and his colleagues did.

The clothes mistress had a little room at the rear of the cloakroom and a door gave her access directly to the north corridor. Access to the playroom was via two sets of double-doors in the north corridor.

The Band Room further along the corridor was where band practices took place.

The clothes racks room had a bench running round its perimeter and it was here that the operation of boot cleaning and brushing was carried out. A tin of black shoe polish would be valued so highly by its owner that it would be kept in his jacket pocket at all times, rather than be entrusted to his locker.

Boots were numbered at the top (e.g. '647') so that the number would normally be obscured by one's trouser bottoms. This boot number remained yours throughout your time at the school; even if you were given a new pair or inherited a used pair. On Saturday mornings each boy had to take his pair of boots, plus his spare pair, to be inspected by the school's engineer and factotum, Ernie Lyons. This ceremony entailed the boy placing his fingers inside the boot and pulling so that Mr. Lyons could see that they were intact and serviceable. Any that were not serviceable would be taken immediately for repair.

Interestingly, Harry recalls that as long ago as the 1930s it was being planned that the school should have its own swimming pool. Several more decades would elapse before this dream could be realised, but trips across The Mystery to Picton Road Baths tided over in the meantime.

Until about 1929, pupils remained in the school over the Christmas period.

In normal circumstances the children remained on the school premises throughout term time and never saw the outside world. Exceptions to this were if a boy was carrying out office boy duties for the school (Harry did this), or if there was sickness in the school and it was considered advisable to keep the remainder of the pupils away from the premises for a few hours. In the latter case they were led on a local walk under the close supervision of a master. Church Road was served by trams in those days, a situation that existed until the early 1950s.

As already mentioned, when he was 12 or 13 years old Harry contracted scarlet fever; indeed he had the dubious distinction of triggering off a fresh outbreak of that illness in the school. In those days, apart from colds, 'flu and the well known childhood illnesses, there was always the danger of an outbreak of a more serious illness, such as the potentially deadly diphtheria.

Harry was taken to Sparrow Hall Isolation Hospital (junction of Lower Lane and East Lancashire Road) aboard the customary 'green fever van'. The hospital consisted of timber huts that had been erected during World War I to house Canadian soldiers, Harry believes. They were demolished many years ago and the area is now a housing estate. After a couple of weeks there he was transferred to Olive Mount Children's Hospital to recuperate before returning to the school. Whilst there, he got chatting to the ward cleaning lady and asked her if he could try using her floor-polishing dummy. She was astonished when she saw how expert he was with it, until he explained that he frequently used one to polish the dormitory floor at the Blue Coat School.

Until about 1936, the school gave each leaving boy a whole set of clothes including a suit and a bowler hat. Thereafter, the hat became a trilby. In the pre-war days the Brotherly Society also provided a set of clothes to a leaving boy. Harry still has the Bible and the Book of Common Prayer that were presented to him by the governors and trustees of the school at the time of his leaving. He left in October 1937 when he obtained employment as office boy to a Liverpool solicitor.

Harry recalls that the Rev. R. Bruce Wilson retired in 1945, by which time the senior master, Mr. Chynoweth, was also close to retiring age. Hence, Mr. G.G. Watcyn was chosen to be the Rev. R. Bruce Wilson's successor and it was he who led the school into the post-war era.

Ray Livingston (1955-59)
Now living in York

A STEP BACK TO THE 1920s! – ALBERT BLUNDELL'S MEMORIES

The writers of this book had no right to expect to find a testimony any earlier than Harry's, but in June 2007 Tony Salmon opened a website for the Brotherly Society and almost immediately found himself being contacted by the son of a 92-year-old Blackpool gentleman called ALBERT BLUNDELL. Alan Blundell explained that his daughter had found the website and drawn his attention to it. His father, a good friend of Danny Ross, had been a pupil in the school from 1923 until 1928.

So far as is known, Albert is the school's oldest 'Old Blue'. He was born in 1914 and his father passed away in 1922. The following year he was sent to the Blue Coat School along with his elder brother Leslie, his younger brother Kenneth and one of his sisters, Muriel. Albert was then only 8 or 9, but this was the typical age of a new starter in those days. Ken was only 6 or 7.

The photograph shows Albert at the school's main door in August 2007.

Some may suspect that Albert's surname makes him a likely relative of the school's founder, Bryan Blundell (1676-1756), but there is no known link. At the start of the eighteenth century, Albert's ancestors were living in North Meols, Southport.

The Blue Coat regime that Albert experienced was similar to the one that Harry described; boys being kept strictly out of contact with girls. However, in Albert's own case he managed at different times to hold romantic trysts with girls who were employed by the school – in one case a cleaner, Ivy Hall, and in another case a member of the kitchen staff whose name he can no longer recall. The agreed meeting place was always a quiet corner of the east corridor; known in those days as 'the spud corridor' because it was the first staging post for the school's potato deliveries.

The headmaster in 1923 was Harry C. Hughes. He was usually somewhat aloof from his pupils ('A bit toffee') but Albert recalls that he formed the new boys round him in a circle on their first day and spoke to them.

Most of the masters lived in the school, but 'Cock' Harling, the school's choirmaster, organist and office clerk, lived outside on Wavertree Road. He had the reputation of being a drinker. The senior teacher, Mr. Chynoweth, a Cornishman, was strict but very good at his job. Mr. Finney was Albert's class teacher in the first year. Miss Hipkiss wasn't there in Albert's day, but he remembers Miss Byers in the kitchen because she was usually the one who gave you your instructions if you were carrying out a task there.

As was also the case a decade later, no one in the school possessed a radio set.

Albert remembers the Rev. R. Bruce Wilson taking over from Harry C. Hughes in 1926, and he also remembers the arrival of a young man called G.G. Watcyn who hailed from South Wales.

The cane was used in the class on older pupils if they transgressed, and on a number of occasions Albert found himself on the receiving end. The school had a good joiners' shop and on one memorable occasion the joinery teacher Mr. Pearson, caught him reading a comic during the lesson.

Although he can no longer remember the tune, Albert confirms that 'Cock' Harling had composed a slow march for the school to use. There was also a fast march. The visiting minister who came to hold services was called Chipping. The school chapel was derisively termed 'the girls' school' by many of the boys.

Arrangements in the dining room were the same as in the 1930s, except that the gavel was not used so much and you simply followed your prefect's verbal orders. It is assumed that the later change from prefects to monitors must have been a decision made by the Rev. R. Bruce Wilson.

Lunch on a Monday was pea soup, and at teatime that day they were given bread and treacle ('n****r's hair oil') followed by 'currant bangers', which the boys also called 'squares' (these were often slipped up waistcoats and taken away to be used for betting purposes).

Lunch on a Tuesday was a sort of scouse. Rice pudding was on the weekly menu but it was disparagingly termed 'rice muck' by the boys.

In those days your parent could deliver a parcel of food at the school office on Saturday evening, and as long as your behaviour had recently been good it would be handed to you at a meeting that took place at about 7 p.m.

Early in his time at the school, Albert opted to join the school band and he played the kettle drum for years. He is the drummer mentioned by his friend Danny Ross in *A Blue Coat Boy of the 1920s*.

The school had an excellent football team and Albert was in it, playing the inside-right position. Arthur Taylor played at right wing and he later became a pathologist and rose to the top at Liverpool University. A chap called Harding was in goal, and despite his large size Albert states that there was no more than twelve months between the ages of the team's players.

Albert became captain of Graham House and he recalls that his name was once inscribed on a trophy shield awarded to the house (perhaps it survives somewhere on the school premises to this day!). He also has the distinction of having been the person who laid out the school's football pitch at the Lance Lane ground.

Sergeant Porter of the 5th King's Regiment gave the boys their marching drill every Monday and Albert remembers him very well – 'a little bandy-legged fellow'. He was good at his job - 'made you drill!' The barracks where he was based was on Stafford Street, which overlooked Lime Street Station. Whenever the Blue Coat boys marched through the city's streets, they would always accompany Sergeant Porter back to his barracks afterwards and be served with sandwiches.

In Albert's day, work commenced on the construction of a swimming pool on the high bank at the north end of the main front, but it was halted abruptly when the pool was a mere 2 feet high and work on the project was never resumed. It is speculated that the bricked-up archway at the far end of what might be described as 'the headmaster's corridor' may have been intended to provide access to this swimming pool, and that the lack of completion of that corner of the premises gave the school the ability to make use of a taxation loophole and thus save on expenditure.

With no pool of their own, Blue Coat pupils had to continue to wend their way across The Mystery to the Picton Road Baths, a feature of school life that would last until the 1960s. In the 1920s, with the exception of those outings and band parades, a child never left the school premises.

The children stayed at the school over Christmas, but this tradition ended circa 1925 and Albert recalls being at home for the holiday in his last two years as a Blue Coat pupil.

Unlike a number of boys who did, Albert never made an illicit ascent of the clock tower. He remembers the chimes that rang out from there, and also the bell on the outer wall of Shirley Hall and that summoned the pupils to various events through the day.

In the 1920s, the school employed cleaning staff ('skivvies') so it did not expect pupils to do such work. Why this situation should have changed just a few years later is open to speculation; perhaps the slump was responsible, or maybe thirty years down the line the cost of living in the large Wavertree premises was being found burdensome.

Albert recalled school trips that he was taken on. They used to be taken to the gardens in Southport, and each summer there was the annual voyage to the Menai Bridge aboard the *S.S. La Marguerite,* provided free of charge by the steamship company. The boys would go on one day and the girls (in their bibs and bonnets) on another. Shamingly, one year a few of the boys were caught with items in their pockets that they had just stolen from the Star Stores in Menai Bridge.

In those days the school uniform included a flat cap. Bioletti was the school barber and Albert describes the location of his shop as 'Penny Lane'. Perhaps this does not rule out the end of Church Road for the whole locality is loosely termed 'Penny Lane'.

Toothpaste was not provided ('If it had been, we would have eaten it!'). A dentist visited the school periodically.

Bedwetters evidently had their own dormitory in the 1920s too, for Albert recalls that that particular wing was colloquially referred to as 'the anuresis wing'.

The school had no examinations for pupils to take. When you were about to leave, you would be asked by the headmaster whether or not you had a Bible, and if the answer was 'no' then you were given one. If your parent was not present you were given money for your bus or tram fare.

Albert enjoyed his years at the school and was 14 when he left to go and work for the builder Charles L. Warren on Green Lane, who was also one of the school's trustees. At the time of his departure, tennis courts were about to be installed on the school's west front.

Although he has not been back to the school since before World War II, Albert returned to it frequently in the first two years or so after he left, and it was there that he met his future wife when they both helped to run the Sunday School.

His old school friend Bob Hall joined the Tank Regiment and Albert was once invited to attend a dinner that followed one of the vehicle trials. He recalls that everyone was shouting - a result of the deafness caused by their working conditions.

Albert was active in the Red Cross before the Second World War and he once had the great pleasure of encountering Sgt. Porter whilst carrying out those duties. It was because of his Red Cross skills that he was posted to Blackpool as an ambulance driver at the time of his call up. After the war he continued to drive an ambulance for the Red Cross, enjoying the social contacts that the job brought. His visits to Liverpool were only to visit relatives, etc., and were carried out on an *ad hoc* basis.

Recalling his good friend Danny Ross, Albert remarked that, unlike himself, Danny had never been the athletic sort. Out of all of Danny's siblings, he had only ever met one of them; a brother.

Some final notes:

In summer 2008 the current headmaster, Sandy Tittershill, will retire, and he is the school's very last link with the Watcyn era for he was appointed as the P.E. teacher by Mr. Watcyn in 1966.

The low wall that used to separate the north playground from the home field existed in Albert's day too. It survived until approximately 2002 but had to go when the school's new extension was built.

The school band was still in existence in the Beaumaris period of the school's history but does not appear to have survived into Mr. Watcyn's time of headmastership.

Albert recalls an incident in the late-1920s when Mr. Watcyn as a young master firmly rebuffed someone who was suggesting that rugby should be tried by the boys - a game that to this day has never been played at Liverpool Blue Coat School.

Ray Livingston (1955-59)
Now living in York

BEAUMARIS – MEMORIES THAT STILL LINGER ON

Who of those who were evacuated to Beaumaris on Monday, 4th September 1939 at the outbreak of the Second World War, will ever forget that day following our school summer holiday? We were due to report back to school later that month, but had been recalled on, I think, 2nd September, to spend two nights at the school.

At about 12 o'clock on the Monday, five special trams drew up outside the school, not on this occasion to take us to the Town Hall, or to a trip on a North Wales steamer to Menai Bridge, as had happened each year in the past, but to take the whole school to Lime Street station, to leave Liverpool on the 11.20 a.m. special evacuees' train to Beaumaris.

After a long journey, during which the train was halted on a number of occasions by other passengers pulling the communication cord, we arrived at Bangor and were then taken by a fleet of buses to Beaumaris. All 270 boys and girls were deposited, along with our suitcases at the seafront at Beaumaris, to be picked up and taken by car to the houses, big and small, where we were to stay. I never discovered how we were allocated to the various houses but remember being on the seafront for quite some time and seeing boys and girls being taken away, and wondering if my turn would ever come. There must have been less than a dozen of us left when an old green Austin Seven arrived and my brother and I were bundled into it and driven out of the town. Up Red Hill, and into the grounds of 'Plas Meigan', the home of Mr. & Mrs. Richard Williams-Bulkeley; later to become Sir and Lady Bulkeley.

We swept into the grounds and were taken into the house to be greeted by Mrs. Bulkeley with words of welcome and saying 'I thought you would have been here hours ago, your dinner has been spoilt.' Nevertheless, after being introduced to the servants, the cook produced a meal of fish and chips for us. After the meal I was shown into the bedroom where I was to spend the night - the bedroom was the largest I had ever seen with a huge bed, magnificent furniture and beautiful ornaments and pictures.

On waking up in the morning I pulled back the curtains of one of the three large windows in the room to see a view which was truly remarkable. Over the top of a wood stood the whole of Beaumaris, with the Menai Straits and Snowdonia beyond. On the lawn in front of the house rabbits were eating, a dog was watching them quite unconcerned and a gamekeeper was walking across the lawn with a gun and two pheasants under his arm; it was like paradise!

When the spring came, a clearing which had been made in the wood and which stood before the house, became a mass of golden daffodils, a beautiful sight. Many happy hours were subsequently spent wandering around the Baron Hill estate with the Bulkeley's dog, an English Setter called Wisdom, who the soldiers stationed nearby were always trying to steal! The woods provided plenty of wildlife and flowers together with a number of birds, the likes of which I had never ever seen and birds' nests were easily found.

Although we were now out of the school at Wavertree, everything was still very much organised. Dirty laundry was collected and clean clothes distributed at the Church Hall on the corner of Margaret Street, and the Parish Church Hall was also fully utilised. At first the school met there for morning prayers and the afternoon was spent on the seafront. After a short while we, the boys, shared the Grammar School with the local children; they attended school in the morning and we in the afternoon, and I think the girls shared the Council School on a similar basis. The Parish Church Hall was also the place for new clothes to be issued and for boots to be inspected for repairs.

Church parades were still held every Sunday when we marched through the town, preceded by the school band, along Castle Street and then up Church Street to St. Mary's Parish Church where the whole school would then become the choir!

Memories of a visit to Bangor when Frank Walker and I were taken there by Mrs. Bulkeley to look around the town and pay a visit to the pictures to see the *Hound of the Baskervilles*: a walk of about 5 miles each way with Frank, myself and a Mr. & Mrs. J.O. Jones, with whom Frank was billeted, to a village church for 'Evensong' one Sunday, where the congregation consisted of the preacher, one other person and us four; a walk to Red Wharf Bay to see the salvaged H.M. Submarine *Thetis*; P.T. on the front; tobogganing down Cemetery Hill on a piece of corrugated air-raid shelter metal in the winter when snow was on the ground. These and many other memories have remained with me throughout the years.

It was with some sadness when in 1941 the Rev. R.B. Wilson sent for me to say there was a job for me in Liverpool and I was to leave the school. His parting words were 'Keep your shoes clean your hair short and respect your superiors, and you should do well.' I wonder, if he were alive today, what advice he would give? At the time of leaving I would have cheerfully accepted, if offered, any sort of position in Beaumaris or the surrounding countryside. How much different my life may have been.

Arthur Martin (1934 – 1941) Written in 1989. Sadly, Arthur passed away in December 2003.

BEAUMARIS – MORE MEMORIES THAT STILL LINGER ON

Lucky me, being billeted in the old Post Office on Wexham Street with Les Cowley and the local blacksmith, Owen Roberts. Even luckier still when my hostess married one of the only two fish and chip shop owners in the town and decided to have me come and stay with her.

This, despite food rationing, always ensured I was well fed and better able to defend the realm when I enlisted in the School Cadet Corps attached to the Royal Welsh Fusiliers.

The excitement of running messages for the Home Guard: mostly my run was to the Catalina factory of Saunders Roe near Llandfaes Church and also the B.B.C. Penmon Radio Station. Being rewarded with a sumptuous meal of sausage and mash at 2 o'clock in the morning in Beaumaris Gaol! (No I wasn't prisoner there; this was the H.Q. of the Home Guard.)

Icy cold mornings with frost-bitten fingers picking 'spuds' for the 'Dig for Victory' campaigns which were part of the compulsory requirements for teenage scholars, instituted by the Ministry of Agriculture.

The regular school band parades in towns all over North Wales for 'Salute the Soldier' week and helping these towns reach their targets of money donations.

Doing 'press-gang' service on the fastest laundry cart in the west! A push cart over-laden with wicker-workbaskets packed tight with soiled laundry, sometimes with a rider sitting on the top tier of baskets, while two kamikaze helpers pushed the cart down the steep driveway of the Bryn School - never lost a wheel or a passer-by, but occasionally our top rider!

Geometry lessons taken at the pace of the brightest spark in the class and for lesser mortals - the answer of course, was always a lemon!

The parade of the Welsh Guards who managed to get back from Dunkirk. In those homesick days, watching express trains on the mainland across the Menai Straits, hurtling along the rails in the direction of Liverpool.

The death of my hostess's mother at 91 years of age and air raid practices when the school would march into the passageways of Beaumaris Castle for protection.

Stan Evans (1936-44). Written in 1989.

CHAPTER 2
THE 1940s

PETER CLARKE RECALLS THE EARLY YEARS

My first recollection of the Blue Coat School was my interview in December 1943 with the headmaster, Rev. Bruce Wilson and Dr. Dickerson who, I suppose, was not only the music teacher but also the school secretary.

Incidentally Dr. F.W. Dickerson, a successful jazz pianist, was affectionately known as 'Fishy' but why I really couldn't tell you! He was however a wonderful organist and pianist – hence the Doctorate. My sister and I paid him 2/6d a lesson to learn to play the piano – after about 18 months Dr. Dickerson wrote to my sister telling her to keep her money as he despaired of me ever becoming a piano player, which was a shame, as my sole ambition was to emulate the late Charlie Kunz who was a successful jazz pianist!

Because the war was on in 1940 and the bombing of Liverpool was extremely heavy, it was decided to evacuate the school to Beaumaris. A short time after, I met up with my travelling companions at the Woodside railway station, Birkenhead to journey to Beaumaris; they were Mr. Dickerson who was in charge and the Crookham family, Eddie, Margaret and Elizabeth. I should imagine that the average age was about 11 years old and we reluctantly said goodbye to our families and set off on the 'great adventure'. When we arrived at Beaumaris, the girls were sent to Red Hill and we were sent to Woodgarth.

One of the things that has stuck in my mind about Beaumaris was that we were permanently hungry. Why? I don't know as we were very well fed at the school, but I suppose, boys being boys, in a very short time we found a way round that.

Being orphans, we didn't have any money to buy extra rations but, Charlie Mills, Lennie Hughes and I soon had a plan worked out whereby we would visit the local bakery and without paying manage to sneak away with a loaf of bread or some scones from the shelves, and we would eat our ill gotten gains on the road back to Woodgarth. Needless to say had we been caught, we would soon have been introduced to the headmaster's cane.

As my mother was Welsh, Mr. Watcyn, the senior master announced to everybody that a real Welsh scholar was coming to the school; what a disappointment I turned out to be. Mr. Watcyn was a South Walian from Swansea and the North Walian dialect of the Welsh language is completely different, so we couldn't converse at all in Welsh.

The discipline at the school was, to say the least, rigid. You could get the cane for practically any small misdemeanour such as a tear in your blazer or the cardinal sin of scuff marks on your boots, usually caused by kicking a stone around. However, to be fair to the school, my mother was a widow, and the Blue Coat School clothed, fed and educated me for five shillings a week so I suppose the regime had to be strict.

Memories of the teachers at the school will always remain strong; Mr. Watcyn, the senior master kept discipline there, Miss Smith the headmistress, who had a wonderful gift of storytelling, she could hold a whole class enthralled during an English lesson as not only was her diction excellent but she would also act out each character. Then there was Mr. Crebbin, it didn't matter what subject he was teaching, if one of the pupils asked him a question which had nothing to do with the subject matter, he would launch into an explanation and before you knew it the lesson was over. Mr. Fowler the history master, and ex Royal Navy man who used to go into Beaumaris on his bicycle and after visiting various hostelries would cycle back parking his bike under our dormitory window talking all the while to the beloved machine and at times even scolding it. This understandably caused a great deal of amusement amongst the pupils in the dormitory.

Incidentally, a small group of ex-pupils have a reunion each year in Beaumaris, Charlie Mills, Sammy D'Eathe, Bill Humphreys, John Woodhead, myself, the late Teddy Taylor, and also our beloved

Mr. Hickman, the first master who turned up at the Blue Coat School who didn't need to hit the pupils to maintain discipline, and we reminisce about old times.

One thing that will always stand out in my memory was, towards the end of the war and after the girls had left the school (they were sent to Wolverhampton), Mr. Watcyn and Mr. Unwin had the whole of the remaining pupils lined up one Sunday night to make an announcement, Bill Laughton broke wind, Mr. Watcyn, horrified asked who had polluted the atmosphere, of course we hadn't the faintest idea what he was talking about; fair enough if he'd asked who'd farted! Anyway after a lot of sniggering, Bill owned up and was ordered to go to the far end of the playground to 'air himself'.

We also had to sit the scholarship and surprise, surprise, only five of us passed; Peter Archer, Keith McLaughlin, Charlie Mills, Peter Broadhurst and yours truly. We were fourteen at the time and ended up in the fifth form in the grammar school under the tutorship of dear old Mr. Hickman; in fact I still have a school report signed by him.

We sat our G.C.E. 'O' levels in 1951 and were not shall we say, Oxford contenders! During this time I had developed an eye for the girls and used to court a girl called Dorothy who lived in Smithdown Lane and as I was a boarder it was rather difficult; in fact it was forbidden to go take a girl out on a date. The only way I could see her was by nipping over the wall. Needless to say, I was caught by Mr. Eade the housemaster who reported me to Mr. Watcyn. I wasn't exactly expelled, but my mother received a stern letter from the headmaster suggesting that as soon as my exams were over she should remove me from the school as I was a bad influence on the rest of the boys.

So in September 1951 I went down to Horne Brothers and was kitted out with shoes, socks, etc. and a good suit and sent packing. I started work in an office but left after three months as I didn't like it; I then went on to serve my apprenticeship as a fitter in Cammell Laird's, Birkenhead, where I again got myself into trouble. A gentleman, called Jimmy Reid called the apprentices on Clydeside out on strike for more money, needless to say, as I was from a 'left wing' family, I got caught up with it.

I became the Merseyside secretary of the strike committee and poor old mother lost her £25 'good conduct money' that she had deposited on my behalf, as in my indentures it was forbidden for me to go on strike; mind you we got a ten shilling rise, which was a lot of money in those days.

I have continued my trade union activities throughout my life and have the honour of being awarded the highest accolade my trade union, Amicus, can bestow; I am the proud owner of the union's gold medal.

What do I do now? Well at 72 years old I am still active on the trade union front, as a delegate to the Wales T.U.C. Standing Orders Committee, President of my local Union Branch and Chair of Amicus Disabled Members Committee, to name but a few.

What can I thank the Blue Coat School for? Well believe it or not in Shirley Hall, during the afternoon service I had to learn and recite passages from the New Testament off by heart and also conduct the service from the pulpit. Believe me this stood me in very good stead, making going to the rostrum and speaking in front of hundreds of people a piece of cake.

There's a lot I have missed out, like Lennie Hughes' nickname 'Mavis' bestowed upon him by Mr. Watcyn, and oh dear me – you can just hear the outcry today; or John Woodhead, a wonderful storyteller after lights out and the wonderful Mayor of Beaumaris, Mr. Taylor from Menai Bridge, who had a magnificent pocket watch whose chimes enthralled the boys whenever they met him.

Peter Clarke (1943 - 1951)
Now living in Wales.

'GET THIS MESSAGE TO HOME FARM'

During the 1941/42 war period the school organised a cadet corps under the command of Captain G.G. Watcyn. The corps was attached to the Royal Welsh Fusiliers. Part of the army training at that time was to have the mainland regular army 'mock' invade the island of Anglesey on a once-a-month basis. The island, for these training schemes, was defended by a few regular army officers and commissioned men, and the Home Guard, the 'Dad's Army' of Beaumaris area. The Army Cadet Corps was required to maintain signals and communications for an area of approximately eight miles radius from the headquarters installed in Beaumaris gaol. The furthermost signal post was at the base of the Bulkeley Monument, between Home Farm and the top road to Llanddonna.

This particular Sunday morning in October, at approximately 0200 hours.(let's be army-like), my name was suddenly blurted out. 'Get this message to Home Farm immediately, take that push bike!'

Now an army issue bicycle is not only built like a tank but is almost the weight of a tank! Even more so when trying to pedal up Red Hill which, in areas, has a 1:4 gradient! Thus after puffing past Henllys Lane, I had to dismount and push the bike up the rest of the hill to the lane-way of Home Farm. Completely against all the rules I left the bike against a tree, after all who at 0300 hours on a pitch-black night would notice it in the dark?

From there I walked through the wet fallen leaves, very conscious of the noise I was creating, petrified that some 'regular army' invader was going to jump on me. As I passed the pig sty I could hear the seemingly contented pigs grunting. Suddenly I stopped – ever had the hair on the back of your neck bristle with fear? I can tell you, it doesn't feel good! I was about to turn the corner of the farm building when instinct told me someone was there waiting for me to move. How I tried desperately to move, and quickly in the opposite direction but, my feet clad in heavy army boots, felt like they were weighed down with lead and prevented me from doing so.

I was not mistaken! I was positive I could hear breathing. First I sweated cobs, then it froze on me, the calls of nature in a frightened state were fortunately suppressed. I began to wonder will I become a casualty of the war. Suddenly what seemed like a huge foghorn bellowed 'Halt! Who goes there?' As much as I wanted to reply, I couldn't! 'Halt! Who goes there?' the voice yelled once again. I suddenly realised if I did not answer on the third challenge, whoever was around the corner had the right to shoot or bayonet me. As much as I wanted to call for help from 'me Mam', I knew she couldn't help it at this moment.

Just as he started on the third and final challenge, I managed to splutter 'It's me, it's me.' Back came the foghorn voice 'Announce yourself under the King's Regulations.' All that I could do was stammer again 'It's me, it's me' at which point a ferocious looking Lance Corporal showed himself shouting 'You bloody fool, you could have got yourself shot. What are you doing around here anyway?'

'Oh Sir, I've got a message for the Monument Signal base.' 'Well you had best come into the house and get yourself together before moving on.' So like a dithering fool I was led into a farmhouse kitchen where I was given a drink of hot cocoa . 'Get this down you, and on your way.' 'Which way to the monument Sir?' 'O.K., finish your drink and I'll take you to the gate.'

On opening the gate he pointed the direction. 'Just about half a mile' he said. The night was still black but very quiet, just such a night the Germans would choose to make a parachute landing I thought. So at a brisk half run I made my way across the field, still no sign of the monument. I thought I heard something so I stopped. No, I was not mistaken, definitely something thudding my way. My, Oh My! Did I run like hell-for-leather; convinced a platoon of Germans was after me. Unmistakably a wall appeared before me and over it I scrambled in desperation, only to frighten the life out of the six cadets and the N.C.O. running the signal post as I tumbled to the ground. 'Who's after you?' they joked. 'I think there's a whole group of invaders coming towards us, we should get moving!' 'Nonsense' the N.C.O. replied, 'What you heard was only some horses that could see you but you couldn't see them.'

Thank goodness, I thought. I gave them the message. It was now approaching 0400 hours and I was only too concerned to find my WD bike and get back to the gaol. I wouldn't want to bore you further with the experience of a bike weighing half a ton, speeding out of control down Red Hill wondering if I could get the brakes to work before arriving at the pier!

Anon.

THE FEMININE TOUCH

MARGARET THOMPSON (née BOND) REMEMBERS

START OF MY BLUE COAT DAYS - EVACUATION

Having passed the interview with the headmaster the Rev. Mr. Bruce-Wilson a few weeks earlier, my mother took my brother Malcolm and me to the Blue Coat Hospital (as it was then called) in Church Road. We were to be dressed in the school uniform and travel to Beaumaris. I had my injured arm in a sling and they refused to allow me to go with Malcolm and the other children. Two weeks later, aged 9 years and 1 week, I was back at the Blue Coat, my mother dressed me in my uniform, gave me some sweets and an apple and kissed me goodbye, leaving me in the hands of a lady whom, I later learned, was Mrs. Dorothy Smith – the headmistress.

We had a carriage to ourselves on the train and Mrs. Smith promptly fell asleep. After we had gone a few stops I woke her up and asked if we were we nearly there. She said 'No'. A few stops later I woke her up and asked if she would like a sweet. She said 'No thank you.' Again I let a few more stops go by and then woke her to offer a bite of my apple, she said 'No thank you.' Once again – well, you get the picture – and this time she sat up and said 'No we are not there yet and you'll know when we are because the train cannot go any further and don't wake me up again.' It seemed a very long and lonely journey.

Waiting at the bus stop outside Bangor station, wearing only my blazer, gymslip and jumper I was frozen. Mrs. Smith opened her bag and wrapped me in a big woolly jumper. When we got off the bus, Mrs. Smith turned to me and said, 'You'll be staying here for a while.' I looked, my eyes were like saucers and I thought I'd died and gone to heaven when she knocked on the door of a sweetshop. An elderly lady answered her knock and I heard her say 'No, you want Mrs. Lewis next door.' Ah well!

Before Mrs. Smith knocked at No.11, she said to me, 'From now on you will be called Margaret not Peggy: we do not allow nicknames.'

Three senior girls, who said that Mrs. Lewis was out and that they had promised to look after me until she got back, answered the door. They washed me, dressed me in my pyjamas, wrapped me in a blanket, sat me in front of the fire and made me delicious toast with dripping and a mug of hot sweet cocoa. As one of them brushed my hair, she said, 'What lovely blonde hair you have, what a pity it's all being cut off tomorrow.' That was the final straw and I burst into tears. As I cried, I told them that not only had I lost my father, I missed my Mum, my family, my home, my friends and my dog, I'd just lost my name and now I was to lose my hair.

Once I'd settled in I learned the names of my three kind housemates. They were Vera Roberts, the head girl, Betty, (surely not a nickname?) Dawson, the deputy head girl and Iris Battersbee, the senior prefect: perhaps my luck had turned at last.

INTRODUCTION

On my first day Vera, Betty and Iris took me to morning assembly. We then walked to Bryn House for lessons and I was pleased to see that I was in the same class as my brother. This was also my first introduction to Miss Hipkiss. During lessons, Miss Hipkiss walked up and down the aisles carrying a large, heavy book with which, at the slightest hint of a misdemeanour, she took great delight in thwacking you on the head. We had deportment lessons and I learnt to curtsey whilst balancing a book on my head. I always managed very well, due no doubt to Miss Hipkiss's contribution.

On the Monday morning of my second week I noticed straight away that my brother wasn't in class. I asked one or two of the boys if they knew where he was but they didn't seem to know anything. Mid-morning, Mrs. Smith arrived and we all stood to attention. She told everyone else to sit down but I was to remain standing and I began to feel a bit uneasy. She then asked me a question 'Did your brother ever play truant at home?' I had no idea what she was talking about, but I tried my best to answer and said 'No Miss, but he did play table tennis.' To my amazement she ran out, followed by our teacher (whose name I can't remember). It was years later, talking to Miss Warren, that she told me Mrs. Smith and the teacher were found in the corridor shrieking with laughter.

Apparently, as a joke, some boys had told Malcolm that it was a bank holiday so he had taken himself off for the day.

SETTLING IN WITH 'AUNT BATCH' & HER PETS

I settled down at Mrs. Lewis's, sharing a bedroom with Vera, Betty and Iris. Our bedroom window overlooked the back entrance of the Bull's Head pub next door and we were regularly woken up by the drunks falling out at closing time. For some inexplicable reason, everyone called Mrs. Lewis 'Aunt Batch' and I never did find out why. She had two cats – Inky and Winky and a dog called Tinker. I love dogs, so every day after school I would take Tinker for a walk. I usually walked up to the castle, then down to the water's edge to let Tinker paddle in the Menai Straits, skirting the empty boating pond, then on towards the pier and the strip of sand on the far side, and always keeping my eyes open for anything unusual.

One day, Tinker got quite excited so I went to investigate what it was he'd found. It was a creature I'd never seen before, dead of course, but I picked it up to have a closer look. Suddenly, I looked up to see Mrs. Smith, out on her regular evening walk, standing at the other end of the boating pond, I said, 'Look what I've found' and she shouted 'Drop it, drop it at once' which I did. She walked over to me and said, 'Never, ever pick up a dead rat again, and go and wash your hands.'

On Sundays, after breakfast, wearing long black stockings and our Sunday dresses (navy blue, long-sleeved with three pleats in the front and three in the back) we assembled in Bryn and put on our tippets and bonnets. If it was cold or wet we would also wear our navy blue cloaks with a large frilled hood to pull up. The boys would be dressed in long navy blue trousers, navy blue tailcoats with silver-coloured buttons and starched white cravats. We would then line up in size order and march through the town to the local church for morning service. The tippets were shoulder-wide, stiffly starched white collars coming to a point at the waist front and back, and then pinned in place. The bonnets were made of straw and shaped a bit like an upside-down coalscuttle and tied with wide navy blue satin ribbons. Our sole pleasure on removing the tippets was to screw them up and scrub the floor with them.

CHRISTMAS 1941 – STAR ATTRACTION

At Christmas 1941, it was decided that the girls would put on an all singing all dancing show at the Bulkeley Arms Hotel. I was asked if I'd like to be in it and I said that I would. I then had to demonstrate my acting, dancing and singing abilities. I discovered that I could act and dance but my singing would have cleared the hall within seconds! So I found myself in the chorus dressed in a sailor suit and dancing the hornpipe. Betty Dawson had the lead female role and Vera Roberts played the male roles and they were very good too.

On opening night, during a break for costume changes, I had to walk across a bridge with a stream supposedly flowing underneath, pulling petals from a daisy and saying, 'She loves me, she loves me not.' Unfortunately my sleeve caught the painted scenery and it came crashing down and the whole audience could see me just standing on some wooden steps. I got down, took off my shoe, picked up the painted sheet and hammered the nails back in. I could hear the audience laughing so I went to the footlights, gave a bow, got a big round of applause then started my petal pulling once again. Afterwards I was asked if I could arrange to do the same for the next two nights as it got such a big laugh. I declined, but the next two nights saw the place packed.

Once I'd settled down into a routine at Aunt Batch's I began to feel happier. It helped that I saw my brother every day and I also met Margaret Pugh and we became best friends. Malcolm was billeted with Nain and Taid (grandma & granddad) in Maes Hyfryd and on my first visit to him I asked about the house on the corner, I wondered why it was totally demolished and was told that earlier in the war a Wellington bomber had crashed there and all the crew had been killed.

Aunt Batch was very excited when she told us that Mr. Lewis was coming home on leave so we all helped to make everything perfect for his homecoming. He looked very handsome in his officer's uniform but all too soon he had gone again. It was some months later that Aunt Batch told us she was going to have a baby. Everything carried on much the same as usual until one day, arriving home from school, Vera told me that Aunt Batch had had a bad accident and was in Bangor hospital and we were all going to stay with Aunt Batch's sister.

The sleeping arrangements were sorted so that Betty and Iris shared a bedroom and Vera and I slept on the landing, which was divided off by a curtain. Vera and I woke up at the same time and we were feeling very itchy. Vera put the light on and we saw what the problem was, we were both smothered in woodlice and our shrieks must have woken the whole street. With great presence of mind, Vera gathered up the crawlies in the sheet and threw the lot over the banisters. We didn't get much sleep that night. Next morning Vera said 'Get your things together, we're going home.'

The three girls coped with everything until Aunt Batch arrived home with her leg in plaster and a beautiful baby girl called Sylvia.

By now, the boys had moved to Woodgarth and we girls were told that we'd soon be moving to Red Hill House. Margaret and I with a group of other friends I remember, including Jean Braithwaite, Thelma Bannen, Beryl Tweedale, Edna Kelly and Josephine Morris, would go up to the top of Mount Field and then roll all the way down, ending up with cowpats all over us. Then we would crawl up to the edge of the cliff and look down on the flying boats being launched from Saunders Roe Works.

I was sad to leave Aunt Batch and the place we called home; she had been very kind to us.

RED HILL HOUSE - WORK ROTAS

When we arrived at Red Hill House, the electricity supply hadn't been connected so to start with we had to make do with oil lamps. We were assigned to our rooms and told to look around to get our bearings. It was a lovely house. The front door opened into a large hall with a huge fireplace on the right and at the back on the left was a magnificent curved, cantilevered staircase which led up to Mrs. Smith's room. The only time we were permitted to use the staircase was when we were summoned to her presence! At all other times we had to use the back stairs. I was in an attic room, in what had obviously been the servants' quarters.

The house overlooked a sloping field, which led down to the bluebell woods (out of bounds of course, but we still managed to sneak down). There were two courtyards, the inner one with the chapel on the left where the feral cats lived and the outer courtyard with stables and coach houses. Once, I had been sent to put rubbish in a bin when I saw one of the cats coming towards me, in its mouth it had a wriggling, squeaking mouse. I hid, as these cats were quite vicious and watched, fascinated, as the cat ate the mouse. It then regurgitated the head, tail, fur and bones all in one neat package. I waited until the cat had gone before I came out of hiding.

We were all given jobs to do on a rota system, such as cleaning, laying tables, slicing bread and peeling potatoes. The best job to be awarded was slicing the bread for breakfast as you never went hungry. The second best job was peeling potatoes, especially in the winter as a fire was lit in a room in the inner courtyard. We threw some potatoes on the fire and once we had finished peeling all the others, we sat and enjoyed the hot baked potatoes.

The overgrown and wooded grounds were perfect for hide and seek, and over in the far corner, where the air was heavy with the smell of wild garlic, were rows and rows of tiny headstones each one engraved with the name and date of the late lamented pet – from dogs to budgies.

Every morning the coaches would arrive to take us down to school. If you cleared it with a teacher, you could walk down instead and we preferred to do that as, halfway down was an Italian prisoner of war camp and we used to shout 'Heil Hitler' at them and we'd all goose-step up and down giving the Nazi salute. The teachers never found out or we'd have been in deep trouble. In the autumn we were in trouble often enough as it was. On the way home we would stop to pick blackberries ending up with purple hands and mouths and tears in our uniform. All our clothes were mended and altered by the seamstress Miss Byers, who was known to all of us as 'Bias Binding'. A group of us went down one day to have our hems let down and as we went in there was a funny smell, she said she was making toffee but had burnt it and was going to throw it in the bin but asked us if we'd like it. Very politely, we said we thought we could manage it and ate the lot. As we were leaving, the second group of girls arrived; we just had to let them know how sorry we were that they were too late.

HOME NEWS – RUNNING AWAY

Arriving in class one morning, my brother told me he had just received a letter from home to say that Gran had died and that our young brother, Douglas, was very ill.

I was sorry to hear about Gran although I had always found her to be a formidable woman who always wore black, and I could never take my eyes off her whiskery chin. I was, however, upset to hear about Douglas and that night I lay awake worrying about him. Next morning, to my horror, I woke up and realised that I'd wet the bed. Later that morning I was called out to the front of the class who were told of the crime I had committed and I received 5 strokes of the cane on the palm of my hand (boys had to bend over).

After tea, I was in the playroom reading when a girl came up to me and started chatting. She hadn't been at the school very long and I didn't really know her. Her name was Flora (well, actually it wasn't, but I'll call her that). She told me she was very unhappy and hated the school and, after what had happened to me that morning, I mustn't be very happy either. I wasn't. She said she was going to run away and asked would I like to go with her and I said 'Yes.'

She said I could leave all the planning to her but the next day I was to save as much food as I could to take with me. She had money and would take care of everything else. I was naive enough to believe her. The following night after lights out, we met in the outer courtyard and set out walking along miles and miles of dark, silent country lanes. We eventually arrived at a village and being so tired I fell asleep in a telephone box. Flora dragged me out and we carried on but I tripped and fell into a hedge and ended up with some nasty scratches.

We crossed the Menai Bridge in a howling gale and arrived at a bus stop at about 5.30am. A bus full of workmen arrived, and as we got on the conductor asked, 'Where have you come from? You look as though you've been dragged through a hedge backwards.' We arrived at Bangor station and Flora said, 'Leave the talking to me.' She asked a porter to take us to the stationmaster's office and told him that we were cousins. She went on to say that our uncle – who had the tickets – hadn't turned up, so could we please get the train to Liverpool and our mothers would pay for the tickets. I was very impressed with her ability to lie so fluently. I arrived home and found my young brother lying in bed. His first words to me were 'You're in trouble.' My mother was at the Blue Coat School with Dr. Dickerson, who had told her that both the Welsh and English police were out looking for Flora and me.

My mother gave me supper then a bath and rubbed cream on my scratches, tucked me up in bed and told me that I'd be going back straight away. Next morning I sat and talked to Douglas for a while and then said 'Goodbye.' It was the last time I saw him as he died soon after.

At the interview with Dr. Dickerson the following morning, he seemed to know all the details and said he understood why I had run away but I couldn't get off scot-free, so I was to be confined to the sanatorium for two weeks under the care of the matron Miss Homer (the dragon) and the kindly Sister Thomas. So it was another silent journey back to Beaumaris, this time escorted by Dr. Dickerson.

I was curious to know why all the girls gave Dr. Dickerson the nickname of 'Dr. Fish'.

Vera and Betty told me that he was called that because, when they were back in Liverpool, he only ever came in to eat with the rest of the staff on a Friday, and what was always served for dinner every Friday? Fish. He continued this habit after the war as well.

Towards the end of my two weeks I heard a commotion and looking down out of my window I saw Flora, she had dyed her hair a startling vivid red. We were not allowed to meet and next morning she left, having been expelled.

After my two weeks were up and I returned to Red Hill House, nothing was ever mentioned about my unorthodox trip home and I think Mrs. Smith must have told all the girls never to speak about it; it was as though it had never happened. Although I was allowed home for my brother's funeral, my mother considered me too young to attend.

A short time later I and some other girls were invited to Mrs. Smith's room, where she handed out toffees and we sat and listened to her reading the chapters of the book she was writing called *Those Greylands Girls*. When it was published, my brother bought me a copy for my birthday and I still have it.

BLONDIE BONDIE

When I first arrived in Beaumaris I had my blonde hair cut short with a fringe (with my surname being Bond I was often called 'Blondie Bondie') and every few months we were sent to have our hair cut – one line of girls with a fringe and one line for those with a side parting. As I got closer to the head of the queue I screwed up my courage and took two steps smartly to the right and slid into the other queue. When it was my turn, the hairdresser said 'But you've got a fringe, you should be in the other queue.' 'No', I said, 'I'm having a side parting.' She was very doubtful, but in the end decided to do it and parted my hair on the side and put a hairgrip in to hold my fringe back. When I got outside I realised I still had to face the music. It wasn't very long in coming; a teacher (Miss Hipkiss I think) soon spotted me and said, 'Come here girl, what have you done to your hair and who gave you permission to have a side parting? Mrs Smith will hear of this.' Mrs. Smith did, and I found myself standing in front of her explaining what I had done and the reason why. I told her that there were several girls younger than me who had side partings, and it would also make me look older. She gave me a long look and said 'Very well, you can keep your hair like that and I'll overlook your behaviour this time.'

DEPRIVATION

Throughout my years in the Blue Coat I existed in a time warp, I only knew there was still a war on when weeping new girls arrived. It wasn't too bad when I was staying at Mrs. Lewis's as I could go out after school and at weekends and I had become great friends with a local girl. Moving to Red Hill House was more restrictive and we weren't allowed to leave the grounds, other than to walk to school and back. We had no radio, newspapers or money. Postal Orders and cash received for Christmas/birthdays etc. had to be handed over and entered in your bankbook. Once a week we could buy four ounces of toffees or one bar of chocolate and the pennies would be deducted from the book. If a girl didn't have money in her book, she didn't get any sweets.

END OF THE WAR – THE RETURN HOME

To celebrate the ending of the war, the Blue Coat School arranged a pageant which was held in the castle grounds. I believe Vera Roberts played the part of Queen Elizabeth I, and I was dressed as an elf and did very little apart from cartwheels and handstands.

At last we were allowed to go home for the holidays and I was very excited at the thought of wearing my own clothes again; I asked my mother where she had put them. She told me she had given them all to charity as they would no longer fit me and there were no clothing coupons to buy me new ones. Malcolm and I had to spend the whole of the holiday in our school uniforms. Arriving back in Beaumaris, we were informed that we would soon be returning to Liverpool for good, not knowing then that what little freedom we enjoyed would soon disappear.

END OF MY SCHOOL DAYS

I was always led to believe that the school in Wolverhampton where the girls were sent after leaving the school in Wavertree was very similar to the Liverpool Blue Coat School. I could have gone there with the other girls. Everyone had to take an I.Q. test and, after the results came through, Mr. Watcyn called me to his study and said he wanted me to stay on and take my exams. He then made me a prefect, with immediate effect, but I refused to stay on and left soon after.

Margaret Thompson (formerly Bond, 1941-1948)
Now living in Cambridgeshire

CHAPTER 3
THE 1950s

SCHOOL INTRODUCTION

As a new boy boarder, in September 1950, I was delivered to the school on a Sunday afternoon by my second father, (having been adopted) and his fiancée, soon to become my third mother. I know this sounds complicated but there seem to be far more complicated arrangements these days!

Anyway, after attempting to settle in to my first term away from home, Sunday tea time arrived and I duly queued with all the other boys, feeling a little strange and perhaps somewhat homesick, outside the dining room to await whatever culinary delight had been prepared for me in the kitchen.

This repast was not to come as quickly as I imagined, as all 120 of us were led not into the pupils' dining room, but into the staff dining room, one at a time, where Mr. Watcyn was standing, ramrod straight, with a cane in his hand. I was told to hold out my right hand and immediately I received a whack from it, which not only hurt but was also a surprise as since arriving at school all that I had done was to arrive, have a bath and be shown where my bed was located.

Worse was to come. Mr. Watcyn then told me to hold out my left hand and he proceeded to whack that one as well! He then dismissed me and told me to queue up again for my evening meal. Trying to eat with sore, weal-marked hands was difficult; innocence of any offence did not help matters.

The food prepared for us did not appease the situation either. It was inadequate both in terms of quality and also quantity.

It was only the following day, after a boy was discovered to have been severely beaten the night before, that I discovered some minor offence had been committed and the culprit had refused to own up. It was the tradition in the school that no pupil ever sneaked on another, so, as the boy refused to own up, everybody received two strokes of the cane and summary justice was dealt out to the culprit by the senior boys. I learned two lessons from that. 1. Never ever sneak on another boy. 2. The cane hurt.

Frank Irwin (1950-1957)
Now living in Wirral

THE RODNEY HALL CHESS TROPHY

In 1955, Rodney Hall, a keen chess player, and some classmates, went abroad to Diekirch in Luxembourg, on a school-sponsored holiday; such holidays usually lasting for seven days. Unfortunately, at the end of one particular day when the roll-call was held, Rodney was discovered to be missing. A search of the boating lake where they had all been enjoying themselves produced the discovery of his body. His mates found him, just beneath the water, drowned.

In memory of Rodney, his parents presented the school with the Rodney Hall Chess Trophy, to be used for an annual competition.

Frank Irwin (1950-1957)
Now living in Wirral

FAIRGROUND VISITS

In the summer, it was the custom for a travelling fairground and circus to visit Liverpool and set up its entertainment centre in Greenbank Park, not too far away from the school. Naturally the glamour and glitter of a travelling fair, with its procession through the city, including elephants, clowns and fire eaters would attract attention even from those of us who were forbidden to go along and experience it at first hand.

Undaunted, boys would bunk out of school in the evenings to go along to see the side shows and hopefully find sufficient money in the telephone boxes by pressing 'Button B' or searching on the floor at the hub of activity, to actually be able to see what went on inside those closed tents.

One particular evening, Tommy Hudson and I sneaked out the rear of the school, across the western front, over the railings and walked into the park. We had a few copper coins and on the way managed to add to our princely collection by the means described above.

On arrival, one particular side show attracted us, the Burlesque! Outside the tent was this 'lady' dressed in fancy clothes, looking back I think she was quite rough, but being fancily dressed in flags, rags and some half-sexy clobber, she got our attention. (That's what happens when you are stuck in an all-male school).

We didn't want to spend our money all at once so we hung around and all the customers piled into the tent, the door was shut and a large burly bouncer guarded the entrance whilst the show proceeded. Suddenly, cheers and clapping rang out from inside! 'Wow!' we thought, 'the show must be great, we'll go in for the next one.'

The clapping and cheering continued for 20 minutes or so as our anticipation and excitement grew, 'We will be able to see her strip off?' asked Tommy, 'Yes', I replied, 'the sooner the better.'

The time came, the crowds piled out and we were first in for the next show so that we could get a good view from the front row. Time passed as others filled the tented enclosure, anticipation grew, patience expired, but eventually the 'lady' appeared and was duly announced by a large man with flushed cheeks, as Madame Fifi.

She stood there and announced that she would remove clothing only in response to applause; the more applause, the more she would remove. We all clapped as much as possible and sure enough, she started to remove some outer items. Then she stopped. 'You aren't clapping enough' said Madame Fifi. She was a Scouser!

However much we clapped, never did sufficient clothes get removed to make the appearance worthwhile. What it did achieve, however, was to have another queue lining up outside waiting to come in. Disappointed, we made our way back to school and returned by the same route.

Although the evening was not what we had expected, the upside was that we didn't get caught.

Frank Irwin (1950-1957)
Now living in Wirral

EATING AS WELL AS POSSIBLE

Having three meals a day was all well and good, but boys being boys and growing up, meant that we really needed meals between meals. Given the strict regime experienced by boarders that was not possible given normal conditions. However, to growing boys at the Blue Coat School, conditions were not always normal.

As I grew hungrier in the evenings, and reading books about survival and daring escapades of P.O.W.s during WWII, books about which where very prevalent at the time, a plan started to formulate in my mind. The staff dining room, located off the corridor to the north of our dining room, was always laid out with food for staff to eat after returning back to school from bible classes, trips to picture houses, gambling dens or places of public hostelry, whatever their personal predilections.

The table was always covered with a blanket type cloth which reached down to the floor. This had been spotted by boys who had been called to the room to either run messages or be scolded, or some other such reason.

Unfortunately, during the evenings, access was not possible for us because the double doors in the main corridor were kept locked until breakfast the following morning. However, following all the tunnelling that had gone on in all those 'Stalags' in Germany, the problem no longer seemed insurmountable.

The school heating system was served by pipework running from the boiler-house to all the various school rooms and corridors that required heating. That pipework ran within a service duct under the marble floor, but for maintenance purposes, cast iron floor grilles were inserted at strategic points to permit access to all the pipework runs.

I carried out an investigation in the daytime and discovered one such floor grill about 20 ft. on the dormitory side of the doors and one on the other, which distance eludes me at the moment, but sufficient to know that it would afford access to the other side of the locked doors. The plan was formed.

Several nights later (the time escapes me but it must have been around 10 p.m.), when the hunger pangs had really set in, a friend and I, with dressing gowns on, crept down the stairs from our dormitory so that we would not disturb the duty master, wherever he may have been at the time. The route had to take us past the staff room door so 'silent running' was the order of the day.

We crept along the corridor and lifted the floor grille, dropped down inside and replaced the grill behind us. The duct was wide enough for us and we crept along under the locked door, removed the grill the other side, climbed out and replaced that grill behind us also.

Listening from outside the staff room all seemed silent! Eventually we opened the door, ever so slowly and finding the room empty (apart from food!), entered. There was not much quality food left. No fillet steaks or lobster thermidore but plenty of bread, jam, cheese and marmalade. To us this was nectar so we set about buttering bread, spreading jam and eating. However, very soon after we heard heels clicking on the marble floor and voices raised and laughing. Oh dear! we had been caught in the act.

What would the P.O.W.s in Stalag Luft III have done? Quickly we slid under the table, hidden from view because of the length of the table cloth and kept very quiet. The staff members were very boisterous and vocal, which perhaps helped our cause. As we sat out their supper time in our 'blanket' tent whilst they moaned that all the meat filling had gone and there was only jam left. They should complain! it was all that was left there for us as well and we were hungry.

Eventually they finished their supper and passed through the locked doors, locking the things behind them. That meant we had to retrace our 'under-the-floor' route back to the dormitory.

The return journey was uninteresting: we crept past the staff room again and managed to get back to our beds undiscovered but with full stomachs. An interesting prank that nobody else was aware of. It was nice to remain undetected, because that way we were able to repeat the exercise later

Perhaps the trip along the heating pipes helped shape my life as an engineer, by giving me an introduction to and appreciation of piped heating systems, amongst other things.

Frank Irwin (1950-1957)
Now living in Wirral

TOPPERS

Evening meal, tea as we called it in those long ago days, consisted of something hot and after that a small piece of margarine about 25mm x 25mm x 5mm, with as much bread as you were able to spread it on.

As generally the crust of the loaf was somewhat thicker than an inner slice, you could make your margarine (a 'butter' we called it) go much further by eating one of the crusts. We called these 'toppers'.

Therefore whilst queuing up in the corridor outside the dining room, we would make our claim, stating, 'I bags the first topper on our plate', priority being given to whoever was nearest the front of the queue.

A 'butter' was a good bargaining tool. If you wanted an extra sausage for example, it could usually be swapped for half a butter. To go one better I used to use the money I made from sweepstakes on the Grand National, pools, etc. to get a dayboy to purchase half a pound of margarine for me, with the express purpose of swapping it in 'half butters' for other boys unwanted food, thereby eating better and still being able to consume my share of bread and margarine.

Frank Irwin (1950-1957)
Now living in Wirral

CATHEDRAL SUNDAY

One year I had the dubious privilege of leading the school into Liverpool Cathedral on what was called 'Cathedral Sunday' wearing the silly 'tailed', 'pale blue' suits. On those occasions, you were officially the school macebearer.

The mace was a beautiful wooden octagonal shaft, in a brittle wood, probably boxwood, topped off by a sensational silver head with lots of engraving on it.

The bottom end, was tapered and adorned with a close fitting silver end. When I say 'fitted', I mean it was a tight fit, not physically screwed or anything like that.

Just before leaving school that Sunday, I was bullied into letting the mace out of my possession for a few minutes whilst some little sod (can't remember who) showed off, trying to emulate American cheer leaders and marchers to John Souser's music. The outcome was that the mace parted from its silver conical end, landed a distance away and the wooden shaft broke into three pieces.

The person responsible then ran off, leaving me to face the music. Remember, nobody ever 'sneaked' on another person in those days.
I repaired it with sticking plaster, supplied by Mr. Derek Jones, and carried the thing into the cathedral anyway. Obviously the repair was not of a good standard, because I was found out and sacked as mace bearer. Now having only just been promoted to that position, the episode cost me a lot of money, because, on Speech Day, the mace bearer got a lot of tips from dignitaries and official visitors and I was replaced by another boy who reaped the rewards instead.

Frank Irwin (1950-1957)
Now living in Wirral

MEMORIES OF A MURDER

There was a little 'ditty' that we used to sing occasionally, after what was known as the 'Cameo Cinema Murders' had taken place.

'My name is Kelly-o', 'I sell ice-cream-io', 'Outside the Cameo', 'I shot a Man-io'.

This double-murder was perhaps the first that had sufficient publicity to come to the attention of us schoolboys. Being a local murder made it all the more interesting in a macabre sort of way. The search for the murder weapon and for evidence to convict the supposed perpetrators was keenly followed by many of us, and perhaps that is why such memories of the events remain so vividly to this day. Picton Road even became known to us as 'Murder Mile'.

The Cameo Cinema murders, took place in 1949; in 1950 George Kelly was hanged for the murders of the cinema manager Leonard Thomas and his assistant John Bernard Catterall. At the original trial, both he and Charles Connolly were charged with murder, but the jury failed to agree a verdict.

At his second trial, George Kelly was found guilty of murder; Charles Connolly was tried separately, charged with robbery and conspiracy, and served 10 years in prison, being released in 1960. He always protested his innocence.

Both George Kelly and Charles Connolly had both been on the wrong side of the law as petty criminals for some years, but not in collaboration with each other. It was probably thought that as a dealer in black-market goods, he deserved everything that came his way.

The father of one of the Blue Coat boys was a policeman at the time and one day he took the young lad to see the Bee Hive public house on Mount Pleasant where it was stated at the time, that the robbery which resulted in the double murder, was planned.

He also showed him the muddy pond just to the west of Edge Hill railway sidings, where the murder weapon was supposedly disposed of but never found. The death sentence on George Kelly was carried out at Liverpool's Walton Prison on March 28th 1950. The Chief Hangman who performed that day was the famous Albert Pierrepoint and he was assisted by Harry Allen.

Who put the story out that Kelly was a petty thief? The Liverpool & Bootle Police Constabulary. How did they know? One of Kelly's best customers was none other than Chief Inspector Balmer. Balmer was also having a relationship with Kelly's partner while Kelly was touring the city centre pubs. So, the family and friends of George Kelly have lived all these years with the knowledge of George's innocence of having been a murderer, but, still having the finger of suspicion pointed at him by those who have not bothered to find out the details of the case and who have chosen to believe the police.

Since then, further evidence has proved both of them were not guilty (in fact, they'd never met and didn't even know each other!) and both of them were subsequently declared not guilty. At the Appeal Court hearing of 2003 that quashed Kelly's murder conviction; Lord Justice Rix said, 'However much the Cameo murders remain a mystery we regard the circumstances of Kelly and Connolly's trial as a miscarriage of justice which must be deeply regretted.'

The Liverpool Chief Constable at that time had had a vendetta against both men (especially Kelly) and had ensured that the evidence given at that time sent him to the gallows when he was still only in his twenties. In addition he failed to disclose information which pointed the finger of guilt elsewhere. As a result of this gross miscarriage of justice, the real killer(s) were never caught.

In the 1980s whilst Charles Connolly was working as a doorman at Litherland Theatre Club, Stan encountered him and found him to be a very quiet, easy-going gentleman who certainly didn't deserve to serve such a large portion of his life in prison.

So much then for the legal system in Britain; Chief Inspector Herbert Balmer was never challenged over falsifying or failing to provide the complete evidence. Law and Order! A bit of justice would do for a start.

Hubert Manwaring, Stan Livingston, Dave Bolt & Frank Irwin

THE CHOIRBOY WHO NEVER WAS

It was a pleasant Sunday evening. The sun had been shining and everybody was generally feeling good and reasonably satisfied after a Sunday dinner comprising roast beef, Yorkshire pudding, roast and boiled potatoes with soggy cabbage as the vegetable of the day.

Having donned my polished shoes, duly buffed up on the back of my trouser legs, and wearing my 'Sunday suit' from the locker room, smartly dressed and well washed, I made my way to evensong.

As we lined up, two abreast ready to march into chapel, Dr. Dickerson's 'Slow March' or 'The Dirge' as some called it, started up. We marched slowly in through the door and, walking past proud (or otherwise) parents who were able to attend owing to the proximity of their living accommodation, we took our pews.

Where I sat that day was directly in front of a teacher's pew at the front of the chapel, slightly to the south of the chancel itself. Mr. G.G. Watcyn who was both the headmaster and also as a Doctor of Divinity (D.D.) the minister, took his place in the chancel with the choir already seated in their designated places. After initial prayers, the first hymn was duly announced and as I intoned the words rather quietly (my singing wasn't up to much), I was amazed to hear Garvey a fellow schoolboy, who happened to be sitting next to me, singing like a canary, wonderfully well.

I naturally continued my low level singing, particularly as I was directly in front of the teacher, Mr. Crebbin, in the pew ahead of me and I didn't want him to hear my inferior intonations.

Hymns and Psalms continued followed by a sermon by Mr. Watcyn and eventually after being treated to this wonderful singing by Garvey, the service ended and those fortunate enough, including myself, were visited by our parents for a short while. I remember receiving some sweets and sixpence. (This was not really permitted, but if you wanted the opportunity to make some money at cards, you naturally needed a stake!)

The next day I was summoned to Mr. Crebbin's room. I was full of trepidation, because for me, such summonses usually meant only one thing, punishment with the cane or the slipper. On this occasion Old Crebbin was smiling. I thought, 'He is a little more sadistic than usual; there could be trouble ahead'. However, to my amazement, he praised my singing in the chapel that day.

Now my singing, as mentioned earlier, leaves a lot to be desired, but me being me, and being glad that I was not after all going to be punished, accepted his praise and said 'Thank you.' Mr. Crebbin then went on to say that with such a voice, I really should be in the chapel choir.

Now at that time, it was the custom, for choir boys to be taken out of school on a fortnightly basis, to see a film at some local cinema. For a boarder, a super treat. Having by now realised that what Mr. Crebbin heard was not actually me, but Garvey who sat next to me, the thought of going to the cinema on a regular basis got the better of me and rather than embarrass him (oh yeah!) I decided to accede to his wish and allow him to put my name forward, which he duly did.

Now for those of you who remember Dr. Dickerson, he was a brilliant musician, even by his own admission. Apparently he came second at Music School to the great and well famed Sir Malcolm Sargent. No mean feat! He composed the school 'Slow March', used not only for chapel, but also for some occasions in the Shirley Hall, like Remembrance Sunday and also, if my memory serves me correctly, Speech Day, which actually was an academic awards day, complete with speeches. This march was also used on 'Cathedral Sunday' when a special service was held at Liverpool Anglican Cathedral, with the congregation being Blue Coat pupils, parents and any other interested party. Again, Dr. Dickerson played the cathedral organ for the service.

However, Dr. Dickerson's 'Achilles Heel' was that he was, as in today's politically correct language, audibly challenged. To boys of our era, he was deaf. For a little while during choir practices I took a full part, and managed to mime my way through proceedings, relying on Dr. Dickerson's reduced capacity to hear. He was such a good musician, that generally he ran proceedings without wearing his hearing aid, thus miming could be a limited success.

Unfortunately, after only one visit to the local picture house at the following practice he must have suspected something was amiss, because he decided that I must perform a solo number in front of the rest of the choir.

The conclusion of this story is that I made no more trips to the 'flicks' and my few days as a choirboy came abruptly to an end.

Frank Irwin (1950-1957)
Now living in Wirral

AN EARLY DISAPPOINTMENT

The scripture teacher, Mr. Slater, has been mentioned a couple of times elsewhere in this book so I thought I would describe how he disappointed me in my earliest days at the school.

It was the 1955 summer holidays and I was due to start at the school when the autumn term began in September – a daunting prospect for any kid who had scarcely ever been away from home in their life up to that point.

How pleased I was, therefore, when Stan (three years older than me and by now a veteran pupil) informed me that he had agreed to go to the school one afternoon and help Mr. Slater do some gardening.

Here was an opportunity, I thought, not only to get a good look at the place and familiarise myself with the layout, etc., but also to get to know one of my future teachers and become known to him; all of which would undoubtedly help to ease me into the new life when term began.

I therefore accompanied Stan when the time came round and I recall that the particular spot where I was put to work by Mr. Slater was the corner of the quadrangle by the 1G classroom. An abiding memory from that day is that Michaelmas daisies figured largely in those flowerbeds. I worked hard and felt that I had succeeded in my aim of becoming a known individual to Mr. Slater; surely a safe bet given that he was a man of God and therefore presumably a 'people-oriented' type of guy?

Not a bit of it! When term began, Mr. Slater took my class (1M) for quite a lot of the time because he was covering both scripture and science, but I never got the feeling that he remembered me. This and other subsequent incidents concerning him taught me that he was a surprisingly 'cold fish' for a man of religion and an ex-missionary, but down the years I have encountered people with a similar background who display the same coldness of spirit. Perhaps the title of a new book just published by a minister offers us a clue to their personality type; he has called it *Behave!*

Ray Livingston (1955-1959)
Now living in York

REMEMBRANCE SUNDAY

As an annual event at the school, Remembrance Sunday was an afternoon service held in Shirley Hall. With the organ to the rear of the stage and behind the boys, a terraced set of long flat benches would be laid out in two halves, with sufficient seating to accommodate the 120 or so boarders in the school at that time.

These benches then faced away from the stage and towards the doors that lead to the entrance used for such occasions by the congregation: the end of the main school entrance hall in fact.

Visitors and parents would enter through the main doors and walk along a, very nice in its day, and extremely traditional for the time, corridor, lined with oil paintings.

I seem to remember Yeames's 'And when did you last see your father?' and Gainsborough's 'Blue Boy' being hung on the wall somewhere, although given the time scale I may well be mistaken. I cannot imagine they were originals so they must have been reproductions, but they well fitted the décor of a traditional boarding school of the era.

On arriving in Shirley Hall, visitors would be directed to chairs facing the set of benches, filling up from the front. I never recall seeing empty rows at the front as is so prevalent today.

The picture shows Shirley Hall as it was then but this service was in 1949 held as a 'service of farewell to the girls.' The seats for the pupils was then to the side rather than how it was in my day.

All being seated and kitted out with 'Order of Service' sheets, the congregation would await the entrance of the boys. Eventually, Dr. Dickerson would take up his position at the organ and begin playing the music for his own slow march, so well known and well practised music, almost second nature to us boarders.

We would enter from doors to the right of the stage as viewed by the congregation, march behind the benches, down between them away from the stage and split off to each side until we were all accommodated within the benching.

The music would stop and the service would begin. The traditional hymns associated with the time, the eleventh hour of the eleventh day of the eleventh month used to be sung by all, but the occasion had some individual elements in it.

Eight boys would be selected each year, not always senior boys, but certainly boys who had powers of recall and reasonable speech. They would take part in a catechism involving set pronouncements and prescribed answers.

I particularly remember 'They shall beat their swords into ploughshares and their spears into pruning hooks, Nation shall not lift up sword against Nation, neither shall they learn war anymore' (Isaiah 2:4) being a part of it. Towards the end of the service would come, as a school tradition the hymn 'O Valiant Hearts.' After the verse that ends with the line 'Who wait the last clear trumpet call of God', the 'Last Post' would be played on a bugle. After that the last verse always seemed to be sung with added vigour, 'Long years ago, as earth lay dark and still, arose a loud cry, upon a lonely hill. Tranquil you lie, your kindly virtue proved, your memory hallowed in the land you loved.'

Somewhere within the service I remember singing the refrain: 'Greater love hath no man than this; that a man lay down his life for his friends. (John 15:13) His memorial will last from generation to generation.' At the end of the service, our parents and visitors would be allowed access to us in the dining room whilst we consumed a meal that had been prepared for them to see the standard of culinary cuisine available to us on a regular basis!!!!

Ray points out that, although I used the genteel word 'consumed', the word 'demolished' would be more accurate and appropriate! He was a visitor with his mother on two occasions before he himself became a pupil and he recalls that she later urged Stan (his elder brother) to grab his fair share of the food at mealtimes as otherwise he would be left hungry and would not grow properly. Latin verbs and the periodic tables had no doubt been successfully grasped by the boys, but table manners had been deferred indefinitely.

Those were the days, with books like R.F. Denderfield's *To Serve Them All My Days* when you were expected to lay down your life for your friends and for your country and to rejoice in it as well. How things have changed. Now for many people, life is about getting as much as they can from the State (not realising it is taxpayers' money) without doing anything to earn it.

The soldier's hat has changed to a hood (hug a hoodie!) and the shiny boots we used to polish as army cadets have been replaced by trainers. Whatever happened to shoes?

We now send soldiers off to fight wars that do not concern us; should we wonder why we forget the defence of our nation during two World Wars? What comes to the fore in our minds is the unnecessary slaughter of our soldiers, airman and mariners in wars for oil and in attempts to force democracy on foreign states that are still living back in the days of the Crusades and who have no wish to become democratic. We send financial aid and protect members of other religions in far away places and in return we are accused of fighting against the same religion we are attempting to protect. No wonder both the public and the armed forces become confused.

We still have the necessary battles to protect our Sovereign states and rightly so, but why do we seem to become embroiled in other people's wars? Schoolboys today, seeing the roles played by our armed forces, cannot truly visualise nor see the reason to remember the essential battles to maintain our freedom and to defend our country from invasion forces who wished to crush us into the ground and to change our valued way of life forever. We should and must maintain the tradition of remembering those who fell in conflicts and continue with war memorials and 'Remembrance' services, despite what the P.C. brigade say about upsetting others. They deserve that much at least for what they gave to our once great country - their lives.

Frank Irwin (1950 – 1957)
Now living in Wirral

RECYCLING

People talk these days of the need for recycling. This of course to any 'Old Blue' of the Blue Coat School is nothing new at all.

Recycling back in the 1950s was not born out of any need to save the planet or for any other altruistic reason; it was purely a matter of survival.

Imagine a hot sunny Saturday; lunch at school was over and a number of boarders are due to walk to the Lance Lane playing fields to play cricket.

Being a hot day, we were rather thirsty and all that was available to us was warm water from the school washroom taps. Lance Lane stadium would not prove to be an oasis for us either as there were no facilities there other than a ramshackle tin roofed shed, which only just managed to keep the rain off our clothes as we changed within. So then, as Tommy and I wandered over, our minds turned to how were we going to get something nice and cool to slake our thirsts.

As we approached Lance Lane, there was for those who remember, a block of shops running at right angles to the lane and the end shop on the corner was a sweet shop. Now that sweet shop had the answer to our prayers, home made lolly ices in various flavours for the princely sum of 1d. each. (Note 1d. not 1p.). So far so good, but we didn't have any money, because it was not allowed in those days, the usual currency used in the school for bartering, etc., was either sweets from the tuck shop or food from mealtimes. (A sausage could be swapped for half a butter.)

The shop had a rear yard where all the returned bottles and redundant packaging, crates etc. were kept. This rear yard was surrounded by a rather high wall to prevent unauthorised entry by miscreants and potential thieves.

In the WWII books we had been reading, high walls and fences didn't stop escapees, similarly, this wall should not stop a determined access. Tommy gave me a 'leg up' and once at the top, I could see that after dropping down on the other side, I would be able to climb back as there were lemonade bottle crates stacked against the wall. I dropped down and gathered two empty bottles, passed them up to Tommy and proceeded to climb back over the wall. Now in those days, in order to encourage recycling it was customary for those persons returning bottles to receive 2d. per bottle. I would guess the 2d. was added to the initial charge, so you weren't actually gaining anything, but it did make you determined to return bottles after use, providing you could afford to buy one in the first place.

Tommy and I duly walked into the shop, re-cycled our bottles and received our 4d. Problem solved. We each had a penny-lolly-ice before the game and sufficient money to purchase two more afterwards.

Frank Irwin (1950-1957)
Now living in Wirral

GRACE

It was the custom, before and after every meal, for a boy to volunteer to say grace. If a volunteer wasn't forthcoming, which would be very unusual, somebody would be chosen by the master in charge. Apparently these graces were unique to the school.

The grace said before meals, was:

'We beseech thee Heavenly Father, to sanctify these thy creatures, to the nourishment of our bodies, and to feed our souls with thy heavenly grace unto eternal life, through Jesus Christ our Lord. Amen.'

The grace said after meals, was:

'Thanks be to thy holy name o most merciful father, for these present refreshments of our bodies, for our daily bread, and for all thy mercies conferred upon us from time to time, through Jesus Christ our Lord, Amen.'

BULLYING TEACHERS.

Thinking back on schooldays in the 1950s, it is amazing now to remember just what we put up with. Reports from all quarters recall, quite clearly, teachers who would pick boys up from the floor by holding their sideboards between their fingers. One Old Blue, who wishes to remain anonymous, reports that, as a punishment, he was hit on both hands with running 'spikes'!

A particular teacher would hit you on the head with a heavy bunch of keys in his hand, drawing blood! Another took great delight in throwing the wooden board duster at the unprotected heads of boys in the classroom.

And teachers who, when about to cane you, would not get it over with quickly but would select canes for use in front of your eyes, whip them about a little, then decide to select another one from the cupboard. Eventually the sadistic little so and so, would proceed to whack you as hard as possible.

Even Albert Pierrepoint the hangman, when capital punishment was in force, got the hanging over with in less than 10 seconds from entering the condemned cell, to the hapless victim being certified as dead.

This torture by delay was probably learned from wartime experiences. It seemed that quite a few of the teachers may have been getting over their wartime problems at our expense, some better than others.

There was a story, distinctly recalled, of boys being caned on their gluteus maximii whilst vaulting over the box in the gymnasium and one particular case where a boy was given corporal punishment in front of all the boarders, in Shirley Hall, presumably as a warning to all.

In fact one ex-pupil stated that when he left school, had he gone to prison or joined the British Army, he would never have known the difference.

There have been many reports of teachers thumping boys for various reasons and not all appear to be justified. Suffice it to say that whilst we, on the receiving end, regarded this kind of treatment as normal at that time, these punishments meted out today would result in those delivering it being incarcerated in Wormwood Scrubs. That is always presuming the government of the day could provide sufficient space for them!

Unsurprisingly, one or two prefects are also known to have behaved badly; probably inspired by the violent methods they had observed being employed by certain masters, but in at least one instance taking things a stage further.

One ex-pupil recalls that one particular prefect formed the appalling habit of standing in the middle of the dormitory holding a book in the palm of each hand. He would then order a misbehaving boy to approach him, and when he obeyed he would clap his head between the two books! The assumed close bond between masters and prefects meant that one knew it would be pointless to attempt to raise a complaint about such matters. *But it must be stressed that only a few masters and prefects behaved violently.*

Frank Irwin (1950-1957), Hubert Manwaring-Spencer (1948-1955) and Ray Livingston. (1955-1959)

THE BEATLES CONNECTION

The school's barber, Bioletti, had his shop a short distance away from the school. 'Bioletti's-toi-oh-letti', we would joke. Subsequently, he and his shop were immortalised by the Beatles in the song *Penny Lane,* and about ten years ago the shop front was used for a scene in the Beatles' video *Real Love.* Several of the things mentioned in *Penny Lane* were actually on Smithdown Road and were familiar to our pupils.

Ray Livingston (1955-1959)
Now living in York

FIREWORKS

Some of us were of a mischievous frame of mind, forever on the lookout for something to do. One of our annual activities, the morning after bonfire night, involved hotfooting it out to the north yard to search for unexploded fireworks left lying around from the previous night's celebrations. These were carefully taken to pieces and the differing explosive contents mixed together. Normally, the resultant hoard was re-constituted into an enormous firework and exploded anonymously, much to our great amusement.

One year we decided to do something special! A piece of string was pulled several times through a tin of boot polish, lit, and the flame then blown out to create a smouldering 'fuse'. This was carefully timed to enable us to create a fuse to give the desired time interval prior to the detonation of the explosive.

We chose a Sunday morning for the detonation, with the fuse timed to take us to the middle of Mr. Watcyn's sermon. The explosive was placed in the south toilets near the chapel. The resultant explosion could not be missed and caused much giggling amongst the conspirators. Later more sophisticated developments, directly resulting from chemistry lessons, led to us making a home-made explosive from sulphur, sodium chlorate and soot. Normally it was used to propel rockets incorporating a copper 'waisted' sleeve (made in metalwork classes!) at the combustion end to avoid a 'blow out'.

These rockets had stabiliser fins and were known to have reached the height of the dormitory block, or as on occasions, blowing up in mid air. These pranks, if that's what they were, took place just outside the staff room albeit at weekends and we were never rumbled. Eventually, one of our enterprising bunch had a spark plug brazed into a copper tube with nichrome wire between the electrodes. A battery, gunpowder, and a wooden projectile were all that were then needed for some very impressive results. I do not touch-type but use two of my ten digits - was I not blessed with a lucky escape?

Eric Woodbine (1953-1959)
Now living in France.

THE ANNUAL LIVERPOOL SHOW

I'd never heard of this event before I came to the Blue Coat, but one day in June 1956 as I played in the yard at the north end of the school I heard a great deal of banging and commotion coming from over the boundary wall and I was informed that it was the marquees, etc., being erected on The Mystery. I also learned that it was an annual event.

The show ran for about three days, I think, so it was still going on Sunday when we boarders were freed for the two hours 2 p.m. to 4 p.m. and many of us seized the opportunity to attend; it made an interesting change from the usual destinations such as Sefton Park and Calderstones Park. It comprised a wide variety of exhibits and you could learn a surprising amount about services like water and gas.

Many commercial firms had stands and they too were enjoyable to visit. The forces were well represented and I remember resisting the temptation to try a simulated parachute drop - a 1950s equivalent of a bungee jump. The nose cone and cockpit of a Hawker Hunter fighter was a highlight for me one year.

About five years ago I made a special effort and took my wife to experience the modern-day version of the event but - perhaps inevitably - it was not in keeping with my 1950s memories; rampant commercialism and raucousness seemed to rule. It was also sad to look across at the school and know that boarding had come to an end several years before.

Ray Livingston (1955-1959)
Now living in York

ANOTHER FAVOURITE SINGING DITTY

There is a prison camp far, far away,
Where we get bread and jam five times a day.
Egg and bacon we don't see.
Dirty great beetles in our tea!
That's why we are gradually, faaaaading away.

THE TWO LAVATORY BLOCKS

There was a block at the end of the tennis courts on the south side of the school and another at the north end, adjacent to the playground, both of which structures are still in existence but used for new purposes. They were basically adequate from the constructional point of view but were not, to my recollection at least, adequately maintained on a day to day basis.

Thus they were not pleasant places to visit and I may not have been the only one who often postponed his visits for hours; or sometimes days.

A much more pleasant option was to use a dormitory toilet, but of course the dormitories were out of bounds in the daytime. Of the two blocks, the one to the north end of the premises was by far the worst, everyone seems to agree.

Periodically, one saw groups of parents being shown those places and I can only imagine that Mr. Flynn must have been deliberately detailed to precede them or the school might have ended up with no pupils!

In fairness to the school authorities and Mr. Flynn, they were up against a few antisocial boys who thought it a joke to, for instance, throw a toilet roll down the pan and block it up, so poor Mr. F's life can't have been much fun.

Ray Livingston (1955-1959)
Now living in York

LIFE-SAVING CLASSES

One of the more popular pursuits amongst the competent swimmers in the school, was life saving classes. For a set number of evenings we assembled in a classroom to study physiology and to learn and practice things like, land drill, release from the clutch of the drowning and artificial respiration as it was called in those days.

After that had been accomplished we spent a set number of evenings each week at Picton Road swimming baths, a nearby Liverpool Council swimming pool, where we learned how to put into practice all the things we had been taught in the classroom.

This actually included rescuing pretend stranded and struggling swimmers and moving them to the edge of the pool. We had to swim to the bottom of the deep end, fully dressed and collect a brick from the bottom, then swim 100 yards whilst still fully dressed. Rescuing the drowning involved the use of a number of methods as did the release from their clutches: all good stuff. The rewards came at the end, though. As well as receiving medals we were awarded contracts for use in all the Liverpool Council baths, free of charge at any time that the establishments were open.

The idea being, there were likely to be a number of qualified life savers on hand should the need arise, as in those days we did not see the risk assessments and all the health and safety requirements that are so prevalent today. There were baths attendants on hand, but nothing like the supervision seen in swimming baths today.

So as well as rewards in two forms, we also got out for number of evenings to swim as after the training we were allowed half an hour to ourselves for enjoyment.

The picture shows the two medals that I was awarded in 1954 & 1955. The Royal Life saving Society's Bronze Medallion and the Bronze Cross.

Frank Irwin (1950-1957)
Now living in Wirral

SCRIPTURE EXAM

It was end of summer term examinations in Class 2G. End of term exams were always the most important as it was that time that determined who was top of the class before moving up a year to 3G.

Grammar School exams naturally differed from those in the secondary modern stream because different subjects were taught in most cases; however not in all. This particular year, 2M had their scripture exam on a Wednesday morning and we in 2G were due to be tested that same afternoon.

Over dinner, the conversation naturally centred on the morning's examinations. One member of 2M, whose name eludes me, was telling a group us about the scripture exam they had undergone that morning. One thing he mentioned was that afterwards the teacher, again whose name I cannot recall but may have been Mr. Slater, passed comment about one question in particular.

It seems that in the question he had asked something like this. 'Who did more to provoke the Lord God of Israel to anger, than all his predecessors?' The teacher passed comment that a one-word answer was all that was necessary, *Ahab!* Then asked why had all the boys spent so much time writing about it. We were then told about all the other questions on the paper.

It seemed likely that there would be some similarity between the paper for 2M and 2G because there was no differentiation required in scripture lessons. The group of us spent the rest of dinner time looking up references to the questions to know just what to write about should there be any repetition.

Luckily our group had a lad called Pettersen amongst us, who always came top in scripture, because when we got our exam paper that afternoon, it was identical to the one that 2M had that morning. The result was that Pettersen came top with 100% and I and somebody else came joint 2nd with 99% each. (I wonder if that report is still at my mum's house). Had Pettersen not come top, there could have been an investigation.

The five of us were congratulated for giving a one word answer to that 'Ahab' question, when most people rambled on. There must have been some suspicion, but I guess had the teacher concerned raised the matter, he would have had a problem explaining how it came about that we both had identical papers.

When I arrived home at the end of the term, my dad read the report, and actually asked me if I wished to enter the clergy when I finished school.

Frank Irwin (1950-1957)
Now living in Wirral

SUICIDE

One day a new teacher, Mr. Moore arrived at the school to teach mathematics. It was rumoured that he had been a criminal lawyer who had had a nervous breakdown and so had reverted to teaching in order to have an easier life. Well he had chosen the wrong school. Firstly, if a teacher has had mental problems, the last thing that should happen, is that the Blue Coat boys be informed about it: all that would do would be to create a challenge.

Mr. Moore duly turned up and was found to have a broad Lancashire accent. His first lesson showed that he had a slight hearing defect, because a boy, at one side of the class made a popping noise by rubbing his finger inside his mouth against his cheek (I am sure you all know the noise).

Mr. Moore's reaction was to look somewhere in the general direction and to ask in his broad accent 'Who made that noise?' to which, somebody else at the other side of the room repeated the exercise to be greeted with 'There it is again! Who is making that noise?' Because the culprits were undiscovered, the popping noises increased. Mr. Moore went blue saying, 'Now I know who is making that noise, and when I find him, I will put my fist right through him.'

To make matters worse, although he did not live in the school, for some reason he took turns as duty master on a rota system. Because we believed he had been a criminal lawyer, his first evening session was a nightmare.

At this time, in the two senior dormitories, boarders slept in cubicles. Senior dormitory, one boy per cubicle, and in the second one, four boys to a cubicle. The cubicles were made from studded partition lined with hardboard sheets and an open space in the front without a door served for access and egress. On one of his rounds in the second senior dormitory, Mr. Moore was greeted with the sight of a boy hanging by the neck from one of the entries to a cubicle. The dormitory lights were out, but those in the toilet block (The Offey) were on, creating a backlit spectacle.

Mr. Moore ran down the dormitory shouting 'What has happened, oh what is going on?' until he arrived at the scene of the apparent execution or suicide. What he discovered was a dressing gown and pyjamas, stuffed with other clothes and a mop sticking through the dummy to resemble a head, all hanging by a dressing gown cord.

That was enough for Mr. Moore, he ran out of the dormitory. The perpetrator then removed the dummy, replaced all the clothes, got back into bed and that was the last we ever heard of the episode.

Frank Irwin (1950-1957)
Now living in Wirral

OUR FAVOURITE SHOP?

Very soon in my time at the Blue Coat – perhaps as early as my very first Sunday Walk - I was introduced to a certain shop down Smithdown Road that sold most of the items that were desirable to a schoolchild; things like Dinky toys, comics and probably sweets as well. I can't believe that there could be a single Blue Coat pupil of our period who did not at some time walk into that shop.

It was located on the north side of the road and at a point, I estimate, opposite Russell Road. Examining the spot with Google Earth reveals that it has now been demolished and the ground that it stood on allowed to grass over.

A particular memory I have of the place was a stand that contained *Classics Illustrated* comics.

These introduced young people to a selection of the great classics of literature and it struck me then, and still does, that it was a good idea. I don't think I could afford them when I was newly arrived at the school but I either borrowed or bought one or two subsequently – Jules Verne's *Mysterious Island*, Mark Twain's *The Prince and the Pauper* and Jack London's *The Call of the Wild* spring to mind. The art work was good and I'm sure many children reading them would have been encouraged to go and seek out the book itself. It's a shame that they are no longer sold.

Ray Livingston (1955-1959)
Now living in York

THE KITCHEN RAID

One evening, feeling somewhat hungry, four or five of us decided to go on a raid in search of any goodies that may have been left out in the kitchen. Maybe this is where I acquired my nickname 'Plum duff' (always thinking of my stomach), anyway, I recall being the first in through the window and putting my foot in a big bowl of rice pudding which had been placed on a table beneath it. Needless to say we were brought to account and got our just desserts (pun intended).

Dave Kennedy (1948 -1955)
Now living in Wirral.

PEG LEG

In the 1950s the 'Western Front', as it was known, was filled completely with air raid shelters, still remaining after giving essential service during the war; an area that was out of bounds to us and was shrouded in mystery. I never ever remember exploring there but somebody must have done, perhaps I was scared!

Anyway, whenever a new boarder started at school, on his first night in the dormitory, he would be told about 'Peg Leg' who had lost his son in the war, lived in the shelters of the 'Western Front', and on first night back at school, would visit all new boys to see if one was in fact his son. This story would be laid on a bit thick, to ensure that all new boys were somewhat nervous of the forthcoming visit.

They would be told that the best way to stay safe was to snuggle down in bed and to cover themselves up with the bedclothes (sheets, blankets and a red coloured counterpane!)

Later in the night, when the new boy was duly hiding in his bed, he would be nudged to ensure he was awake, then 'Peg Leg' would arrive. A boy using a brush handle as an artificial leg, would walk down the dormitory, using the brush handle as alternate steps, with a definite bang, sounding just like Long John Silver from *Treasure Island*. As he approached the new boy's bed, all the others would jump on him and punch him through the bed clothes so that he thought he was being punished by 'Peg Leg'.

The next morning, the new boy would tell everybody that he had been visited by 'Peg Leg' to which everybody else would reply, 'We never heard a thing.'

I learned recently, that the east corridor, which in our time was always in darkness and unused, is now known as 'Peg Leg's corridor as he used to 'live' there! Obviously some traditions do not die out, but merely move on to a new phase of myth and school lore.

Frank Irwin (1950-1957)
Now living in Wirral

FOOD

We ate some odd things with, occasionally, doubtful provenance. Scouse was a good example, in which any meat might be used and the diner certainly was kept in ignorance on that score. I don't share Frank Irwin's recollection of margarine since I'm sure we always had butter, particularly at breakfast time. This was 'extended' by mashing in with ones syrup portion to make it go further, due to the fact that extra bread was normally forthcoming if the head of table allowed a boy to ask the duty master. Also, our occasional banana was mashed up for the same reason. My favourite meal was scalloped potatoes with baked beans. Subsequently I have never found a batter thick enough to create the thick, crunchy coating which 'Ma' Byers managed to achieve. It is a source of angst to me that I have only tried it twice since school and both times the batter would not pass muster!

As said before, extra bread might be forthcoming if there was something to put on it. Furtive movements were often to be observed as some people opened a hidden jar of jam or Bovril. I persuaded my mother to let me take a jar of jam back to school after one holiday. Initially she refused, being a stickler for the rules without actually knowing what they were! Imagine my horror, some weeks into term, when a hairy, white growth was perceived! Penicillin perhaps! Given that the jam was home-made thus lacking in antioxidants etc., I should not have been surprised. Once scraped off, the jam still tasted good.

One time, Tan Tan was the duty master and he hit a boy who was sitting down at the table (had he been standing up, Tan Tan could not have reached him). This caused silent outrage amongst the 100 or so of up there present. What could we do? We were helpless. Strangely, someone walked out with a plate and asked for more bread (a bit like a better dressed Oliver Twist). Granted permission, the boy headed off to the kitchen to see the matron whereupon another boy asked the same and another and so on. Tan Tan went apoplectic and forbade further bread rations. It was, as I saw it, a spontaneous silent protest.

Once per week, we were allowed a quarter of sweets which was paid for out of the pocket money lodged with Mr. Walter Crebbin at the beginning of term. Inevitably, there were boys lurking about waiting to be paid in kind for debts incurred. For some strange reason, I decided to collect sweet papers and, over time, was able to create a remarkably unimpressive collection. However, I was able to sell it to someone later! Again, some boys were given items by their parents not available to most of us. One chap had a record player and several Lonnie Donegan EPs. I well remember the B.B.C. banning 'You've been digging my potatoes.' It's amazing how lines like 'I thought you was my friend until I caught you in my bed' and, 'I love you in the winter and I love you in the fall, but between those blankets, I love you best of all,' could offend the system.

Eric Woodbine (1953-1959)
Now living in France.

THE AMMONIA CAPER

It was the last period in the morning and we were in the chemistry laboratory with Mr. Unwin, the chemistry teacher. The laboratory was then on the second floor on the west wing. It was early in the summer term, close to dinner time, when Mr. Unwin told everybody to clean up the benches and put things away. This was duly done and we were ready for our dinner when suddenly we all heard the question 'Who is making ammonia?' Nobody replied.

'Somebody is making ammonia!' still no answer! Mr. Unwin then proceeded to go around the laboratory sniffing all the benches, which by that time were all as clean as whistles: there were no traces of ammonia being made, but we could all smell it.

We left the laboratory and proceeded down the three flights of stairs, by the time we reached the ground floor the smell was much stronger. As we got closer to the dining hall, we noticed that the smell intensified and was absolutely awful! There, in a sight to behold was Mr. Watcyn, standing in the middle of a group, all of whom had tears in their eyes.

Mr. Watcyn was shouting at a student called Baker-Bates. He was a secondary modern student that I had known quite well because we were both in the school Army Cadets. He was a big tall lanky guy, and always keen and enthusiastic.

That morning, his class had a gardening lesson in the quadrangle and apparently, Baker-Bates had been given the job of mixing the compost heap. The school had bought some chemicals to help the composting process and if my memory serves me correctly, it was a 100lb. sack of ammonium nitrate and a 100lb. sack of lime. These chemicals are supposed to be layered alternatively with the soil and rotting vegetation, but it seems that Baker-Bates had just cut the sacks open and dumped the two chemicals into the pit and mixed the lot with his spade.......

The resultant reaction immediately produced a cloud of ammonia gas and, once started, there really was no way to stop it.

I am sure that the food in the dining room that lunchtime was ammonia flavoured and therefore tasted terrible.

I will never forget Mr. Watcyn's comments, which he shouted out in a clear, loud voice. 'Bates you fool! You shouldn't have done it.'

Dave Bolt (1951-1957)
Now living in Vancouver, BC

THE RAP

'Rapping' is not just a modern day thing, we used to sing a little ditty to a rap beat, as school holidays drew nearer, obviously the first word changed dependent upon how many days of term were left.

Three more days and where shall we be? Out of the gates of misery.
No more Latin, no more French, no more sitting on the old school bench.
No more dirty bread and butter, no more water from the gutter.
No more beetles in my tea, making goggly eyes at me.
No more spiders in my bath, trying hard to make me laugh.
If the teacher interferes, knock him down and box his ears.

Frank Irwin (1950-1957)
Now living in Wirral

FOOTBALL POOLS

Each school summer holiday, I would purchase a small book that used to be available, showing all the Football League fixtures for the duration of the following season and more importantly the fixtures for the following winter term at school.

Laboriously, I would write down the left hand side of a piece of foolscap paper, all the games to be played in what was then called, the 1st division, (Now the Premiership) for each forthcoming Saturday. In those days all games then had a common kick-off time of 3.pm, no Sky T.V. then. On the right hand side, I would draw columns, which along with the rows already there, would create boxes in which a forecast of each result could be placed.

Once back at school, each Saturday, instead of buying sweets with my pocket money, I would invite boys to forecast the results of the 1st division matches by placing either 1 (Home win) 2 (Away win), or X (Draw) in each of the boxes. There were no 'score' and 'no score' draws in those days; all were just draws.

The entry fee for this was two sweets. That was to say 'proper' sweets, not mint imperials which were twice as many in a ¼lb. compared with the real thing. The person who correctly guessed the most results was the winner. In the event of two people winning, the prize would be divided equally between the two. The prize available would depend on how many entered. I would deduct my management fee first and what was left over became the prize kitty. As the pools were always well subscribed, I always managed to have more than enough sweets for myself without having to buy any from the tuck shop.

In an attempt to make some actual money, I ran a sweepstake for the Grand National Steeplechase for quite some time for day-boy participation; with cash stakes (naturally I was to make a profit). Boarders only used sweets as per the football pools.

This was successful until during what was I think my last year at school I was summoned to Mr. Unwin's office and questioned about it. (It transpired 50 years later that Mr. Hulford was responsible for this and he has since apologised. However given his integrity I feel sure that he would do the same thing again, given the same circumstances). I was told in no uncertain terms that that this practice was to cease forthwith, but as I had taken money for this year's race, I could continue for the current year, but after that the gambling was to stop immediately.

Meanwhile Mr. Unwin asked how much the entry fee was and immediately bought a horse for the weekend's race. Had my revenue been curtailed like that today, perhaps I could have taken out litigation under E.U. rules on restriction of trade, rather like a schoolboy Bosman ruling!

Frank Irwin (1950–1957)
Now living in Wirral

NOCTURNAL ACTIVITIES

Night time was often used in summer as cover for expeditions around the school. This was usually aimed at a visit to the masters' dining room to scout for food. We never found a thing. Having read other accounts of similar activity (probably a couple of years before us), I'm not surprised since the practice must have been rumbled. One night, approaching the steps either side of the library, I looked up to see a 'ghost' on the stair and received a heart stopping jolt- stories of Peg Leg in earlier years had had some effect upon us. However, since the wraith disappeared as quickly as it appeared I had to investigate. We eventually discovered somehow that the moon projected itself to appear almost as an entity half way down the steps- a feverished young mind had been at work no doubt.

Another of these nocturnal affairs was used to prepare for the following morning - April 1st! At the side of the aforementioned stairs was the large, red school bell used to signal lesson changes etc. We taped the clapper such that it could not be moved. We hung around that day (not too close mind you for fear of giving ourselves away by smirking or whatever) 'till gone 9am at which point silence! The corridor was full of boys looking somewhat bewildered. Mr. Unwin eventually came thundering down the stairs to find out what was going on!

It was not the same year but two friends of mine (Geoff and Stan), in preparation for April 1st, ascended the school tower at night and draped a sheet from the balustrade above the clock face on the west elevation suitably painted with 'APRIL FOOL'. If my memory serves me correctly, they were both caned on bare backsides in front of the assembled boarders by Mr. Watcyn. I also believe that they were expelled!

Eric Woodbine (1953-1959)
Now living in France.

SCHOOL MACE BEARER

I and many others considered it to be quite an honour to be appointed as the school mace bearer, with the bonus of not having to sit through the whole service.

Well I decided this was the year that I Dave Kennedy, alias 'Plum duff' would carry the mace and lead his honour the Lord Mayor into Shirley Hall with all the pomp and ceremony that it entailed.

Well the first part went fantastically well and feeling a great deal of self importance, I retired to the side entrance (the stairway down towards the dining room) to read my *Hotspur* comic.

Soon after this Mr. Watcyn passed a message to me through the door to say that the Lord Mayor would be leaving the service early and that I was to be on hand to escort him out. Although I could not hear his message clearly, I thought it wise to just say 'Message understood' and then go back to my comic. The next minute, Mr. Watcyn was at the door, 'Come on' he cried 'he's going,' you can just imagine the Lord Mayor half way down Shirley Hall being chased by the mace bearer in a manner that lacked a certain amount of decorum. Alas I would not be mace bearer again, not for all the comics in the world.

Dave Kennedy (1948 -1955)
Now living in Wirral.

THE LAST BOARDER?

I wonder how many school leavers were in the same category as me - i.e. not 'marked out' in the Board Book, owing, presumably, to a faulty clerical system. Perhaps I can lay claim to being 'the last boarder' because of this oversight! I wonder where my bed is to be found nowadays. What time is breakfast?

At least it explains why I never received a Bible.

Ray Livingston (1955-1959)
Now living in York

THE CREAM CAKE RUN

One Sunday along with Peter Grand, (my best mate), I was summoned to the kitchen by Miss Warren, who you may remember was the head of catering at the school. On presenting ourselves, we were informed that she had chosen us, being honest and trustworthy characters, to perform what to us became known as the 'cream cake run'. Now, the run entailed collecting cream cakes from the kitchen on a Sunday afternoon and escorting them to the headmaster's house, which if you recall lay on the far side of the sports field.

As a reward for this service we each received a rather nice cream cake for our own consumption. I often wonder whether it was noticed that on some occasions the cream cakes we delivered were a wee bit short on cream, as now and again the temptation to take a finger-full of cream from each one was just too much to resist.

Dave Kennedy (1948 -1955)
Now living in Wirral.

HOMESICKNESS

My brother Stan had been at the school for three years when I joined him there in September 1955 so I was relatively well acquainted with its traditions and style, but regardless of this I found myself struck down by homesickness immediately and very badly that first evening (which was a Sunday as usual). The reasons were: (a) the strangeness and the scale of everything, (b) the evident iron discipline of Blue Coat life that would brook no soft, homely ways, (c) the fact that we were completely shut away from the outside world behind those walls, (d) the gloominess of the building. As some of our contributors have already remarked, being a boarder at Liverpool Blue Coat School was in some ways similar to being a prisoner in jail. That first traumatic evening formed a clear and abrupt dividing line between my two states of childhood - early and late - but I didn't know it at the time.

The tour I was given of the school by Stan included such places as the wardrobe room on the top floor, where our grey suits and our navy blue jackets were housed. The wardrobes, under the care of Mrs. Piperno, smelled of mothballs. He also showed me where the lockers were to be found (already described by Frank Irwin) and I selected one. We had been ordered to bring from home: a toilet bag, pyjamas, a Bible, a Common Prayer Book, a woodwork apron, a small padlock and a shoe-cleaning kit. These and any other personal items you had brought had to be crammed into the tiny locker space allotted to you and the padlock deployed to keep them secure. I was also shown the dormitory I was going to be in (Bingham, situated on the second floor) and the stark reality of that, and all the bustling activity going on, was unsettling.

A mug of the dishwater-quality tea in the dining room (remember those square-profile, pale-blue plastic mugs?) was not reassuring. Within an hour of saying goodbye to my mother I was pleading with Stan 'I hate being shut away from the outside world! Where can I go to still be able to see it?', whereupon he and his friend Andy Wilson took me to the tennis courts and over into the corner, where there was a pair of large wooden gates. 'Peer through the centre crack', they told me, 'and you will be able to look up the drive and glimpse cars passing along Church Road.' This was the best they could offer, and my feelings of imprisonment and homesickness grew still further – almost to a state of panic. By now I was realising what a strange, limited life I had embarked on in this place, and if I could have elected to vamoose right then and there and attend some other school instead, I'm sure I would have done it. When bedtime arrived, kindly Andy Wilson arranged for me to have the bed next to his own and I remember this being one of the few reassuring factors in the whole experience.

Of course, within a few weeks I had settled into the school and was little troubled by homesickness on a day to day basis, but I always found that going back after any holiday was a miserable experience for me all over again, and this never changed.

In about 1957, a little fellow called 'L******' arrived at the school and I still remember to this day how badly he suffered from homesickness. It hit him so badly, and apparently permanently, that I remember thinking that he really ought to be removed by his parent or parents. To my recollection this never happened, however, and I'm sure that the poor fellow must have been permanently traumatised by what he went through. At one stage I considered befriending him in the hope of helping him, but he was two or three years younger than me so I don't think I ever acted upon it.

Ray Livingston (1955-1959)
Now living in York

THE SATURDAY EVENING FILM SHOW

These ranged from the sublime (e.g. *Great Expectations*) to the dire (e.g. *The Shop at Sly Corner*) but usually you could rely on a good evening's entertainment. Westerns were frequently screened, reflecting their general popularity in Britain in that era. The film *Boys' Town* has been mentioned elsewhere in this book and rightly so, for it could have been made for an audience like ours.

By the way, a statue outside the actual school in America inspired The Hollies' famous 1969 hit *He Ain't Heavy – He's My Brother*. The statue depicts a boy carrying a younger boy on his back.

I am pleased to say that whoever it was who was choosing the films in 1955 when I first arrived had the good sense to show *Great Expectations* at a special morning film show, presumably at Christmas, and the unusual timing lent extra kudos to the film and made you devote proper attention to it. It remains to this day a serious contender for 'Britain's greatest film' and is certainly in the Top Ten. Many films were seen, of course, but I would single out the following for particular mention: *Young Tom Edison* and its partner film *Edison the Man, Dr. Jekyll and Mr. Hyde, Random Harvest*. Not only were these and many others enthralling as entertainment but also instructional about life, for it has to be remembered that we were impressionable youths and in need of a bit of culture.

The film show room was on the first floor, where the Scout Troop also convened, and was reached from the north corridor. The walls of the room had ancient paint that was bubbling and flaking off everywhere, but I quite liked that and would often sit admiring the shadows being cast as I waited for the film to begin. In 1978 when Stan and I visited the school, I was delighted to come across a surviving example of such paintwork that I could photograph; it was on the staircase leading up to the chapel. It seemed to be the result of dampness coming through the walls for one could also see salt stains that must have been coming from the bricks.

Ray Livingston (1955-1959)
Now living in York

MORE ON MOVIES

Apart from the Saturday evening movies for boarders, I remember that once or twice we were treated to a quite different type of film, shown to the whole school in an upstairs room directly above the gymnasium, the same room as described by Ray Livingston.

The films were in colour and presented by The Moody Bible Institute, this was some American group that I had never heard of before.

The films, although educational in a way, had a bit of a religious ring to them. I do recall, amongst other topics, seeing open heart surgery in vivid colour and being quite shocked at the time.

Well thirty years later, Sheila and I were down in Arizona and met a couple who were wearing Tee shirts, across which was blazoned, 'The Moody Bible Institute.' We had a chat and I understand that the institute still exists to this day; some things you never forget.

Dave Bolt. (1951-1957)
Now living in Vancouver, BC

THE MYSTERY MILE

The 'Mystery' was the name given to the Wavertree Playground, to the west of the school, across Prince Alfred Road from the 'Western Front'. It was given the name 'The Mystery', because it was donated to the city in perpetuity and the name of the donor was in fact a mystery. It was the site of the Annual Liverpool Show which was a major event in the Liverpool City calendar.

Annually, the boarders of the school competed in a race utilising the mystery and its footpaths called the 'Mystery Mile'. The race was for boarders only and was a compulsory event for all ages without a handicap being awarded to the younger boys. Naturally some boys were competing and others just wished the whole thing was over and done with.

The path of the race is shown in red on the plan and started to the rear of the school in Prince Alfred Road. After a mass start the boys would run like the 'clappers' for the gate opposite Holy Trinity Church, turn left and proceed down the footpath until they reached what was then a small circular timber built shelter, without walls. By this time the stragglers had begun to form their own little sector of, 'if we have to do it, we will do it slowly' runners.

At the shelter the racers turned left and ran across the park, again following the footpath up a slight incline until they reached a fairly large pavilion to the left. It was about this point that those runners who had been struggling to maintain a pace, beyond their standard, began to experience a 'stitch'. After the pavilion, the path became a slight decline until the gates at the bottom of Grant Avenue were reached. This gave a little respite for what was yet to come.

Running down the slight hill boys started to consider their positions; those who were tired simply attempted to completed the course (or got collected by staff if they had fallen by the wayside) but those trying seriously to win the race made their minds up about their strategies.

From the gates at the corner, Grant Avenue was a long sharp uphill track and it required some guts to decide to make a move from this point, but if the race was to be won, that was what was required. As the competitors reached what seemed to be the top or the end of Grant Avenue, a final sprint was called for. However, that was not the end of the matter, at that point, just when competitors felt the end was near, they turned a corner back into Prince Alfred Road only to discover that after that sprint, there were still another 200 yards to be covered to complete the course.

Prizes and also 'house points' were awarded for the first four boys to finish, regardless of age or size. The certificates were presented as part of the annual sports day.

All in all it was a rather gruelling race covering about 1.3 miles, I believe: I was fortunate enough to have competed in the event on five occasions from the age of 10 to 15. At the age of 15, I managed to achieve 4th place which I considered an achievement given that there were two classes of older boys in the sixth form competing.

In my latter years at school, it was decided to create a 'Mystery Half-Mile' race to cater for the younger boys, it seemed to us that the 'new dykes' were not considered to be as hardy as we were.

Frank Irwin (1950–1957)
Now living in Wirral

THE ANNUAL SCHOOL PLAY

The annual school play was a source of diversion, perhaps more particularly, for the boarding fraternity ever content to miss prep. in favour of a rehearsal. *The Torchbearers* was not particularly suitable for the hard-bitten members of the Blue Coat but probably selected for the parents who attended. It was I think, first produced in 1923, in London, with dialogue much connected with that time. '...a concomitant enactment of a human life' as sprouted by the leading lady. It was a play within a play but enough of that. In this production, the leading management was 'Scogs' Scarland and Mr. Perry.

Eric Woodbine (1953-1959)
Now living in France.

A STROLL ALONG THE SOUTH CORRIDOR

As it is no more, I thought I would take you all for a stroll down the old south corridor. The period is the mid-1950s, before the four dormitories were renamed Earle, Macauley, Stythe and Tinne in the spring of 1957.

We begin by walking down the L-shaped service road and entering the school at the right-hand half of the double doors. This, I am sure, must have opened inwards. We find ourselves looking down a long corridor with a flat ceiling and a set of double-doors (indeed a double set of double-doors) visible in the far distance, daylight shining through their upper halves. It is a distinctly Edwardian scene (unsurprising given the school's vintage), the lower half of the wall comprising well-glazed brown bricks and the upper half painted plaster. At regular intervals a pendant light fitting descends from the ceiling, each has its own plain white glass hemispherical lampshade. The floor is interesting; it appears to have been made from multi-coloured stone chippings set in concrete and then polished. The effect is almost mosaic-like and it is obviously extremely hardwearing. (See sketch on Page 326).

In this half of the corridor there are doorways on both sides, the ones on the left being built into deep, bevel-shaped recesses. A few windows on the right-hand-side give illumination from the south quadrangle in the daytime. Immediately to our left is a well-polished wooden staircase that comprises the fire escape route for the Graham and Bingham dormitories (and also the route occasionally taken by marauding bands of inter-dormitory attackers, who would mainly be armed with rolled-up or knotted towels).

A little more light comes into the corridor from a window halfway up the stairs just mentioned. A large door on the right-hand-side of the corridor gives direct access to the service yard (e.g. the cobbler's room, the laundry room and the boiler room).

The first door that we come to on the left-hand-side is the playroom or common room used by boarders of the younger age group - say 11 to 13. It is extremely basic, so the boys are to a large extent forced to make their own amusements. There is a fireplace in the corner of the room but I don't think it was ever used to provide heat during the years I spent in the school - probably because the building had recently been fitted with central heating.

The second door leads to 'the shed' - an open space, more or less square in shape, that gives access to the two tennis courts via three big arches. The 'shed' also serves the purpose of providing shelter during break-time when it happens to be rainy. A line painted on the wall at tennis net height enables boys to practise their tennis shots.

Moving further along the corridor, we find that we have doorways to left and right. The ones on the right are not accessible to boys, the first of them leading to a room that is used by the cleaning ladies for storing their brushes, mops, etc., and the second being a washroom and toilet for visitors' use. Across the corridor, a door leads into a small room that may once have functioned as a washroom but is now derelict; this is the natural choice of venue when two boys wish to fight one another as there is little chance of their being disturbed. Within a year or two it will be converted into a common room for the boys of Earle dormitory. The next doorway along leads into the boarders' washroom, which has washbasins all around its perimeter, and down the centre of the room are lines of metal frames with hooks for briefly hanging towels and clothes on.

Moving on, we pass a drinking fountain mounted on the right-hand wall, and a few feet farther on we see a corridor going off to our right, identical in style to the one that we are in. This is the Secondary Modern classroom corridor and it leads us to most of the remainder of the school, but we are not going that way.

Next we find ourselves in a hallway with a set of well-used stairs off to our left - the route to the four dormitories, Blundell, Bingham, Graham and Shirley. The stairwell space is occupied by a hoist for moving heavy or bulky items to or from the two landings above, and it is normally out of bounds to boys. There is the entrance to a little corridor immediately to the right of the hoist and it turns the corner behind it. A door there can give access to the tennis courts but it is normally kept locked. Boarders seeking a bit of peace and quiet will often go to this little corridor, but it can't comfortably fit more than, say, six. Just left of the well-used staircase there is a staff room, and opposite to it across the hallway a room for the use of older boys.

Passing beyond the hallway, we enter the next wing of the south corridor. The same arrangements as the other wing still apply here - doorways mainly to the left and windows giving daylight to the right. The first door leads to the common room used by the older boys - say 13 to 15. Unlike the other common room, it contains a few comforts! There is a half-size snooker table, comfortable chairs, and a bookcase. I well recall seeing several Arthur Ransome books in the latter, e.g. *Swallows and Amazons*.

Our tour of the south corridor is now nearing its end. To our left we see a large number of wooden lockers set against the wall, each locker made secure by a padlock of the owner's choice, several of them being the new-fangled combination locks. This is the meagre storage provided by the school for a boarder to keep his personal belongings safe.

We have now arrived at the far end of the south corridor and there is only one door left to explore. This is a playroom available to the older boys and it comprises table tennis tables. On the far side of the room is another door and this leads into a tiny room used exclusively by the most senior boys. I personally never made it here because I left school at 15, but in 1958 I remember hearing Buddy Holly's music emanating from it so there must have been a gramophone or record player in there.

We have now completed our tour. The south corridor ends at this point and we are standing next to the double set of double-doors mentioned at the beginning. These lead to the school's west front – an area that is permanently out of bounds to pupils because it contains dilapidated and therefore possibly dangerous air-raid shelters. To maintain security, the two sets of double-doors are kept permanently locked.

Ray Livingston (1955-1959)
Now living in York

THE SÉANCE

During the summer holiday period, my parents had allowed me to attend a séance held in our home. They must have now considered me old enough to be able to handle the occult, as this was the first time that I had ever been invited to participate.

Without boring you or attempting to make false claims, there was an awful lot of truth appearing and things were mentioned that nobody else could have ever known. Therefore I knew that there was something in this 'thing' but could not understand it or where it was leading me to. It and further experiences eventually led me away from spiritualism, because of occurrences that both frightened me and gave me cause for concern. However back to school days.

In our common room, (the one across the ground floor area from the staff room) I had been recounting to my school friends what had happened during the séance without telling them everything, but ensuring that they all knew there was something in this thing.

Because of that it was decided to hold a séance the following night in the very room where we were holding the discussion. This meant that my reputation (or 'street cred' it would be called today) would be called into question if something significant didn't happen. I made some secret arrangements to ensure the success of the occasion, we synchronised our watches!

The following night arrived and the assembled five sat round the table. We placed an old mirror, found in the cubby-hole, on top of the quarter sized snooker table. A further ten or so schoolboys watched in awe and anticipation from outside the circle. On the old mirror we had placed pieces of paper bearing the letters of the alphabet in a circular fashion.

From my memory of what had happened at home, we made some short cuts, more bits of paper with the words 'Yes' and 'No' and we placed them within the circle of letters.

We had taken a beaker from the dining room at tea time, especially for the purpose and turned it upside down within the circle of letters. I requested each person present at the table to place one finger each on the top of the inverted beaker.

Somebody asked me 'What do we do now?' I replied 'We all keep very quiet and one of us asks are there any spirits in the room.' Somebody then intoned very slowly and deliberately 'Are there any spirits in this room?' Nothing happened. The question was repeated and still there was no response, the beaker didn't move an inch.

I looked at my watch, a Newmark watch. If you had managed to get your parents to buy you a watch, the chances were that it was of Newmark manufacture, what we all called a 'Newmark never-right'. My reputation was fading as nobody believed that a response could be obtained from the spirit world beyond the grave.

I looked again at my watch and said 'If there is anybody there, please make a sign.' Within a few seconds, there was a ringing tone to be heard, 'ping' 'ping' resounding throughout the room from the central heating pipes. Somebody with his finger still on the inverted beaker said, 'Give it a start.' I said 'You don't do that, it will move of its own accord if anybody is there.' 'Ping' 'ping' again resounded in the room. Surely it was a sign! However that was the end of the matter; nothing further happened.

After we had finished the séance I got hold of my mate and asked 'What did you bang the heating pipes with?' He replied, 'I found a bit of iron bar, did it sound all right?' 'Yes' I replied 'but I was getting a little worried that your watch had gone slow again.'

I mentioned in an earlier description about the little room (the cubbyhole) within that common room, well the following night, some of us walked into our private area and found all the lights out. As we entered we could hear intonations coming from within the cubbyhole, 'Move o bottle, move o bottle.' On looking inside, Harrison was squatting on the floor, lights out, with his right index finger on the top of a lemonade bottle, the letters from the previous nights séance were spread out in a circle on the floor, attempting to contact the spirits either to keep him amused or for company, I never found out.

At home, having attended a number of one-to-one sessions with a well known medium, things were said that made me realise that there was an awful lot to spiritualism and that secrets could be unlocked. Many years later in a telephone call from my mother, I was asked had I changed my car. I said 'Yes, I bought another one only last week, why do you ask?' My mother was nervous in her reply but she had been told by a medium that my new car would 'give up the ghost!' I told her never to involve me again in such matters, but I immediately changed the car for another one because of it.

My advice to all now is; do not knock what you don't understand. Because something seems far fetched does not mean it can't happen. In defence of this I always quote my father-in-law. In an early 1960's discussion about space travel he was asked did he think we would ever visit the moon. His reply, based on the technology of the day was 'Don't be so daft that can never happen.' Well it did soon after, during that very decade.

Frank Irwin (1950-1957)
Now living in Wirral

MORE ABOUT MASTERS – GOOD AND BAD

I remember Mr. Frank Hulford very well. He is the teacher adding his memories from the teaching point of view and a very much needed addition to be able to see that things were not only rather spartan and unfair to us boys but to a certain degree similar conditions applied to them. I found Frank very fair and he was one of my favourite teachers, (honestly Sir!) along with Ron Scarland and a couple of others.

When I first joined the school in 1952, I always had respect for the teachers but subsequent events over the next five years, meant much of that respect was lost towards a minority of staff members who, for the most trivial reason, clearly took great delight in meting out undeserved and unwarranted violence against pupils who they had taken a personal dislike to.

One who still stands out in my mind was the red-faced Mr. Edwards who demonstrated violence on many occasions. Apart from canings and slipperings (usually administered for the most minor of offences), when he was on early morning duty he would prepare a cold bath for any boy he found to be still in bed on his second round of the dormitories, and took great pleasure in carrying the struggling lad from bed to bathroom and dropping him into the freezing water amid pleas for mercy that were totally ignored!

He especially, of course, took even greater pleasure in this activity during the coldest periods of the year. He was obviously bullied when he was at school and should never have been allowed to work with minors.

Another bully (although he was not a teacher who I had personal experience of) was 'Tan Tan' Rowlands, (mentioned elsewhere in this book) who met his Waterloo when he attempted to drag one of the boys from the back of the class to the front by holding on to the hair of his temple just above his ear. The lad (I forget his name) was rather larger than the bullying midget, and retaliated by smacking him right in the mouth; I don't know whether or not he broke any teeth but the blow sent him flying to the ground and certainly gave him a bloody nose. The boy was, not surprisingly, expelled that very day!

As far as bullying by pupils was concerned, I remember a lad named Alec Pearce who was the 'cock of the school' at the time that I arrived in 1952. On one of my first nights in the dormitory away from home and missing my family for the first time I was summoned to his bedside, and, for absolutely no reason other than King Pearce asserting his authority, he took me totally by surprise by punching me full in the face as an example to anyone who may be considering stealing his crown. I punched him back and was dragged off by a couple of his henchmen, but my response to his attack had earned me a degree of respect and he never bothered me again.

We became quite friendly sometime later.

Stan Livingston (1952-1957)
Now living in Ormskirk

PUNISHMENT

Apart from the normal punishments meted out to us naughty boys, i.e. beatings, detentions etc. occasionally alternative methods were used, sometimes the beatings were supplemented by 'lines' and on other occasions 'lines' themselves constituted the total deal. We don't hear much about 'lines' these days, perhaps such punishments and detentions are now a figment of the dark and dismal past. Teachers are either unable, or are not permitted to dole out such punishments for fear of upsetting the Politically Correct brigade.

'Lines' as we called them, was a punishment whereby we were instructed to write a specified number of lines pertinent to the offence that we were supposed to have committed, like, 'I must not talk in class.' To make life easy we would generally scrawl down the blank page to create a column comprising the word 'I', followed by a column of the word 'must' until we had achieved the set number of sentences the prescribed number of times. Because of this, I well remember Mr. Perry decided that this was not sufficiently literate for Blue Coat boys and he required a different sentence, but again to be pertinent to the crime committed, that went like this. 'Talking in class is my most besetting sin, and I must do all within my power to eradicate it.' Naturally this sentence could not easily be fitted into one line of a standard foolscap sheet of paper, so each line had to be written out individually. Mr. Perry being Mr. Perry, I suppose we were fortunate not to have to write it in Latin.

Frank Irwin (1950-1957)
Now living in Wirral

CONVERSATIONS WITH A PHILOSOPHER

Although academic expectations were not set very high in the Secondary Modern side of the school, there were one or two compensations for this, the best example being my class's contact with the wise and friendly veteran teacher Mr. L.S. Price. I always looked forward to his lessons, which I fear may have been largely classified as 'university of life' rather than rigorous academic training. This at least is my recollection of his lessons so I hope I am being fair to his memory.

I confess that I was always biased in his favour, because when I was eleven he carried my suitcase the length of Church Road. The school had just broken up for Christmas and he had noticed that I was struggling to keep up with Stan as we walked to the bus stop opposite the Abbey Cinema. Big suitcases and little lads are not a good match.

A boy once fell asleep on the front row during one of Mr. Price's lengthy homilies (usually delivered sitting down, by the way) and we were amused to witness his novel way of dealing with the situation. A disciplinarian would have stormed over and whacked the poor chap, but Mr. Price's *modus operandi* was to walk across quietly with a little smile on his face and very lightly brush the lad's cheek with the back of his fingers. After several seconds the boy woke with a start, and I'm sure the embarrassment of finding himself the butt of everyone's amusement was every bit as effective in deterring a repetition as would have been achieved by the disciplinarian.

If his class was ever noisy, he would just continue to speak with his normal volume and you could hear the decibel level of the 'opposition' falling off dramatically in order that they could pick up what he was saying; within seconds he would be in charge once more. I realised at the time that he must be employing an old trick here, but it was still impressive to witness.

Not all of his 'hobby horses' were valid, I have found. He swore, for instance, that the cure for a bad stomach was to drink lemon juice, but it hasn't worked on my wife who often suffers from that complaint.

I recall that when he lost his father he was not averse to bringing even that sad private event to the classroom for discussion. 'Life must go on!' he philosophised to us.

The last time I met him was on Dale Street as I carried out my office boy duties for the solicitor. He was visibly surprised when I remarked 'I thought we would bump into one another here one day!', and one could imagine him making use of the incident when chatting to a class ('Have you ever experienced *déjà vu?*' etc., etc.).

A lot of Mr. Price rubbed off on me, so if it was the intention that such a man should become an influence on fatherless Blue Coat boys like me, then in my case it succeeded.

Ray Livingston (1955-1959)
Now living in York

BROTHERS

One of the group of brothers that I well remember were the Lyon brothers, Chris, Michael and Peter. The story was that the J.S. Lyon metal workers factory at the Rotunda was the family business. I don't know how true that was, but every time I went past on the bus it would come to mind.

Talking of brothers, George and Charles Buckle, or the other three Hughes brothers, Arthur, John and Eric, two of them moved to Southampton with the Cunard Line. Regarding the Archer twins, they would always stop Griff and I fighting (as brothers do), and tell us to remember about brotherly love! Five minutes later they would be fighting each other.

The only other brothers I can think of were the Hays brothers, but I cannot remember their Christian names. I do, however, recall one night, along with one of them, getting the slipper from Mr. Jackson. We also got a couple of extra strokes for being caught out of bed. He laid in to us to such an extent, that we both ended up with black and blue backsides. Sister Thamos spotted this and reported the matter to Mr. Watcyn. As a result, following being questioned about the reason for the punishment being inflicted, we both got a cup of tea and a piece of cake.

Kenneth Hughes. (1945–1953)
Now living in France

THE BIRDS AND THE BEES 1

My widowed mother largely avoided the embarrassment of telling the four of us (girl, boy, girl, boy – of which I was the last) the facts of life by nonchalantly leaving a book kicking round the house when we had reached that certain age. It was written by an American lady and bore the enticing title *It's Time You Knew*. I suspect that all of us read it without discussing with the others that we had done so.

Long before that, I was given the most basic facts by my two sisters when we and their friends were out playing one evening (I'm talking really basic basic here!). I was about nine years old and must have gone into denial of such weird concepts, because I had to be given them all over again a couple of years later by Stan; by that time I had joined him at the Blue Coat and we were out together on a Sunday walk. I recall that our chat took place on one of those public seats just inside the gates of The Mystery, off Smithdown Road. At the age of eleven I was much more ready to absorb the knowledge than I had been the first time round, and it felt good to have gained a more realistic understanding of how the world functioned.

The closest thing to a sex lesson that I can ever recall receiving at the Blue Coat, was one day in a scripture lesson when Mr. Slater cryptically tried to explain to us what the phrase '... and he went in unto her .' meant. It was clear that he expected us to know what he was driving at without being too overt and explanatory.

Ray Livingston (1955-1959)
Now living in York

THE BIRDS AND THE BEES 2

Unlike modern times, in our day at the Blue Coat we didn't have such a subject as sex education on the curriculum: I suppose the nearest we got to the birds and the bees was in chapel one particular Sunday morning. Mr. Watcyn was delivering his sermon, which involved somebody explaining how he was able to know which children were boys and which were girls, given that the length of ones hair was no longer a distinguishing feature. The answer was that when they washed their hands was the time to discern one from the other. The boys only washed their hands, whilst the girls also washed their wrists and forearms. I suppose that was true of the boys, but what of the girls?

Frank Irwin (1950-1957)
Now living in Wirral

MORE OF THE OLD SCHOOL TIE

I was extremely keen to escape from the school in the summer of 1959 - even to the point of academic recklessness, for I had no qualifications at all (I was 15, and would have been in 5M if I had returned in September - something I was determined to avoid if I could because Mr. Watcyn had told us in no uncertain terms that we would not be allowed to take O-Levels, and would instead be studying for a new set of exams called 'U.L.C.I.' - written by the Union of Lancashire & Cheshire Institute).

Guided by the Youth Employment people on Edge Lane, I attended a few interviews at offices in Liverpool and eventually met with success at a small solicitor's office on Stanley Street. What sticks in my mind was that it was on hearing that I was a Blue Coat boy, that made the solicitor (Kenneth Maxwell Brown - a product of Merchant Taylors' School in Crosby) take me on. He remarked 'Boys from there don't expect life to be a bed of roses!'

I think he told me on that occasion, that every solicitor in Liverpool admired one of their number who also was an ex-Blue Coat boy – Mr. R.H. Vyner-Brooks - who was renowned as being the richest solicitor in the city. I never met this man in my 4-year career in solicitors' offices, but I occasionally passed his office on Lower Castle Street.

Ray Livingston (1955-1959)
Now living in York

THE FIRST DISASTER

I remember what perhaps was to be my (and possibly other boys) first experience of both a mystery, and also a major disaster. Events of the war were alien to us as we were too young to have understood at that time just what transpired, but this to us was very vivid.

At the time, it was 1951 and I was sleeping in the most junior dormitory, Blundell: although I cannot remember how we heard about it, as there were certainly no crystal sets at the time in the school, the events remain well implanted in my memory.

We had heard somehow, perhaps via a teacher, about the H.M. Submarine *Affray* being lost somewhere in the English Channel, (Portland meant very little to us at the time) and we were updated on a regular basis just how many hours of air were left on board to be able to sustain life. This went on over a number of days until eventually we were told that there was no hope for anybody on board.

I remember, lying in bed, as the hours reduced and no good news was forthcoming, we all sang 'Eternal father strong to save,' and imagined being trapped in such a small vessel, perhaps in darkness waiting for death to arrive. It took 59 days of searching for the *Affray* to be located, involving the investigation of 161 wrecks before the right one was discovered.

The story is well documented now, but at the time no reason was apparent for the catastrophe and to date that remains the case, although speculation has it that the snort mast was of faulty manufacture, having been found broken off, and that a battery explosion took place. The true reason may never be known.

The submarine lies 282 feet below the surface, which means effectively that the wreck will remain undisturbed for posterity. Although there were no hostilities at the time, she remains a war grave and the final resting place of 75 naval personnel. I suppose this memory may have been more poignant to me as I have always been led to believe that my birth father met the same fate, but early on during World War II.

Frank Irwin (1950-1957)
Now living in Wirral

MORE DISASTERS

A troubling question in the early 1950s, including amongst many of our boys, was 'Why are so many De Havilland Comet airliners crashing with huge loss of life?' The answer was eventually given that something called 'metal fatigue' was responsible and the aircraft was susceptible to it because of its square windows. Boeing's answer to the Comet (which had been designed in 1949 and was the world's first jet airliner) was the Boeing 707, and as it had oval windows it had a much better safety record. This is why American airliners 'won out' in the long run and have dominated passenger aviation ever since.

Of course, it is now easy to see that this era was the fledgling beginning of the mass-aviation that we have today, and that it was not entirely a good thing.

Ray Livingston (1955-1959)
Now living in York

MIDNIGHT FEASTS

Taking the expression 'midnight feast' literally, I don't ever recall attending one, but I do recall accompanying my friend Peter Greig on a couple of evening episodes that one or other of us dreamt up. The first was in 1957, I believe, and it took place one particular evening when Peter, or perhaps both of us, had somehow managed to assemble a few edibles.

Where to go for the exciting escapade? I believe it was me who provided the answer in this instance, for I had noticed that our woodwork master, Mr. Holiday, had recently begun to store his wood on a short landing at the top of a staircase in the east corridor and the planks had been leant against the wall, thereby creating a very convenient triangular space where we could insert ourselves and lurk in the dark.

At one time in the school's history the landing must have had a purpose, for it was adjacent to the sanatorium ('San') and a pair of doors (always locked) gave access to the school's main front on Church Road. It seemed a splendid choice.

The appointed time arrived and we made our way to the venue – separately, if we had any sense. The discreet festivities began and we were greatly enjoying ourselves, but sadly we had reckoned without the possibility of our being given away by the slight sounds we were making, and who should happen to pass along the east corridor but Mr. Holiday himself!

We knew we were in big trouble, and we also both knew what it meant to receive a caning on our finger ends. How much worse was it going to be now that we had qualified for the same on our bottoms! I don't know how the overnight worry affected Peter but I know that it badly affected me.

Next day we were greatly relieved when we reported to Mr. Holiday to learn our fate and were told that, in this instance, our punishment was that we must spend the next Saturday morning tidying and rearranging his woodpile.

A few weeks or months later Peter proposed another feast, but this time he was equipped with a solid-fuel camping stove so it would be a hot meal! The chosen venue was one of the air-raid shelters on the east side of the playing field – dangerous territory because it was perilously close to the headmaster's house.

Miraculously we got through the session undetected, but I seem to remember that the cuisine was less than perfect owing to various unforeseen technical difficulties (no decent tin opener and the stove was troublesome to operate, for example).

A couple of other memories of this good Blue Coat friend of mine before I end this account. Peter Greig was renowned for carrying a small screwdriver in the top pocket of his blazer and bringing it into service whenever he happened across a piece of technical apparatus that intrigued him. Sadly he did not display the same skills when it came to reassembling whatever it was, so it was later found in bits by its owner or person in charge.

His home was in Dovecot, and one memorable Sunday I accompanied him when he attempted to walk there and back within the two-hour Sunday Walk period (quite a tall order as the distance was about 2½ miles each way). This, by the way, was an illicit act, for we were not supposed to go more than one mile from the school and always in a southerly or westerly direction, not northerly or easterly.

Lo and behold, no one was at home when we arrived so we could not enter the house!

Ray Livingston (1955-1959)
Now living in York

HOLIDAY SCHOOLING

Whilst having one of our granddaughters stay with us recently, a situation arose which gave rise to a further memory of the school.

Over dinner I asked her about her progress at her school and suggested that she brush up on her Spanish vocabulary during the holidays, learning just five new words each day: being quite normal she showed a polite quiet opposition to the suggestion.

It reminded me of towards the end of my time in 1G when Mr. Eade must have been the French teacher. (I cannot really remember that but others have stated he preceded Tan Tan). Mr. Eade had left the school for pastures new and Mr. Watcyn entered the classroom at the end of term and told us about our new teacher to be, Mr. Rowlands. He went on to tell us that the series of text books we had been using was not as advanced as the new set that Mr. Rowlands proposed to introduce us to, and so we would have to learn something like 120 new words of vocabulary during the summer holiday in order to be prepared for year two of the new series.

Well nobody likes to have to work during the holidays do they? Unfortunately once at home my father discovered this list of French – English words and asked me what it was all about. I just explained that they were words we had been using during the past year. Not being as daft as a Blue Coat boy imagined, he asked me what was the French word for this and what was the French word for that, soon realising that I didn't know any of the answers at all. He therefore decided that I must learn twenty words each day, and I was to be tested each evening at dinner time, if I failed to answer all the questions correctly I would not be allowed out the following day and the test would be repeated until I achieved success. The result was that when we returned to school I knew off by heart all the words that we were supposed to learn.

The first French lesson arrived and we met Tan Tan for the first time. A short, moustached, very smartly dressed, somewhat dapper in appearance little man with a vicious temper. He proceeded to test us on the words to be learned during the holiday to make sure we were all up to date and ready for the new text books.

Well, at the end of the test I had full marks for the twenty questions asked and nobody else had any more than five correct answers. The whole class with the exception of yours truly was made to attend detention that evening, which made me very unpopular. Explaining the reason for my doing so well cut no ice: I had been swotting and nobody else had. All the class except me was in detention for most of the week because we were tested on a daily basis: I was labelled a swot just because my father had accidentally discovered the list of vocabulary.

My dad made it a habit during holiday periods of setting me work for daily completion, not every day but certainly for a fair coverage of the period; I hated it at the time but later in life I realised the benefits of just giving a little of the holiday time to the pursuit of learning, I just wish my grandchildren felt the same.

Frank Irwin (1950-1957)
Now living in Wirral

ABIDING WITH ME FOREVER

When my elder brother Stan left school in February 1957, (earlier than that if his voice broke) it left the post of head choirboy vacant, and as I was by then a member of the choir myself I was eligible to apply for the post.

Dr. Dickerson auditioned me and others, and I could tell that he had his doubts about my suitability because, he said, I didn't sing loudly enough. Nevertheless, he ended up giving me the job and I did it until my voice broke. The most enjoyable part of it was that I was the one who lit the altar candles before the service, and snuffed them out afterwards.

During chapel services I was, of course, quite close to the organ and was able to watch Dr. Dickerson as he so expertly operated it and got the best out of it; he really was a craftsman.

Mr. Watcyn was only a few steps away too, and I can hear his singing voice in my head to this day – in particular the hymn 'Abide with Me'.

Anyone who is today familiar with the tone and style of Aled Jones (a fellow Welshman) will be surprisingly close to knowing what our old headmaster used to sound like.

Ray Livingston (1955-1959)
Now living in York

THE WELCOMING COMMITTEE

Four or five months into my time at the school, I and the other new boarding starters were taken to the city centre to be presented to the school's governors. The meeting took place on the first floor of the Royal Insurance offices on Cumberland Street.

It was a slightly awkward, one-sided occasion for we just stood there before them and were scrutinised; albeit they had benign and friendly expressions on their faces. Rembrandt would have enjoyed recording that line of worthy faces, I'm certain.

A few words must have been spoken to us but they were evidently not memorable enough to have stuck in my mind so I can't pass on what they were.

A few years before my arrival, my brother Stan had an encounter with one of the governors and after shaking hands at the end of the short conversation he found a two-shilling piece in the palm of his hand.

Ray Livingston (1955-1959)
Now living in York

THE SECRET CORRIDOR

The school, being an old building, had many passageways which, perhaps because of their age, were sectioned as 'out of bounds'. You knew that if caught in these corridors you would be severely punished. One such corridor ran from the school to the chapel, and as this corridor was sloping downhill it must have gone underground, to what I believed must be a way into the crypt.

Being inquisitive boys, our imaginations would run wild. For a start, anything out of bounds meant that it had to be investigated! It was like a magnet; we were drawn. The crypt meant bodies, perhaps bodies buried with treasure, like the pyramids (after all, it was the 1950s and buried treasure was being found); or perhaps there were knights buried in their armour! We were only 12 or 13-year-olds, with vivid imaginations. We had to 'suss' this out.

My best friend at school was Reginald Johnson, Reg to his friends. Reg was a bit wilder than I was and he was also one year ahead of me. Most of the school had locked areas, and master keys were sought by the boys because they could be copied during metalwork lessons and sold or exchanged for some worldly goods or the major prize - food. But also, we learned how to pick locks - or at least Reg and I did. (Thinking back, I never put that talent to any good use! I could have been a jewel thief like the criminal character in *The Pink Panther!*)

Anyway, we sneaked out of the dormitory one night and made our way across the school to the corridor. We successfully got through the first door but couldn't get past the door leading to the crypt. We made it back to the dormitory but, disappointed, we resolved to try again another night; we would not be defeated. On our first visit, we had noticed another corridor leading off. This corridor was some way down the main corridor but not as far as the door into the crypt. It was underground so we thought it might be an easier way to get into the crypt. Anyway, we thought we would give it a try.

So, once again we made our way carefully out of the dormitory, across the school and into the old corridor. This old corridor was very much neglected; there was dirt, masonry and spider webs along its full length. There was no lighting, but we had small torches (most of the boys owned them in order to be able to read under the bedclothes. Remember, in those days boys as young as 12 and 13, had to be in bed by 8.00 p.m., whether they were tired or not!)

We made our way along the main corridor until we came to the turning. There was no door barring our way, but partway along the corridor we found that it began to slope upwards. We started to panic as we thought we might suddenly come back into the school and be caught. We were just about to turn round and retrace our steps when we came to a wider section, with a huge wardrobe up against the wall. It was an old cupboard, probably made of oak. It looked very plain but very solid, and it had a clasp with a padlock securing its double doors.

At first we thought that the cupboard might be concealing another way into the crypt and we tried to move it, but it was solid so we set to work on the lock. We soon had the padlock sprung and we gingerly opened the doors.

Now, in order to empathise, you have to understand that it was like finding the tomb of some ancient emperor buried with all his wealth. This cupboard was full of tins of condensed milk! I am not a big lover of the stuff, but teenagers are always hungry.

We helped ourselves to two tins each, hoping that it would not be noticed and arranging the other tins so that it did not look as though anything was missing. We then waited, and waited. Weeks went by and nothing happened.

By this time we were getting hungry again, but in our mind's eye, we had a vision of someone waiting for us, ready to pounce and capture us. Nevertheless, we decided to chance it and go back. We did, and collected two more tins each. Indeed, this cupboard supplied us with tins of condensed milk for the whole time we were at the school and it never looked empty.

We never mentioned this to anyone until now. Reg and I met up many times after we had left the school and I am godfather to his son, and he to my daughter. We always assumed that, at the start of the war in 1939/40, the cupboard was stacked with the milk for emergencies but later lay forgotten. How old the tins were is anyone's guess; tins then did not have to have 'sell-by' dates and we reckoned that they were at least 17 years old when we found them. I like to think we 'liberated' them; they certainly kept two boys happy for the rest of their time at the school. I often wonder what happened to the cupboard after we left.

Brenton Williams (1955 – 1959)
Now living in Liverpool

THE WILLIAM T. BOWDEN STORY

I was born on 22nd July 1941 at Walton Hospital in Rice Lane. My mother and father lived in Tintern Street, off Walton Road. In 1942 my mother gave birth to a little girl called Florence, but after three months of fighting for life, the baby girl died, from toxaemia. My father, William Thomas Bowden R.N. was killed in June 1944, whilst, serving in the Royal Navy aboard H.M.S. *Cabot,* in the Mediterranean Sea. My mother was a supervisor at Marks & Spencer's store in Church Street in the city centre. In her spare time she was quite well known as a ballroom dancer, her partner was a chap called Billy Bullen. They won many major championships together but unfortunately my mother had contacted tuberculosis after getting caught in the tramlines and falling outside Fusco's, latterly Aindow's American ice cream parlour in Spellow Lane. Defying the doctor's advice, she regularly removed the iron support from her leg and went out dancing: this resulted in her premature and unexpected demise. As a consequence she died in June 1947 at Walton Hospital at the age of 28.

That just left the boy!!

As a one-year old baby, I was christened at St. Lawrence's C of E Church in Barlows Lane, Walton. My father and his large family of brothers and sisters, who all lived in the Spellow Lane area of Walton, were staunch Protestants and my mother was a Dublin girl, so very much a Catholic. As my father was on leave from the Royal Navy it was decided that I should be christened as a Protestant. After my father's death I went to live at my Aunt Nellie's in Royal Street. It was decided by my mother's family that I should attend at St. John's R.C. School in Fountains Road, where I was subsequently christened and baptised in the Catholic faith. When my mother started to become very ill I had to go and live at my grandmother's very large house in Spellow Lane: once installed in the house of the doyen of the Bowden clan, it was obvious that I would have to attend the local school, St. Lawrence C. of E.

In 1948, a lady from the War Office (Naval Section), approached my grandmother and explained that there was a scheme available for the children of servicemen who had been killed in action and who had also lost their mothers, thereby making them orphans. This scheme involved the joint financing by the child's family (if they could afford it) and the Ministry of Pensions (War Dept.). It was agreed that if my grandmother paid my annual tuck shop fees (15 shillings), the War Dept. would pay my school fees, plus all school expenses (clothing, annual trips and any extra equipment needed for school).

After my school interview I remember Mrs. Williams, the head of the Ministry of Pensions at Orleans House in Edmund Street, next to the Liverpool Stadium, taking me to Horne Brothers in Whitechapel. This really snooty chap with a waxed moustache and hair plastered down with brilliantine came over and asked with a certain amount of distain 'Does madam have the correct shop? This is a *gentlemen's* outfitters,' to which Mrs. William's replied 'My young charge has been accepted as a boarding pupil at the Blue Coat School and we require a complete uniform for him.'

Believe me, only somebody who has gone through the 'kitting out' process of a boarder at Horne Brothers knows what it is like. If I were to make a comparison, the army process is very similar, but not as extensive.

A typical shopping list would be:

Navy blue blazers with school badge x 2
Grey double breasted suit x 1
Grey flannel short trousers x 4
Navy blue knitted tie x 1
Royal blue knitted tie x 1
Trouser belt x 1
Grey shirts x 6
Boots – lace up x 3
Cotton vests x 6
Navy blue raincoat x 1
Cotton underpants x 6
Gentlemen's suitcase x 2
Grey woollen stockings x 6
Braces x 1
School peaked cap x 1
Handkerchiefs x 12
P.E. Shorts x 2

Toilet bag x 1
P.E. vests x 2
Boot Brushes and polish x 1
One pair black plimsolls
One pair football boots

When you further consider that Horne Brothers is probably one of the most exclusive and expensive shops in Liverpool, this lot wouldn't have come cheap, but I can assure you that this list is pretty accurate.

So now I am booted and suited and raring to go. It has been arranged that as I am virtually on my own, a member of Mrs. Williams' staff from the Ministry will take me for my induction at the Blue Coat School.

Upon arrival at the school a most formidable entrance hall greeted me. This hallway led directly to the magnificent Shirley Hall. To my left was the daunting boardroom with paintings of former governors and dignitaries associated with the school, an enormous, magnificently polished table surrounded by chairs was the centrepiece. The ceiling was a masterpiece. I am going to have to stop there because I think I am going to give people the impression that I actually liked the place and that would really ruin my story. To the right and next to the headmaster's study, there was a window, this was the office and on arrival we rang the bell. Mr. Rees, the school secretary greeted us.

I think the first person I met was Mr. Crebbin who was the boarders' master as well as being the housemaster for Bingham House, the house that I belonged to. A prefect took me to the locker room where I met Mrs. Piperno the seamstress. She could write better with a sewing machine that any boy could with pen and paper. She did all our clothing repairs and ran the laundry room. She was also in charge of the locker room. Everything you owned had your name written on it in double writing done on Mrs. Piperno's machine. In this room each boy had a locker in which he kept his Sunday morning suit and his best blazer, plus an array of other clothes.

THE BLUE COAT RAMBLERS CLUB.

The first bit of school activity that I can remember was walking hand in hand down the road to Mosspits Lane Primary School from the Blue Coat. I liked it there because the *other* kids at the school used to bring sweets in and we would cadge some from them. Funnily enough, when I started metalwork lessons at the Blue Coat we had to walk to a school on Queens Drive, near to Childwall Fiveways, to use their facilities. We also had to walk to Picton Road Baths for our swimming lessons and we had to walk to Lance Lane for all other sporting activities (great on a Saturday, we used to watch Earle F.C. over the fence).

SCHOOL DAYS

I liked the common room after school. I always managed to get a game of chess or table tennis there before prep. In the summer I played tennis with a good pal and doubles partner called Ian Davy, he was from St. Agnes in Cornwall. His father, reputedly, owned a tin mine there.

Night times were often the most amusing because it was bath time, and this entailed each dormitory filing into the bathroom to be greeted by matron and her sidekick Miss Burgess. The bathroom consisted of eight baths, four on each side of the room. These are the baths that people are paying a fortune for nowadays; the massive, white roll topped ones with the claw-footed supports.

Matron was what you would expect a matron in a boarding school to be; large, rotund and austere in every way. She was a Scottish lady whose voice carried with a lot of authority. Miss Burgess had also been hand-picked to serve as matron's assistant. This woman could give you nightmares, she was poker faced with a large mole on her upper lip. The mole itself was comical enough, but this beauty had hairs growing out of it, which made it much more derisible. This facial feature was to get me into lots of trouble during my tenure at the Blue Coat (the lady could not take a joke). Matron and Miss Mole, sorry Burgess, would patrol up and down the bathroom suggesting which parts of the anatomy would benefit most from a good scrubbing and quite often they became involved in demonstrating how this was best achieved, believe me this was a painful experience. You're rubbing away with this giant block of carbolic soap, whose edges and corners are like razors, and all of a sudden this giant figure dressed in a blue uniform with a white starched pinafore and a white starched handkerchief on her head would appear at the side of the bath saying in a brogue Scottish accent 'Between your legs Master Bowden, between your legs.' Miss Burgess was always one step behind matron, gesticulating and nodding her head in agreement with every word or comment the matron uttered.

Miss Burgess was dressed in a formal white laboratory-type coat. Her stocking were made of the same fabric and worn in a similar fashion to that popular style icon, Nora Batty. Her hair was plastered down and formed into a bun at the back. This look made her even more prone to satirical comments from the residents. These ladies were definitely hand chosen for their respective roles and placed in a perfect environment to suit their talents.

The time that I felt most depressed was bedtime. I remember in our dormitory we had a guy called Alec Pearce: this guy was a bully! I make no apologies for this accusation. He would instigate, even order slipperings (a form of torture). A boy would have to start at one end of the dorm and work his way down one side by sliding along the highly polished floor, under the beds and as he did so each boy who occupied the bed would hit the him on the back or backside and then he would have to do the same down the other side of the dorm. If at any time the chap failed to complete his task, bully-boy would take him, usually with a couple of his cohorts, into the ablutions and give him a beating. Another of the practices carried out was to make a boy hang down from the hot water pipes in the ablutions and get others to twist wet towels up into a type of cosh and beat the boy on his legs and back. This was a vicious thug who, I am proud to admit I took to task one day in the playground, much to the delight of many of the lads and masters, I suspect. After his humiliating defeat he seemed to change a little, but we were never going to be pals and that suited me fine. Incidentally, I made sure that his 'minders' got their comeuppance soon after.

One privilege that we boarders were afforded was our weekly two-hour walk. This walk had to be taken within a certain perimeter, which took in Sefton Park, Calderstones Park, and Penny Lane. Conditions for this gesture of goodwill were that you only walked in the suggested areas, that you never removed any part of your school uniform and that you returned to the school before the two hours had elapsed.

On the few occasions when I was allowed the freedom of the two-hour walk, I used to enjoy myself by spending the time with my pal Stan Livingston.

Firstly, I should explain why I say 'the few occasions'. If as boarder you committed any sort of misdemeanour it could be decided by either your housemaster or the headmaster that you should be 'gated'. This punishment could be for any length of time, depending on the seriousness of the misdemeanour. You could also receive a mixed punishment of being gated and losing your movie privilege. Mr. Mugglestone, the scoutmaster, showed a movie in the scout hall every fortnight. These fabulous, never to be missed epics included great titles such as *Kid McCoy fights again* these were advertised by wonderful posters painted by Mr. Scarland, the art teacher.

Due to my behavioural problems, of which there were many, I very rarely had the opportunity to enjoy the benefits that the other boys did. *I did not go for many walks and I was never destined to be a film buff.*

Stan and I would run down to Penny Lane and get on the 501 bus to Walton. This bus took us right to the bottom of Spellow Lane, where my grandmother lived. We would sit and talk to 'Nana' for about ten minutes, she would give Stan and I a few bob and we would run down Spellow Lane to catch the 501 bus back to Penny Lane. Most times we would have to sprint up Church Road to just make it on time. Stan and I always knew that if we needed a few bob and I had managed to keep out of trouble, we could rely on my Nana coming through, but that bus only just made it each time.

I think that I was punished by every teacher at the Blue Coat School. Punishment meaning; being caned, slippered, in detention, gated or losing film privileges. I even managed to rile masters who had reputations for being decent, unflappable and cool. The only good thing that came out of this was, teachers had developed the art of duster throwing, ruler flicking and ear twisting into perfection, due to the practice I provided for them.

THE FINAL IGNOMINIOUS ACT

I had on many occasions been sent to the office of Mr. G.G. Watcyn, the headmaster, to receive punishment, normally in the form of a caning, for a variety of misdemeanours. On this occasion I had well and truly overstepped the mark. Mr. Watcyn was furious. I am certain it was about Taffy Davies striking me in the corridor outside the dining room after him accusing me of stealing a boiled egg from a table that had been pre-set for supper. I retaliated by threatening Mr. Davies, suggesting what I was going to do to him when the time was right. Mr. Watcyn asked me to be seated; he then spoke to me calmly, in his charming Welsh drawl about how much disruption I had caused since my arrival at the school. He spent the following half an hour explaining to me why he thought I had developed into the kind of child that I was. He explained that he should have expelled me before this incident, and was certain that this time he would expel me from the school. However, he went on to say that this would be a defeat for him personally and he did not want to appear as though he could not change my attitude.

He touched on the subject of my being an orphan and not having anybody to visit me. The fact is that at the end of term I was taken down to Surbiton in Surrey to stay with Commander and Mrs. Williams from the Ministry of Pensions; and at half term I would have to stay with a relative who barely knew me, and who had drawn the short straw at a family gathering. On many occasions I was invited to stay at the home of a Mr. Kenny, who was the owner of Orleans House, in Edmund Street, the building that housed the Ministry of Pensions. He had been a long time friend of Mrs. Williams and she had discussed my situation with Mr. Kenny. This gentleman and his wife had no children of their own and they lived in a lovely bungalow in Upton. They treated me as if I was their own son.

At the end of this conversation Mr. Watcyn called a number of teachers into his office; they were Mr. Unwin, the deputy headmaster

Mr. Crebbin, senior master for boarders and Mr. Rees, the school secretary.

Mr. Watcyn informed the collective in the room that he did not intend to expel me from the school, but had decided that the accusation against me was so serious that he intended to make an example of me. He said 'I have decided that you will receive twelve strokes of the cane, six on your hands and six on your bottom, which will be exposed. This punishment will be carried out on a certain day at 09.00am in Shirley Hall in front of the assembled school. It will give me no pleasure to carry out this punishment, but the school standard has to be maintained.' I was asked to wait outside the office. Ten minutes later Mr. Unwin and Mr. Crebbin asked me to go to Mr. Unwin's office, where they explained the procedure for the punishment to be carried out.

On the day in question I attended outside Mr. Unwin's office at 08.30am. There was a flurry of activity in the corridor, two boys were carrying sections of the horse from the gym and Mr. Tait was supervising them. At 08.55am. Mr. Unwin and Mr. Crebbin came out of the office and told me to follow them into Shirley Hall. Those few steps up to the hall seemed like I was climbing a mountain. When we went inside, the hall seemed so big, especially as I was in front of a large audience.

The horse was only two or three sections high, standing around it were the matron and Mr. Crebbin on one side and Mr. Unwin on the other. Behind the horse (vault box) was Peter Hornby the head boy, another full prefect and Mr. Tait. Two minutes later Mr. Watcyn came sweeping into the hall, cape in full flow as he approached the front of the assembly. He had about four to six canes at the side of the room. He proceeded to select one, at first rejecting one, then trying another. Satisfying himself that he had selected the correct weapon, he stepped over to where I stood trembling, he turned to the assembled school and explained the purpose of this regrettable action and then swiftly asked matron to assist me in removing my trousers and underpants.

Mr. Watcyn then told me to extend my left arm upon which he brought the cane crashing down onto my hand, the pain was really excruciating, then he alternated until he had completed his six strokes. My hands were numb. He told me to lean over the horse and I felt the hands of the prefects gently pressing on my shoulders. The first stroke caught me plumb in the middle of my bottom as did the second, the third struck me low, across the top of my thighs, the fourth and fifth went were they should but the sixth caught me right in the small of my back. I could even hear the matron in the background uttering some kind of disapproval.

When the flogging was over, I was quickly helped out of Shirley Hall by the prefects and matron, who half dragged and half carried me down the corridor to the sanatorium, which was opposite Mr. Watcyn's study. Once inside they placed me on a bed, and I remember the head boy, Peter Hornby, an officer in our Army Cadet Unit and really big chap, saying to the matron, 'That, was barbaric.' I had welts on my hands and backside for weeks following the flogging. The one on my back lasted for months. I even detected a little sympathetic tenderness from matron: she really looked after me for three or four days after the punishment. Two or three times each day she would apply a soft cream to my back and rear.

Only one teacher ever mentioned the punishment to me and that was Mr. Tait: he said to me some weeks later, at an Army Cadet meeting 'At least you took your punishment like a man', nothing else, just that!!! I thought to myself 'Yeh! but I'm only a kid!' I did a lot of growing up after that episode.

That was the final punishment for me. I had learned my lesson; you cannot beat the establishment, so why try!!!

I knuckled down and started to enjoy the benefits of being a normal, reasonable, well-behaved pupil. The benefits were great; I was allowed to go on school trips. I went to Zandvoort in Holland, I went away with the cadets to Barrow-in-Furness in Cumbria, I also went to Lake Bala in North Wales, but my most enjoyable trip was to Castle Rushen School, on The Isle of Man.

The next most memorable moment for me was in May 1956 when I was told that I was mustering in June 1956.

Arrangements were made for me to meet a representative from the Ministry of Pensions who would take me to Horne Brothers in Whitechapel, Liverpool to select and purchase my leaving outfit. This was as extensive as the first time; they bought me a complete gentleman's wardrobe: a navy blue double breasted suit, a blazer, a sports jacket, a trench style raincoat, a variety of shirts, underwear, shoes, suitcases etc. Mr. Moustache was in attendance once again, but this time he adopted a completely different attitude towards me, I even detected a little courtesy was being proffered as he muttered the occasional 'Sir', to me or 'May I suggest this item for the young gentleman's approval' directed to my charge, from the Ministry of Pensions.

I remember we were allowed to wear them on the final day at school. I went to the locker room and remember asking Mrs. Piperno, the seamstress, 'What do we do with our uniforms when we leave?' She replied 'You can leave them with me and I will have them cleaned and then they will be given to any pupil whose family cannot afford to buy them from the suppliers.' This is what I agreed should happen.

THE BIG WIDE WORLD

I was offered an apprenticeship in electrical engineering by a friend of Mr. Kenny's, my mentor. His friend was the owner and Managing Director of a company called Electric Power Installations, which was based in The Inner Temple, off Dale Street. It was actually in the basement next door to the Temple Bar. I worked in many locations on Merseyside and Wirral.

In the late 1950's I found myself homeless after disagreements with the sons of my aunt with whom I had being living since leaving school, and so I decided to enlist in the army. I signed on for three years at Pall Mall in Liverpool. Originally I joined the Royal Artillery but was later seconded to the Military Police. I was stationed for a year in Hereford before my tour of duty to many parts of the world and eventually I left in 1962.

In 1963, having returned home to Liverpool, I found it very difficult to find employment so I accepted a job in Maidstone, Kent. I worked for Reed Medway Sacks, a subsidiary of The Daily Mirror Group, as a pulp analyst in the company's Elmsford plant, laboratory. Whilst living in Maidstone I met my first wife. She was a student from Valencia, Spain. We have two daughters. Both of our daughters were born in Liverpool at the Oxford Street Hospital, the first was born in 1964, the second 1965, both girls were pupils at Maricourt High School in Maghull.

My younger daughter is married and lives in Valencia, Spain with her husband and her son. My elder daughter now lives in York after living in Malaga and later Madrid for many years, two of her five children were born in Spain; fortunately, my daughters and I are reasonably fluent in the Spanish language.

In 1963 I returned to Liverpool after securing employment with The Ford Motor Company at Halewood. We bought a house in Green Park, Maghull, where we were resident for the next twenty years.

I then applied for a job as an electrician but was offered a position as a Quality Control Inspector at the company's transmission plant. I worked in that capacity for 21 years before leaving in 1983 to buy a restaurant in Fuengirola, Malaga, on Spain's Costa del Sol.

I have not been in contact with many Old Blues since leaving school but was really surprised when one day in the early eighties as I walked onto the shop floor and saw an old face from the past, Ian Bentham. He had just started as a production operator on one of the machines lines. I spoke to him on a few occasions but our paths did not cross that often. The last time I heard anything about him was that he had been elected by his colleagues to represent them as a shop steward. I am sure anybody who knows Ian, would agree that he would be perfect in his new vocation.

Ironically, one of the other pupils that I did meet was Ian's brother, Geoff. He had been a full prefect at school and like his brother, was a boarder. He was a brilliant footballer and a good cricketer, but it was at football he excelled, playing at club and international (Liverpool schoolboys and England schoolboys) level and later as a professional at Liverpool Football Club. Injury caused Geoff to leave the football career he loved so much. He then moved to Llorett de

Mar on Spain's Costa Brava where he opened a large and successful bar called 'The Londoners Bar'. I heard that he was living there so I called on him and his family at their apartment in the town.

For many years I drove from my home in England to my mother-in-law's home in Valencia, so it was easy to visit him and his family on the way down. We did this on a few occasions, but lost contact when I moved to live in the south of Spain.

Unfortunately, my marriage broke up whilst I was in Spain so I decided to return to the U.K. Before I left Spain, however, I met my present wife, Carol. We met through a mutual friend who introduced us; Carol had been a guest of this friend on many occasions and both ladies were from York.

On returning to England we took up residence in York and bought our first public house in a place called Pocklington, some eighteen miles away.

A year later I was admitted to Killingbeck Hospital in Leeds, having being diagnosed as having angina (narrowing of the arteries). My condition was regarded as serious and the coronary heart specialist said that I had to undergo an emergency heart operation. A triple-by-pass operation was performed successfully, and to this day I continue to enjoy good health due to the wonderful expertise and care afforded me by the hospital and its dedicated staff.

Five years later we bought another pub in the centre of York, reputedly one of the most haunted pubs in Britain, 'The Anglers Arms' in Goodramgate, starting point for the famous 'Ghost Walk'. Two years later we expanded to our third pub, which was in Leeds. 'The Buffers' had been transformed to a large pub from the railway station in a village called Scholes. It was part of Dr. Beeching's railway closures in the sixties. The restaurant area of the pub was a luxury Pullman railway carriage which had been integrated into the building: the whole theme and decor of the pub was its former status as a railway station.

In 1997 we sold our pubs and bought a retail unit from a firm of solicitors in York city centre. We converted this unit into a high class licenced tearoom/bistro - 'Kings on the Square'. This was aptly named, as it was situated in Kings Square. Like all businesses in York we suffered from our rents and rates matching those of London, but without the income that the capital generated.

We sold our tearoom and bought a mobile catering unit from the manufacturers in Preston. We called our new enterprise 'The Hogroast'. We specialised in lovely big, hot, pork, beef, lamb and chicken rolls. We were based in the city centre open market, for six years; it was by far the best little business we had ever had. York being such a large tourist city, benefited from millions of visitors every year and also many famous celebrities performed at the theatres there. The very popular 'York Races', which are held on the Knavesmire, involves several meetings each year which are attended by hundreds and thousands of people from all over the world. We were very fortunate to have met some wonderful people during our tenure in the market.

I retired last year 2006, at the age of 65. My wife and I now enjoy ourselves by entertaining our friends and families, which include our joint total of thirteen grandchildren and three great grandchildren.

I consider myself very fortunate that I have had a wonderful schooling, which prepared me for the world that I was about to enter after my schooldays. I have faced many hardships and difficulties throughout my adult life, but without having the sound grounding that a boarding school gave me I would not have survived as I have.

I remember my first day in the army; a big strapping sergeant took us into a storeroom where a guy behind the counter weighed me up, purely for sizing purposes, and then threw a bundle of smelly khaki clothing at me. This was followed by one pair of navy P.E. shorts for the use of, one cap badge, one set of mess tins, one kit bag for the use of, etc. etc. The only difference, this wasn't Horne Brothers! I went into a long room called a billet. In this room, down both sides, were lines of beds and lockers: it could have been a dormitory. A corporal came in shouting and bawling about making your bed in the morning, cleaning your bed-space (Oh no! not with Ronuk and a bumper!) getting to the ablutions at six o'clock in the morning (will the matron be there?), then present yourself in an orderly queue at the cookhouse, (normally called a dining room), marching in and forming lines at the tables that have lance corporals and corporals sitting at the ends to ensure your silence throughout the meal.

A breakfast of porridge and a piece of bread. A corporal coming around giving out mail and parcels from home, from Mum and Dad, brothers and sisters and worst of all, wives and sweethearts.

That high-pitched, terrifying screech at night, 'Lights out!' The whimpering from beneath the bed clothes as homesickness takes over, the threats emanating from the newly self-appointed bully about what he is going to do if his orders and demands are not carried out, the noise of creaking springs as the self-abuse kicks in, the morning when the assembled troops are informed 'We have a bed-wetter in our midst'.

Yes, it is true that the young of today may find all these trials and tribulations hard to get accustomed to.

BUT AT THE LIVERPOOL BLUECOAT SCHOOL FOR BOYS WE DID ALL THESE THINGS AND MANY MORE ARDUOUS TASKS AND - WE WERE ONLY EIGHT TO FIFTEEN YEAR OLDS.

We all stuck together and lived by our school motto:

'NON SIBI SED OMNIBUS' 'Not for oneself but for all'

FOOTNOTE

For anybody to think that the article about my flogging in Shirley Hall besmirches Mr. Watcyn's character in any form could not be more misguided. Although it was quite normal in those days for Blue Coat boys to suffer corporal punishment in many guises, in my particular case Mr. Watcyn did everything he could, and tried every method available to him to bring me into line, but somehow I always managed to frustrate him.

No, this is more about how great the man was as a headmaster; nobody got the better of him; and also what we must never forget is that this man was a devout Christian, a lay preacher. The truth is that I will always feel that I owe a big debt of gratitude towards Mr. Watcyn and a lot of his colleagues for bringing me around from the brat that I was, to the young man they sent out of the Blue Coat School in 1956. If only we had a school full of teachers like Mr. Watcyn nowadays, just think how this society would be. Can you see him standing in front of a pupil who was ranting at him 'You touch me and I'll sue you,' or maybe 'I am going to report you to the police for assault?'

William T. Bowden (1949-1956)
Now living in York.

THE BLUE COAT SCHOOL & GROUNDS IN 1950

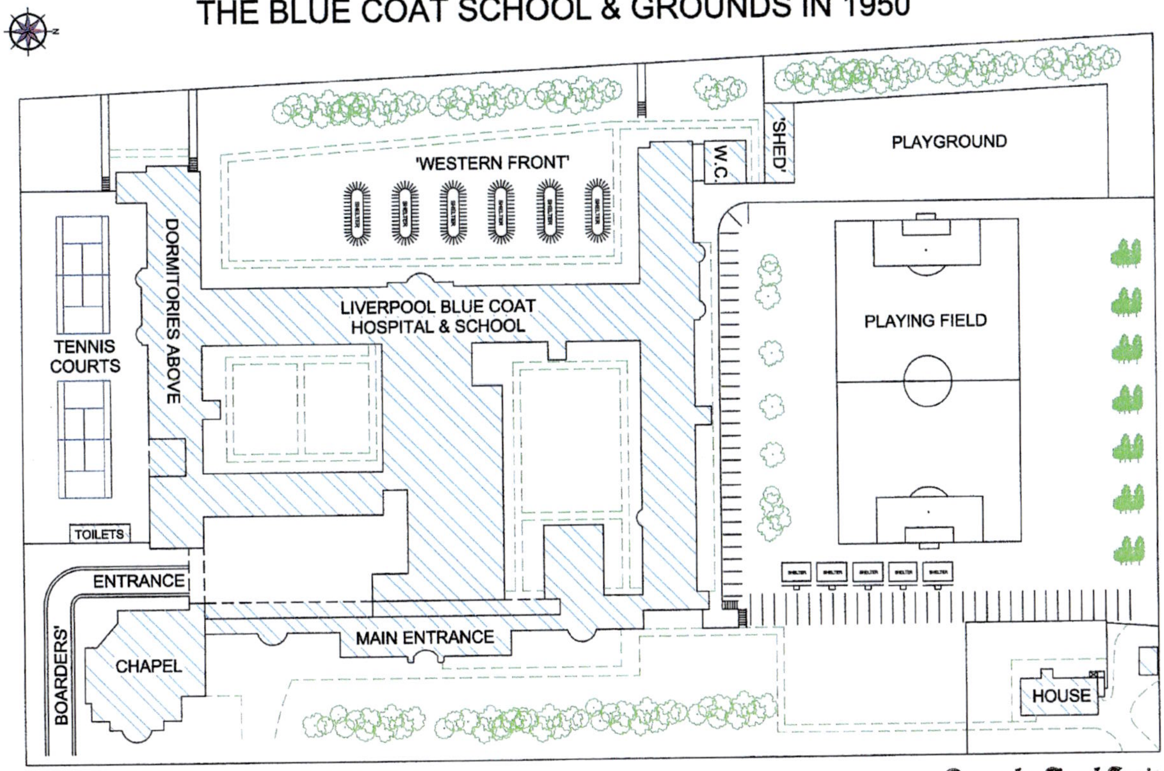

Drawn by: Frank Irwin

CHAPTER 4
OLD BLUES' PERSONAL MEMORIES

HUBERT'S MEMORIES

On leaving the Blue Coat School in 1965, I went to live in Preston and did three years at Preston Art School followed by another two years at Blackpool Art School. At the age of 21 I commenced working on motorways and on building sites/farms/factories/offices, wagon driving etc., you name it I did it. At the age of 38 I met my wife (a customer on my market stall) and soon after moved up to Skye, to a stone built house with 17 acres of land and a small trout stream. I have 3 children of my own and also 2 step children.

We started a small local museum in 1988, and later incorporated a nearby bagpipe museum which had recently closed down. Life has turned out O.K. after my early start, slow marching to Dr. (Fishy) Dickerson's dirge.

I remember a lad called Kelly and him telling me that he had scaled the clock tower. If I remember rightly, I went with him once up into the roof space up by the old chemistry laboratory. We didn't have a torch but went a fair way along! I think the same guy had one or two pet mice in the crypt. As some of you will recall, the place was chock-a-block with pews, chairs and god knows what else.

Kelly was well in with the caretaker, who we used to call 'Dewdrop' because he had a constantly running nose. Remember the cobbler in that courtyard? I was sent to him one day to have my shoes stitched. They looked and felt horrible. Mr. Watcyn also sent me to have my trouser pockets sewn up, (another cure that didn't work with me as, I still keep my hands in my pockets to this day).

Also I remember being hit on the head with a cricket ball and being given an aspirin! The large bump was treated by being dabbed with a cloth filled with stuff called 'Dolly Blue'! It must have worked, but can you imagine it being used today?

I remember two school trips. The first was to London to see the decorations for the forthcoming coronation and I got into trouble with 'Mousey' Hamilton in the Tower of London; we got lost on purpose and found ourselves in a large room where people were cleaning suits of armour! There was even an escapologist outside the Tower, stripped to the waist and bound over with miles of chains with a sack over him? What a way to make a living!

The second was a coach trip to Beaumaris in Anglesey, stopping on the way back at Betws-y-Coed, where some kid fell down a waterfall, (probably the Swallow Falls). Sitting there, seeing him covered in blood, and with the smell of sick all over the floor didn't make for a pleasant journey home. We had been given some cheap pop which was such a rare treat that we drank every last drop.

One night with another kid, being caught out of bed in the dormitory, we were made to stand outside the staff room with bare feet on the marble floor, arms outstretched and with a Bible or prayer book on each hand. After a while, when we started dropping them, a change was made and instead we were made to stand some distance from the wall supporting ourselves with our fingertips. Many years later I believe this punishment was given by the army to members of the I.R.A., until it was deemed inhumane conduct!

As far as I remember, I was not punished when attending Mosspits Lane County Primary School, (children were sent there if they were under age for attendance at Blue Coat) and things got a bit better when the dayboys were admitted. I think there was some realisation by the teachers that they sometimes overstepped the mark, we being virtual prisoners. Another incident, clearly in my mind and never to be forgotten, was when Mr. Watcyn, the headmaster, helped by Mr.

Unwin, the senior master tried to turn me into a zebra using canes; the blue marks lasted for a week at least. They surely knew it was unacceptable and actually tried to console me when they realised they had gone too far. It still rankles after all these years!

🏛

A few memories about the food: my mate and I used to open a door of the small room used by the cleaners/caretaker to store their equipment. One particular day, when we switched the light on, there were a few medium sized cockroaches, but also hundreds of tiny ones that with the pattern on the floor gave an hallucinatory effect. This, I suppose, was acceptable and quite entertaining, but one night, on a raid to the kitchen, and only finding some half-rotten carrots, I lifted the lid on a large cauldron which was absolutely thick with massive cockroaches on the surface of the following morning's porridge. After that, I was even hungrier because I would never eat the lumps off the skin that was served! And indeed, for all my life since, I have observed a policy of never eating out.

🏛

I don't know when the trams were replaced by buses, but I remember the last leg of my journey to the school from city centre on a No.8 tram. I was always full of wild ideas, like should I run away or face again (in my mother's words) that fine school and that very nice gentleman Mr. Watcyn. Under the constant uncertainty of the mood of those in charge of us, we created our own little world.

🏛

A lad in our dormitory (I can't remember the year) had a battery operated radio in a (then modern) white rexine-type box. His name was Derek Prince. Another lad in the dormitory was Charlie Puckey, who fancied himself as another Al Martino (a singer). I had a small crystal set (about 4 x 3 inches) in a pink plastic case, with a very cheap pair of earphones with a metal frame that went over my head and caught my hair every time I moved. They cost about 30/- (£1.50 in today's money) and more than one boy had one of these.

I don't remember the armoury even though we did rifle drill in the cadets, but there must have been two doors opposite Mr. Unwin's study. The small room I went into (I think with Kelly) had a full-size antique blunderbuss, also a set of handbells and all sorts of other gear, but I had to make a quick retreat when somebody said 'Douse!' I admit I did take one of the bells and I had to keep it for years afterwards because I was never able to put it back.

When people were expelled, it didn't matter what time of the day it was, they just seemed to disappear off the face of the earth never to be seen again. Like the lad who was beaten on a Sunday afternoon in the dining room for reading a Hank Jansen book in the chapel.

Does anyone know the name given to the type of collar we wore with the old uniform? They were not what you would call a dog collar as a vicar would wear! I ask this as I remember when I first started they were always kept in a laundry basket (just like the dirty sock basket! That was a horrible experience if you had the misfortune to be thrown in it!). The collars were all starched and ironed: the problem was that if you were unlucky enough to get one of the last ones, they tended to be those that nobody else wanted because they had shorter cords on them - not long enough to tie a bow.

On one occasion I was assisted at the last minute by some older boy, who resorted to tying the ends in a knot, very tightly round my neck. After the 'slow march' into Shirley Hall, kneeling on the tiered platform and not being able to breathe properly, I fainted and collapsed onto the kids in the row in front. I vaguely remember being carried out through the double doors and, believe it or not, NOT being punished for this disruption.

At one point our Saturday night movie must have been a film about the war, because a craze developed of making parachutes out of our handkerchiefs. Remember we used to tie a knot in each corner and attach string with a weight at the bottom for stability? We would fold the completed article up with great care and then proceed to throw the thing out of a high window, usually a dormitory window, and then watch it land.

☖

Another time, my mate Chingo and I got hold of some cycle inner tubes, which, when cut, made very strong elastic bands. These bands and two bits of wood, together with a nail, could be made into a gun. On a Sunday walk we found a house with pebble-dash, and were able to fill our pockets with good ammunition. I seem to remember they were confiscated.

☖

There were both good and bad memories of teachers. Mr. Scarland inspired me to go to art school after leaving the Blue Coat. He did this by showing me a large oil painting of his wife undressed! He was a very entertaining teacher.

On the other side of the coin, there was Mr. Eade. His main hobby seemed to be dipping into our pocket money without our consent and presenting us each with a nail file and a comb (no doubt everyday items to him, but not to us).

I remember Mr. Slater was a cold fish. I remember his face, not a pleasant memory, and a Mr. Dodd (who had a wooden hand) regaling us with his memories of landing a plane on an aircraft carrier in rough seas. If I remember rightly, the wooden hand (fist) on some occasions came into contact with boys' heads.

☖

One day at the end of term, Mr. Watcyn assembled us all in Shirley Hall, (we sat there in trepidation wondering what we had done wrong!). He announced that next term there would be a new boy starting at the school who suffered from alopecia, his name was Davidson. He then went on to describe what that particular disease involved – having no hair, baldy as we schoolboys would call it.

We were also informed however, that he was perfectly capable of looking after himself, so we were not even to consider the possibilities of either poking fun at him or bullying. Now there was a challenge!

Anyway, next term duly arrived as did Davidson. As far as I remember, on his first night in the dormitory the door was swung open by a master (Mr. Edwards, I think) to see what the commotion was. He found Chingo Chandler using the wig like a Frisbee to the delight of everyone else! Punishment was severe.

⇧

Another memory from that dim, murky past; was getting a printed invitation from the Lord Mayor with my name on it. I can't remember how many of us went to the Town Hall, but when we entered we handed the card to a guy who then announced us. Our invitation was as a result of the Lord Mayor's attendance at the school annual Speech Day, and there was some real food laid on.

Also a trip to the deaf & dumb school (I think down Smithdown Road) with the school choir (the deaf ones were lucky). We couldn't understand why we were singing to the deaf but still, it was a trip out.

⇧

I well recollect the day that the Bristol 'Brabazon' aircraft flew over the school. I was with some friends and we were aware of the time to be watching the sky - so it must have been advertised as a flypast to promote it - it was bloody big! Not like the ones that scream over our house now, whilst having dog fights below radar level!

On the subject of aeroplanes, I well remember making a model of a Kiel Kraft SE5 bi-plane, powered by rubber-band, and a Hawker Hunter powered by a Jetex engine. I can still remember the smell of a Jetex engine, even in the large dormitory where we had our 'craft club': in there the window sills were wide enough to work on. I believe now the Kiel Kraft kits are highly collectable (you get the odd one on eBay). In addition there was the Cadet Glider with a wingspan of about 2ft. available. One boy older than me and with a lot more money, made a Chief or Chieftain glider - quite a massive thing, but I think it crashed badly on the playing field!

Hubert Manwaring (1948-1955)
Now living on The Isle of Skye.

FRANK'S MEMORIES

I left The Liverpool Blue Coat School in 1957 to train as a Marine Engineer with Shell Tankers Limited. I was sent to Birkenhead Technical College full-time for 2 years to obtain a Diploma in Mechanical Engineering, after which I travelled the world for a few years to complete my apprenticeship before marrying in 1961. We bought a house in Prenton in Wirral and later moved to Thingwall also in Wirral. At that time I worked as a senior engineer in a multi-national pharmaceuticals company for 27 years before being made redundant when the factory was shut down in 1996, leaving only research operational. I decided to become self-employed and set up an engineering consultancy business. (F.I.E.S.) Still living in Wirral, I semi-retired in 2001, and retired fully in 2006. Happily married now for 46 years, Barbara and I have two daughters and 4 grandchildren.

🏛

First night back at school for a new term, we had to arrive on a Sunday afternoon and have a bath prior to going to bed. The bathroom was a large, first floor room decorated throughout in marble and tiles. It contained to the best of my memory 10 cast iron baths, five on each side of the room. It was always freezing cold in there during the winter terms, which was not helpful for new boys on their first day away from home as it only helped add to the general feeling of homesickness.

The first set of boys to bathe were each given a piece of red carbolic soap, chopped off from a long bar, naturally each piece had sharp corners and edges. Best practice was to throw the soap into the bath repeatedly until all the sharpness had been removed. Then we would fill the bath with the lukewarm water available and proceed to wash with it, whether in fact we needed a bath or not.

One particular teacher, Mr. Edwards, used to take great delight in scrubbing the back of every boy with a floor scrubbing brush until it was red and sore; this as he said he believed we were all dirty; which was purely fictional, for most parents, like mine, ensured that we were bathed before we left home for school.

Slightly earlier than Ray's experiences, during my time (1950-57) it was 'crystal sets' that were used to provide the dormitory entertainment. Favourite then was still Radio Luxembourg and I well remember listening to 'Valentine Dial The Storyteller' who recounted tales of murder and mystery, and 'The Black Museum', which I believe still exists in London. It was a museum containing souvenirs from famous murders; each time the show was on, the story surrounding one such piece of evidence was told. Another such favourite was 'Perry Mason', and his able secretary, Della Street, from the books written by the author Erle Stanley Gardner.

One had to hide under the bedclothes with the crystal set, and 'tickle' a crystal with a 'cat's whisker' until the best reception was obtained. What a difference from today's digital radios!

During Sunday afternoons between 2.00p.m. and 4.00p.m. we were allowed out of school to walk at liberty, but within a bounded area. This area included both Calderstones and Sefton Parks. Calderstones Park had a hothouse full of tropical foliage and shrubbery, whilst Sefton Park had a nice lake and at the edge of which was 'Old Nick's cave.'

I well remember one Sunday, Tommy Hudson and I were feeling a little peckish and so we went into the kitchen and asked for some bread with which to feed the ducks on the lake. We were given a fair amount and it was fairly fresh and certainly edible.

Anyway it was never intended for the ducks, because as mentioned earlier, we were somewhat hungry, so we ate the lot ourselves, saying 'Sod the ducks!'

An aunt of mine, Vera, my Dad's sister, presently in 2007, 92 years of age, reminded me recently, that on a regular basis I used to hop on a bus at Picton Clock and visit her during my Sunday afternoon walks, for tea and chocolate biscuits. On one occasion that I was found out, it was she and not my parents who were summoned to Mr. Watcyn's office to face his displeasure. I asked her if she could recall the conversation and if she was aware of why she and not my Dad was summoned, but at 92 she just said it was far too long ago. It would have been nice to have known the content.

She also reminded me that one Saturday afternoon I arrived with four schoolmates to watch the F.A. Cup final on her black & white T.V. That visit however, remained undiscovered.

⇧

When you wanted to look your best, which was very difficult for a boarder, the first priority was to have creases in your trousers; the correct creases that is, front and back.

Now trouser presses were a feature that school funds couldn't manage, (see the Board of Parsimony) the money had to be spent on electricity for the teachers to be able to keep warm rather than on personal street credibility for scruffy boarders.

What we used to do to create these creases was to lay the trousers down on a towel, (if I remember correctly the towels were green and white), wet the edges where we wanted the creases to be, then fold over the overhanging edges of the towel and place the completed combination under the bottom bed sheet so that we could lie on it. Lo and behold!, unless you had a restless night, the next morning you had a pair of well creased trousers.

I do remember the amateurs who were frightened of rolling over in the night and making a mess of things. One placed the towel and trousers under the mattress; the next morning the trousers were well pressed, but with the outline of the diamond shape of the bed springs deeply engrained and making a nice 'Paisley' type pattern all over.

⇧

It was a condition of school attendance that all boarders were confirmed, in the school chapel, into the Church of England. As a result we all had to attend confirmation classes in which we learned the responses to the catechism. In a final instructional talk prior to actual confirmation, we were told not to wear 'Brylcreem' on our hair because the Bishop didn't like getting his hands greasy.

On a weekly basis, it befell dormitory residents to carry out a thorough clean of the floor, which included a final polish. I forget the day on which the cleaning took place, although I seem to remember it was a Saturday and immediately before breakfast.

Each dormitory, before the construction of 'the cubicles' (studded timber clad in hardboard to provide some degree of privacy to either a single boy, or a group of four boys, dependent on seniority of age) consisted of two rows of cast iron framed beds on opposite sides of the room, alongside the walls. The floors were tongue and groove timber with a highly polished finish. (See photograph, Page 326).

The drill was for the nominated three boys to each perform a task of moving beds, brushing and finally polishing the floor.

Firstly, the beds from one side would be pushed into the beds on the other side leaving a long strip of floor exposed.

This was then brushed to remove all the dust and fluff, and then the 'dummy', a large heavy block on the end of an oscillating handle, was moved manually along the floor with a side-to-side swinging motion, applying a polish called Ronuk to the exposed area.

Finally a large soft cloth would be placed underneath the dummy, and the swinging action repeated to give a final polish to the area.

This having been done, the beds would be pushed over to the other side of the room and the operation would be repeated. Finally the centre section would be completed then, following a satisfactory inspection, we could all have breakfast.

⇧

At some significant point in time, we learned that the staff had posh breakfasts, i.e. their toast was served up with the crusts removed (perhaps to aid mastication when eating with old-style dentures). We boys were never served toast as far as I can recall, so on discovering this we asked could we have the crusts ourselves to supplement our morning diet. As a result we were served the off-cuts in a large bowl and we used to butter them. (Remember butter was margarine for six days of the week, but was always known as 'a butter'). We use to call this special treat 'crispies'.

⇧

One time, I had an idea to supplement my diet by planting radishes in a small plot of soil in the easterly corner of the north quadrangle, close to what is known today as Peg Leg's corridor. On my return to school after the Easter break however, I was disappointed to discover that builders had deposited a pile of rubble directly on top of my anticipated yield thus rendering it useless.

⇧

One school holiday, some of the boys in our class were invited to go potato picking on a farm in Childwall. The farm was owned by the father of one of our classmates and we were to be paid 10/- per day each; a wonderful amount of money in those days for a schoolboy.

I remember cycling there each day for a week from my home in West Derby, some 4 miles away. When we got there we discovered that the ground to be picked was divided up by the use of wooden stake markers, into 12 equal sized plots.

We were each allocated a plot and were to dig the ground with a fork without spoiling the spuds and were to place them in piles ready for collection by the farmer; which he did regularly with his tractor to keep the area clear for more digging.

Being grammar school boys, in order to keep ourselves educated and occupied mentally, we translated into French, (as best we could as we didn't have a French-English dictionary to hand) the song *Davy Crockett,* maintaining the theme tune from the film. It worked out quite well actually, 'Davy, Davy Crockett, Roi de la frontiere.' We did have to employ what is now called 'Franglais' to enable us to sing the words that we failed to translate.

At the end of the day we were allowed to take a few spuds home in our saddlebags to contribute towards our dinner, and perhaps to enable us to maintain our strength for the next day's work.

The second day started and things seemed to have changed; my area to be picked seemed to have become longer than on the first day. To remedy the situation I moved my markers closer to me, reverting my area back to normal. What I didn't realise at the time, was that the next guy, on noticing the same thing happening to him also moved his markers. This continued down the line until the poor guy at the other end had twice as much as everybody else to work in. He then started moving the markers back and so the thing progressed until the boy who had started the ball rolling had too much ground to cover himself and so eventually things calmed down.

The work lasted a week, during which we each made £3.10s.0d., developed our muscles and learned to sing *Davy Crockett* in French. To add to all that our parents had a few bob's worth of free spuds. I, like the others, was sorry to see the work finish as the money earned was very acceptable.

One of our more competitive sports played at school was chariot racing. This was carried out in the dormitories during the early evening and acted as a soporific inducement, helping us to get to sleep more easily (although that was not the reason for the sport).

To participate in the event you had to be a jockey, a horse or a spectator, the chariot being formed by laying a dressing gown on the floor with the sleeves laid out at the front to act as chariot shafts.

The race would be over a distance, previously agreed, something like four lengths of the dormitory. The chariots would be lined up at one end of the room, in the centre where the beds were not located, and where the floor had a nice shine from the Ronuk polish that was applied weekly. The jockeys would sit on the dressing gowns and the horses would pick up the sleeves, one in each hand, and at the word 'Go' all hell would break loose, as the charge commenced down the dormitory to the first turn at the wall at the end.

There were no rules, other than the first chariot to complete the course with the jockey still on board, was the winner. There was no prize to be won; the excitement was the event and the fighting to win that continued until everybody was so tired that they were ready for bed. If the arms came off the dressing gown, well it was much cooler then when it was worn in the summer. Teachers did not seem to bother themselves with the activity; it was either too much trouble to intervene, or they considered it good healthy fun.

Frank Irwin (1950-1957)
Now living in Wirral

RAY'S MEMORIES

After the Radio Officer phase of my working life, I left the sea and did 28 years in the Telecoms Section of British Rail; finally being made redundant. I did part-time clerical work for nearly four years, but then decided to call it a day and retire properly. I must say I've had a great time since then.

Mr. Perry was one of those teachers who had evidently gone 'through it' in WW2.

One afternoon I excused myself from my class and decided to use the toilets at the north side of the school for a change. As I walked along the Grammar School corridor I was happily whistling to myself, but suddenly a door opened behind me and Mr. Perry quietly called to me 'Come here, Livingston'. Unaware of my danger I obeyed, but he told me to come closer. When I was suitably within range he uttered the words 'You will write out 500 times, I will not whistle in the CORRIDOR!!', and with the last word he thumped me hard across my left ear. It ruined my day, as you can imagine. He simply couldn't stand whistling and someone later told me that it dated from a bad experience during the war.

⇧

In my early days at the school, Saturday mornings were a bit hard to get through because I didn't yet know people very well, and after the hurly-burly of the week I craved a quiet corner where I could be by myself for a while. A recce soon revealed that the most promising place was the polished fire escape staircase that served the Graham and Bingham dormitories, so up I went.

Some way up I came across two boys who were sitting chatting. One was called Murray Brown and his brother, much younger than he, may have been called Ian Brown, but was at that time known to all as 'Little Brown'. It turned out that Murray was an expert on naval matters and was passing on his knowledge to his little brother. It was a topic I knew very little about and it sounded interesting, so I got their permission to join in. For the first time I got to know what the differences were between battleships, cruisers and destroyers, and what their various theoretical roles amounted to in wartime, etc., etc. He knew a lot of naval history too.

A few years ago I was browsing in a library and glanced at a book called *Jane's All the World's Trains*. The author was one Murray Brown, so it is possible to speculate that he went into the famous 'Jane's' organisation on the strength of his naval knowledge and had a long career there.

⇧

Once per week, the school served peanut butter to the boys - a product I was previously unfamiliar with. Visually it was not enticing, but hunger and the fact that there was nothing else on offer encouraged bravery. The first mouthful was a shock for it dried up ones mouth juices and became almost intolerably cloying, but it wasn't long before a liking for the peculiar substance had taken over and you looked forward to the next occasion. I don't recall anyone ever enquiring whether or not we were allergic to peanuts.

⇧

One winter's day I decided I didn't fancy spending my lunch break in the cold yard so I hunkered down beneath my desk in the classroom and got on with my book. A few minutes later the door opened and Mr. Rowlands and a boy he was tutoring took over the teacher's desk at the front. I lay doggo for about twenty minutes but eventually tired of the situation (perhaps the book wasn't holding my attention or I simply lost my nerve). What happened next? Mr. Rowlands suddenly saw a figure rise from a desk near the back of the erstwhile silent room and heard it say the immortal words 'Please sir, I'm here'. He was completely flummoxed and could only reply 'Oh, well, clear off then!', or words to that effect. I promptly left the room and that was that.

Given this man's violent reputation, described elsewhere in this book, I know that I had a lucky escape here. I must have been saved by the element of sheer surprise.

⇧

The naughtiest thing that I got up to was a spin-off from the stargazing sessions that Eric Winterbottom and I used to have on the tennis courts. After one of these, it suddenly dawned on us that if we went into the corner by the double gates, we could climb over the wall and get into the rear garden of the Conservative Club. Then we could walk down the cul-de-sac Barnhill Road and reach the 'chippy' on Smithdown Road. This proved so successful that it became quite a frequent escapade and others soon joined us.

We were never caught, but we had a couple of near-misses when our exit coincided with a meeting at the club and people came up Barnhill Road and into the garden. We had to dash into the flowerbed where the street lights didn't shine, and on more than one occasion I had to hide my face and hands in my navy-blue jumper while people passed just a few feet from me and I worried about whether they might spot my shiny shoes. Back at the school it was a wonder that no one rumbled us from the smell of our chippy breath!

⇧

I could weep when I think about poor Mr. Hugh A. Gibson and the hard time he was given at the Blue Coat School. He was such a lovely bloke - kind, generous and wanting to do his best for everyone. Unfortunately, the hard types picked up on the fact that he had a low 'breaking point' and they could gain amusement at his cost. I witnessed quite frightening scenes in the classroom when the poor man was goaded by these bullies to the point when he turned violent; every boy in the room receiving a hard thump on the middle of his back. I don't think I was so much frightened of Mr. Gibson but rather the willingness of the fools to continue the goading process when the terrible damage they were causing was already clear. I have always assumed that his problems must have stemmed from difficult wartime experiences (I judge that he would have been in his late teens towards the end of World War II).

Aware of these difficulties, I was shocked one afternoon to overhear a spat with Mr. Slater just before Mr. Gibson walked into our classroom. This suggested to me that his tormentors might not all be boys.

I hope he found peace in his next appointment, which I recall was a school in Plymouth. He had a greatness of spirit, so I hope this saw him through and brought him much better things. He deserved better.

⇧

One Saturday morning, Eric and I were loafing around on the landing outside Stythe dormitory - a place where we were not really meant to be at that time of day. Suddenly we heard sounds of people coming up the stairs from the ground floor, so we flew into the dormitory and threw ourselves under the bed in the prefect's cubicle on the right-hand side. To our dismay, the people came into that very cubicle and began to hold a conversation. Eric and I silently took steps to ensure that we had shrunk back as far back as possible so that our presence would not be detected. We were amused, or should I say bemused, to find that we were overhearing a conspiracy - the intention of Nigel Baker-Bates and his friends (for that was who the people were) was to ascend the clock tower that night and hang a cheeky banner over the parapet.

Everything happened as per the planning and Eric and I were careful to keep silent about what we knew. Despite this, the group were found out and punished; Baker-Bates even being asked at a later stage to leave the school, although it was not just for this one escapade.

⇧

We lived in Huyton, and during one Sunday Walk I took a chance and walked to Childwall Fiveways, where I caught a Crosville bus. I got aboard and looked forward, and to my dismay recognised the bluff shape of Mr. Crebbin's head! Surely he must have seen me as the bus drew to a stop?

I nipped upstairs smartish and sat in the corner seat, from where I could look down and watch him get off.

To my relief he eventually did, and I was able to get off at my own stop and dash home. I thought I had got away with it, but that evening as I chatted to my mother after the chapel service, someone summoned me to the vestibule where Mr. Crebbin wanted to speak to me.

He had evidently bided his time until this moment, no doubt to also involve my mother if necessary! I escaped with a warning after I explained that I had been threatened by the woodwork master, Mr. Holiday, not to attend another of his classes without my apron.

⇧

A popular target for adventurous boys who wanted to go somewhere illicit was the crypt beneath the chapel. I never got there myself but I understand it was full of junk. A chap called Bob Kelly claims to have climbed the tower via a drainpipe!! At the school's Open afternoon in 2006 he pointed out the window where he started the expedition; the first in a line of windows above the kitchen.

🛆

Another dramatic incident that I remember, involves staff bullying. One evening, a Sunday I think it must have been, we were queuing up for tea along the Secondary Modern classroom corridor and the dining room tables were full of hard-boiled eggs in eggcups. Suddenly 'Taffy' Davies stormed along the line of boys shouting out in his Welsh tones 'Somebody has stolen a hard-boiled egg! Own up! Who was it?' This was fine so far, but suddenly, without any proof, he landed on a boy called 'Bowdo' Bowden, who was quite a tough guy, and smacked him repeatedly about the head whilst shouting 'Was it you, Bowden?' The poor lad, who may well have been innocent, was in tears. This was one incident that did not reflect well on 'Taffy', who was a hero in so many other ways.

🛆

Transistor radios! They were the equivalent of today's iPods and laptop PCs, and a steadily increasing number of boys acquired one during the four years of my time at the school (1955-59). I suspect they were contraband in the dormitory, but it was mainly there after 'lights out' that you heard them being played (always 208 metres Radio Luxembourg, of course). I have no specific recollection of anyone having a transistor radio confiscated, but I guess there must have been some instances.

🛆

Somebody had a transistor radio playing in Bingham dormitory in January 1956 as I helped to polish the floor with the dummy, and that day proved to be a seminal moment in my life for it was when I first heard the sounds of what came to be known as skiffle music (Lonnie Donegan singing *Rock Island Line*). Nationwide, a huge craze stemmed from this; many thousands of youngsters forming groups, but by the summer it had been overtaken by rock 'n' roll because American artists like Elvis Presley and Buddy Holly had arrived on the popular music scene.

By about 1960, two of the school's Old Boys, Billy Hatton and Brian O'Hara were themselves involved in the local music scene, their group achieving national fame as the Fourmost two or three years later; part of the Merseybeat phenomenon that flowed from the unprecedented success of the Beatles. Like the Beatles, the Fourmost were managed by Brian Epstein, and Lennon and McCartney penned a song especially for them.

My only involvement with Mr. Tait (Captain Tait) was the P.E. lessons he took us for from 1955 until 1958. When he left the school his replacement was a Mr. Weedall, I think, and we were all startled to discover that Capt. Tait had let us down in one aspect of our physical development; he had failed to develop our arms! Neither did we like all of Mr. Weedall's solutions to the crisis - one of the things he did was make us don boxing gloves and knock the stuffing out of one another!

I remember how there used to be a tradition that your parent(s) could take you away from school on the Saturday following your birthday and treat you to an outing in Liverpool (sadly it was dropped in about 1958 and I never learned why this was). The first time it happened to me was in February 1956 and my mother took me to a pantomime. Who did I find sitting a few rows behind me in the stalls? Mr. Tait and his family (leastways, I HOPE it was his family!)

Come the interval, an ice cream, or perhaps a lolly, appeared over my shoulder and someone informed me that it was a gift from Mr. Tait. Kids of twelve years of age don't forget an unexpected act of kindness like that, as this account proves.

Dai Davies gave me a shock one evening. I had been misbehaving in Bingham dormitory in some trivial way and he took me onto the landing and hit my bare behind with his hard-soled slipper. Really, it's strange that we look back with fondness to our Blue Coat days!

In 1958 a certain girls' school (presumably Olive Mount) contacted the Blue Coat and requested that my class retime its visits to the Picton Road Library in order that we would not coincide with one of their classes. The headmistress went on to explain that their girls had become excited and therefore uncontrollable. Going at a different time was a nuisance to us for it prevented a natural connection with our trip to Picton Road Baths and gave us an added journey, but nobody minded because the incident had been good for our egos.

⇑

Another memory I have of Mr. Tait was in the spring of 1956 when my class (1M) had just had a P.E. lesson that comprised a football session somewhere. For the first time, he applied some pressure on us to drop our shyness, strip off and get into those so far unused communal showers! As he no doubt well knew, we were at that borderline stage of development when some had started puberty and some hadn't, so at the time it was quite a big deal to us little 12-year-olds. Nevertheless, under his cajoling we managed to overcome the initial awkwardness and were thenceforward able to enjoy the facilities without embarrassment; and we were less smelly too.

The most enjoyable P.E. sessions that I can ever recall having were when Mr. Tait had us all playing something called Crab Football. It was a bit like soccer, except that you played it in the gym in teams of five players and you sat on your bottom and shuffled round the floor with your arms behind you supporting your body weight.

It was lively action and great fun, but I had never heard of the game before nor heard of it since, which seems a shame.

⇑

On two occasions I received four strokes of the cane from Watcyn - and boy did it sting!! The wretch was incredibly skilled at it and could be sure to hit the fingerprint area every time without fail. The first occasion was only a few days into my time at the school; some observant master having spotted that I had failed to brush my shoes for assembly. The cruelty was overwhelming to a kid whose only experience of corporal punishment had been a female teacher at primary school lightly brushing his knuckles with a plastic ruler. It didn't help my struggle against homesickness either.

⇧

I would like to describe the scene in Mr. Unwin's study on the day that I received my second caning. I can no longer recall what I had done to earn it, which in itself is probably indicative of how slightly one had to transgress in order to earn such a thrashing.

It was like a scene from hell, because that day the room was pretty much filled up with boys who were there to be dealt with. Before he thrashed one particular boy, I actually heard Mr. Watcyn say to him 'This hurts me more than you!' I'm sure he meant it, but it seemed strange to hear those words said in a serious context when they were normally used in jokes.

Of course, in the old days the guiding light was 'Spare the rod and spoil the child' so we have to make allowances.

⇧

Remember how Mr. Perry used to be the school's unofficial watch-mender? One day my mother bought me my first ever watch and it broke within the first week or two. I copied others and took it straight to Mr. Perry, but he returned it to me very quickly and remarked (with diplomatic phraseology, of course) that it was a cheap thing and not worthy of his time.

⇧

As a schoolboy I used to enjoy reading things about the two world wars and found it all exciting. What a shock I got in October 1956 though when the Suez Crisis blew up and rumours abounded that our masters were likely to be called up! For the first time in my life I found myself looking at a war whose outcome was NOT known, and the experience taught me not to glorify the thing in future; there is a world of difference between reading a history and looking forward into an abyss!

The visit to the Town Hall recalled by Dave and Hubert elsewhere in this book may not have been an isolated occurrence. I remember my class (4M) being taken there in the spring of 1959 and being shown around by the then Lord Mayor, Mr. Harry Livermore. He was extremely friendly, attentive and inclusive, so one did not at any stage feel intimidated.

I don't think I ever saw him again, but he was a solicitor in Liverpool so his offices at the extreme eastern end of Dale Street were an occasional destination for me in my first job. His warm, welcoming performance that day has never been forgotten by me, however, for it was a civic *tour de force* and a very positive experience for budding citizens like us.

In about 1958 I remember being told that an American negro singer was coming to sing to us in the chapel. I looked forward to it eagerly because I jumped to the conclusion that he would be just like Little Richard and would sing a few lively rock 'n' roll numbers. Of course, the reality was far removed from that and he only sang negro spirituals and gospel songs.

Bath night! When I first arrived at the school there was little supervision and you could be 'got at' by bullies and almost drowned by being forced down in the bath while they sat on boards laid across the top (or so Stan told me at the time).

In my later years at the school, I and my age-group were slightly perplexed to find that the two school nurses - Mrs. Bowcock and Miss Allen, had commenced a new habit of standing on duty in the room as we bathed. They stood by the door looking, I thought, slightly uncomfortable, so it may well be that it wasn't their own idea and they were merely obeying fresh orders. Perhaps they enjoyed it, despite appearances.

In 1958 a revolutionary innovation was the arrival of a TV set! It was installed in a room opposite to Mr. Watcyn's office and the school office, and there was room enough for about twenty boys to cram in and watch, I think. Amongst many other things, I can remember watching the Johannson v Patterson boxing match there and the B.B.C.'s answer to the I.T.V. pop show *Oh Boy!*, called *Drumbeat*. No doubt its use was mainly confined to weekends, but I can't now recall. You certainly had the feeling that a quantum leap had been taken and the school had dipped at least a toe into the modern age.

One bright, sunny, Saturday afternoon in the spring of 1959, I happened to be standing in one of the two high dormitories, probably Earle dormitory - which until a couple of years earlier had been called Blundell dormitory - when two exciting crags about ten miles away to the south-east caught my eye. Much later I would learn that one of these loomed over the village of Frodsham and the other over the village of Helsby on the southern bank of the Mersey, but from the moment I first noticed them they came to represent in my mind the freedoms I would be able to enjoy when I had at last left this place; an event that, excitingly, might be just a few short months away.

A similar experience had been inadvertently provided a year or two earlier by our esteemed Mr. Hulford, for during one particular geography lesson he had issued each boy with a copy of an Ordnance Survey map that showed the Lairig Ghru area of the Cairngorm Mountains in Scotland, his object being to draw our attention to the awesome scouring power of the ice ages and tell us about moraines, etc., but it did not escape my attention that the area shown was a dramatic and exciting one that one day, when I was at last a free agent, I might become familiar with.

On leaving, I was quick to act on these spurs, and like so many others I have enjoyed many years of exploring such marvellous places, but my old desperate desire to escape from the confines of the Blue Coat School has been interestingly reversed and, like others, I take enormous pleasure in returning to the old buildings as frequently as I am able; just as though I am coming home.

In these pages we have sometimes been a little critical of Mr. Watcyn, but I think we should also acknowledge that in our boyhoods we felt secure and happy in his regime - because his leadership was so strong and he laid down such clear boundaries between acceptable and unacceptable behaviour. This largely explains why we all have such happy memories of our time in the Liverpool Blue Coat School.

In adulthood, I have always regretted my lack of involvement with at least some of the special interest groups during my time in the school. Chess is the prime example, for although I was intrigued by the sight of an adjourned position that Dave Williams showed to my brother in the dormitory in 1956, six years would elapse before I learned the game myself.

A similar case was classical music, for I recall being impressed by the ornate front cover of a Grieg piece that Mr. Jamieson had lying next to him in the film show room one day, and thinking to myself 'If the artist who drew that was trying to do justice to the music inside, then it must be worth hearing!' Years later when I became familiar with the music, my guess was shown to have been absolutely correct; but what a shame that the process had taken years! Finally, taking part in debates or being introduced in some small way to public speaking would have been good for the development of my confidence, but such a notion was evidently alien to those who were deciding how the Secondary Modern pupils should spend their time.

Does this mean that I and my classmates were neglected? Certainly it is a fact that grammar school pupils were treated very differently from we secondary modern ones, so failing the 11-plus was very like shooting myself in the foot.

I was a child who would have benefited from a Comprehensive education. I only recently learned that, in the 1950s, the disparity in the funding of a grammar school pupil over a secondary modern one was approximately ten-fold.

Ray Livingston (1955-1959)
Now living in York

STAN'S MEMORIES

I was a boarding pupil at the Blue Coat from 1952 to 1957. During that time, I became head choirboy and was a sub-editor for the school magazine *The Squirrel*.

After leaving the Blue Coat School in February 1957, I became an apprentice in the printing industry and worked for Eric Bemrose Limited in Aintree until being made redundant in 1990. The company finally closed in 1991 after operating for 53 years. From there, I opened my own music shop in Ormskirk in January 1991 but closed it down in January 1998 following declining sales brought about by unfair competition from pirates illegally copying music to sell at car boot sales, and music being downloaded for free via the internet. I currently work as an administrator for an engineering company in Skelmersdale.

🛱

I'm not sure exactly what year it was, possibly around 1954, but I remember the major installation of the gas boiler system that caused great disruption in the boiler house and in all other areas of the school.

I particularly recall workmen threading endless lengths of piping so they could be fastened together to supply hot water and heat the building.

My two favourite subjects were English and art. Ron Scarland, the art teacher, was one of my favourite staff members and my memories include one day during my final year when the weather was particularly bad and it was time to go out to the yard for the mid-morning break. I think Mr. Scarland could tell from the look on my face I didn't fancy going out and getting drowned, so he suggested I stay in the warm classroom and continue with my painting. Once the other lads were out of the way he lit a cigarette and offered me one which, of course, I sensibly declined.

🛱

Captain Tait, the teacher who was in charge of the school Army Cadets, had occasion to visit the dentist for emergency treatment. The dentist obviously had the impression that the Blue Coat's model soldier was tough enough to withstand a greater degree of pain than ordinary people and suggested a tooth be extracted without the support of an anaesthetic! Not wishing to be labelled a sissy, the captain agreed and returned to the school with a seriously swollen mouth that was clearly causing him considerable distress and pain. Surprisingly, there wasn't too much sympathy for him from his pupils!

While I'm on the subject of Captain Tait, it seemed he and Derek Jones had a mutual dislike of each other. At supper time one evening I remember Derek Jones was the duty teacher as the Captain arrived a few minutes late with a number of cadets. Derek Jones made a comment along the lines of 'Been playing soldiers again, have we?'

The comment clearly outraged the Captain; his face turned bright red as he lashed out verbally and struggled to control himself from physically attacking a shocked Derek Jones. The event lasted only seconds, but provided considerable entertainment for the pupils present

.⇧

Further to the mention in this book of pupils' holding séances, experimenting with Ouija boards was a regular activity to while away the evenings for some of the boarders at one time. I remember one occasion when we got through to the dead brother of one of the pupils; he had apparently died or been killed at a very young age and his message came through with loads of spelling mistakes indicative of someone who had possibly only just begun to learn to read and write. I can't remember the pupil's name, however.

On the subject of spiritualism, I can understand that some people are wary - even frightened - of dabbling in such activities. I've personally had some very interesting experiences both during and since my Blue Coat days and can assure sceptics there can be some very positive and reassuring results.

⇧

Some of my contemporaries may remember that towel fighting often included the wetting of the twisted or knotted end of the towel to add weight to the business end of the weapon. The chances that the victim would be most likely to receive a bruising when the towel connected were increased significantly, to the great satisfaction of the sadistic little horror administering the punishment!

⇧

I well remember the departure of Mr. Derek Jones, a.k.a. 'Delvante'. I had been on a hospital appointment that particular day and, as I returned to the school entrance adjacent to the chapel, Messrs. Jones and Perry were standing in the driveway apparently saying their goodbyes. They were both clearly in a serious mood, Mr. Jones had luggage with him and I seem to recall that Mr. Perry had his arm around his shoulder in a consoling manner. I said hello to both teachers as I passed by them, but it wasn't until I went into the school that I discovered exactly what had happened. I personally felt saddened at the whole episode; Derek Jones had been an entertaining and popular member of staff with many of the pupils and teachers alike, and we were sorry to see him go. He apparently went from the Blue Coat to Skerry's College in Rodney Street, but I don't know what happened to him after that.

⇧

In 1953 leading up to the Queen's coronation in June, I entered a poetry competition through the school for schoolchildren across Merseyside to compose a ditty about the event. I won, and went to Liverpool's Picton Library to receive my prize from the Lord Mayor. The prize was a book all about the Royal Family and I still have it to this day.

⇧

As I was returning to the school alone from a football match at Lance Lane late one afternoon in 1953, I was accosted by a man who had stepped out from a back entry on one of the roads leading down to Church Road. He had conveniently dropped a packet of photographs as I approached him and, being a well mannered Blue

Coat boy, I stopped and helped him pick them up without once bothering to check their content.

Once he had them all back, he suggested I stop for a moment and have a look at them. Although I wondered at the time why on earth anyone could think I would possibly be interested in pictures of people I'd never met, I didn't want to appear impolite and followed him into the entry to view the photos as he handed them to me, one by one.

The vision of pornographic poses of both men and women left me momentarily stunned; never in my life had I seen such filth. At the tender age of twelve, I had only the vaguest knowledge of sexual matters and, for a few frightening moments, I was frozen to the spot. I fortunately pulled myself together and had the presence of mind to turn and run like mad out of the entry and down the street, across Church Road and into the safety of the school gates.

I related the incident to one of my friends (possibly Peter Barr), who suggested I immediately inform the duty master who, I seem to remember, was 'Taffy' Davies. He went straight to the headmaster's house and told me I may be called later to recount the tale to the police.

At that time I still hadn't washed or changed from the football match and was still dressed in my soccer kit but, as is always demonstrated in detective stories, I felt it better not to disturb any of the evidence, so it was an unwashed and scruffy twelve-year-old who visited the headmaster's house later that evening!

I related every detail of the incident to the officer who was introduced to me by Mr. Watcyn. The interview lasted about thirty minutes, after which I returned to the school and washed away all the 'evidence' before going to bed.

It was during assembly the following morning that Mr. Watcyn (who clearly had no idea of the imaginative workings of the mind of a youngster) prattled on about cleanliness and personal pride in one's appearance that all pupils should practice. He quoted an incident of only the previous evening when one of the boarders had visited his house in an unwashed, dishevelled state to meet a visitor. He expressed disappointment that the offender should have known better, but at least our unimaginative headmaster was diplomatic enough not to name the pupil, nor go into the reasons for the visit!

As to the incident itself and my report to the police, I never heard of any progress being made in relation to the pervert being apprehended.

⇧

In 1955, as head choirboy, I was chosen along with two other choirboys to accompany a couple of our masters (I think one of them was Mr. Sephton) to an evening seminar in Liverpool city centre attended by teachers from other schools in the area.

The main reason for the seminar was for participating schools to demonstrate new inventions and ideas to each other that were considered to be potential new teaching aids for the future; the modern invention chosen for demonstration by the Blue Coat was a reel-to-reel tape recorder!

It was certainly not a portable piece of equipment, being the most gigantic, heavy, cumbersome piece of furniture you could imagine.

Microphone stands were assembled in front of the gathered audience and, to a piano accompaniment, we three choirboys sang two or three songs that we'd rehearsed during the previous week.

We never found out whether our teachers had got the wiring connectors mixed up or if they'd simply forgotten to adjust the recording level, but it was to the utter embarrassment of all concerned that the tape recorder failed to reproduce a single note and the demonstration ended with the reddest faces!

Stan Livingston (1952-1957)
Now living in Ormskirk

DAVE BOLT'S MEMORIES

I was studying at The Liverpool College of Commerce for what was then a degree in Export Practice. In 1960 a colleague was going to emigrate to Canada, it sounded to me like a great idea and in 1960 we arrived in Montreal only to find that my five years of French were useless; I could not even read a parking sign. I eventually got a job in a Canadian textile company in their export dept. as they were selling lots of products in England and I knew how to calculate the currency. I was subsequently married and started a family but in 1972 the politics and anti-English sentiment in Quebec was too great so we moved to Vancouver, where I ran a sales office for a Canadian textile company that was a subsidiary of Carrington Viyella of England. I was with them for 30 years and retired in 2002.

Now we live in the west coast rain forest and have a wooden house with a creek but no fish. We are planning to visit England next year; It will be the last time that I will return so I have to make it worthwhile.

⇧

I disliked the school cap intensely. It had a big peak and the wearing of it was mandatory going to and coming from the school. Mr. Watcyn had been known to hide up the side streets leading up to the Blue Coat School, as I and half a dozen others had spotted him as we rode our bikes home to Childwall, which involved cycling along those nearby roads and past Mosspits Lane Primary school. On the last day, on leaving the school for the last time, I impaled the cap on one of the spikes on the back gate. It felt very good.

⇧

I well remember another incident which happened when I was in 5G. A bunch of us were riding home one sunny afternoon, maybe six or seven of us, and I was the oldest. One guy, doing something stupid, crashed into a parked car with his bike and caused a small scratch. The car owner rushed out and played hell with us, and I spoke for the group but he didn't like what I said to him so he took my name and the next day in school I was told to see Mr. Watcyn. I was apprehensive to say the least and discussed the matter with my dad (the cop) who told me to tell Mr. Watcyn 'With respect sir, this is not a school matter'. I did as I was instructed and to my surprise it worked. Mr. Watcyn backed down and I didn't get the cane as expected.

🏛

I recall the Parry brothers were twins, and in fact I met Nigel after we had left school whilst taking a night school course in Export Practice at the Liverpool College of Commerce. He had, what I thought, was one of the best employers in the world at that time, 'Guinness', which had a bottling plant in Liverpool and exported the bottled beer around the world. Each employee, he informed me, was allowed to drink six bottles of Guinness a day 'on the house' which, I thought at the time was marvellous. However, some months later when we next met, he had stopped drinking the beer as it ruined his stomach. It proved that in this life there can be too much of a good thing.

The name of Banks cropped up recently and reminded me of a Robin Banks, who was a member of my class and who was at that time reading aloud from a text book during one of Mr. Edwards history lessons. The topic involved was the Roman occupation of Britain and in particular, how they heated their dwellings during cold periods.

The line in the book stated that the houses were heated with fires, in baskets, beneath the floors and that the baskets were called braziers. Banks read the word as 'brassieres' which caused an uproar in the class room. I can well remember Mr. Edwards' reaction which was to splutter out 'They heated their homes with what?'

🏛

In the summer of 1958 the Army Cadets were supposed to go to a camp at Leek, and for reasons that I cannot recall it was left to me as the R.S.M. to issue the letter to the twenty or so attendees. With some trouble I had a letter typed on a Gestetner form (no photocopiers in those days) and ran off enough copies on the duplicator to mail them out. I also had to get the travel warrants from Major Carr's office on Lime Street. One way or another we managed to make it to Leek.

My efforts must have impressed Major Carr because several months later I was advised that the Army was going to sponsor me to go on an Outward Bound Course in Aberdovey in North Wales. I had just started a new job with Kraft Foods in Kirkby and didn't think that I could politically ask for the time off and so eventually I declined the offer.

40 years later our youngest son was also sponsored to go on an Outward Bound course in the winter in the coastal mountains of British Columbia. I did get a tee shirt, but I should have gone on that course

Dave Bolt. (1951-1957)
Now living in Vancouver, BC

KENNETH HUGHES' MEMORIES

After leaving school I did a six week course at the Gravesend Sea School, after which I joined the Merchant Navy with the Canadian Pacific Steamship Company. During the course of which I sailed on all the company's 'Empress' Liner's, starting as a bell boy and finishing up a third barkeeper on the *Empress of Canada*.

Leaving the Merchant Navy I took up a career in contract catering with Gardner Merchant Limited, mainly on the Ford Motor Company contract (Dagenham, Halewood and Southampton), eventually moving to Hampshire, but still with the same company. I then worked for J. Sainsbury and a couple of other firms before retiring to France in 2004 at the ripe old age of 68.

During my last year at school, I was allowed out to go to night school to learn shorthand and typing. Mr. Watcyn thought it would be a good idea for me to learn these skills as I was planning on taking an office job of some kind on leaving school. That career path managed to get forgotten as I ended up in the Merchant Navy!

The shorthand course was at Broadgreen School but I am afraid I didn't find it very interesting, so instead I used to go to the pictures. I am happy to say that I didn't get caught!

The nearest cinema was The Grand on Smithdown Road. The typing course was at a school near Breck Road and I remember that on returning to school I had to ring the bell to get back in. Dependent upon which master was on duty, I would sometimes be rewarded with a cup of tea and a cake.

On a visit to the school a few years ago, I observed that they were knocking down the north side boys' toilet block. I did have memories of this block as I once hid in the cubicle that Ted Farrell used to keep his cleaning equipment in. I was running away at the time but got caught before I could get home so I had to face the wrath of Mr. Watcyn and his 'friend'. I can still feel it.

Kenneth Hughes. (1945–1953)
Now living in France

DAVE KENNEDY'S MEMORIES

I seem to recall that the room next to the cleaners was used by the school cobbler for the weekly shoe inspection. We used to assemble there, and as our turn came we had to shout out the number that was stamped on our shoes, whereupon the cobbler would inspect them for any repairs they might require.

This brings to mind another memory never to be forgotten by myself. On my initial introduction to the school it was in this same room I recall, that I was introduced to Mr. Flynn the maintenance man. On the top shelf in this room stood a quite magnificent cruise ship in a glass case and Mr. Flynn obviously noticed that my attention was drawn solely to this treasure. Now during my school days I suffered from a quite serious speech impediment, so in his wisdom Mr. Flynn decided to try to give me a motive to rid myself of this problem and proceeded to say 'Once you can talk properly, the ship is yours.' By the time I left school I was cured of the speech impediment but did I get the cruise ship? 'Sail on boy,' in the words of Nelson, 'I see no ships.'

I remember my first encounter with Mr. Eade, the French teacher being quite hilarious. I think he had only just begun teaching at the school, three of us were tempted at the sight of seeing his study door being wide open and sheer curiosity got the better of us. We just had to take a look inside: on spotting his mortarboard on his desk we all had a go at wearing it, only to be caught by his sudden return. Now we feared the worse but were amazed that he took the whole thing in good part and sent us giggling on our way.

On one occasion we attended a trip to see an American aircraft carrier which was moored in the River Mersey, another big event that springs to mind was the trip by the whole school to London to see the preparations for the coronation which included tea at Lyons' Cornerhouse. What a sight we must have made scoffing our food to the strains of the violinist who was trying to play above the din we created.

Concerning football: I recall that one particular year the school progressed to the semi-final of what I think was called the Grammar Schools Cup. The game was organised to be played during the school holiday period. At the time Mr. Tait (Captain Tait) was the sports master and he had in his wisdom picked me to play as the team's goalkeeper on a few occasions, so I was quite chuffed to be chosen for this semi-final. Unfortunately, we were well and truly beaten and so I chose to 'forget' the final score, but what hurt me the most was that the venue for the final was to be Anfield; to be one game away from playing on the hallowed turf really hurt.

However, all was not lost as I went on to have a second career after leaving school - yes football - 14 years in the local district of Southport during which we had the pleasure of receiving medals from both Billy Liddell of Liverpool F.C. and also Nat Lofthouse of Bolton Wanderers F.C. I finished my playing days in the Lancashire Amateur League. Happy Days.

Dave Kennedy (1948-1955)
Now living in Wirral

ERNIE FOULDER'S MEMORIES

I was one of the first grammar dayboys and we tended to keep together as a unit and mixed together outside the school. We looked on the boarders as a sad lot, with the odd breakdown in tears for homesickness, and they were always hungry and broke, whereas we day-boys had access to the outside world and its freedoms. In fact, I joined the junior Old Boys and with Arthur Haygarth and Peter Heatley, helped restart the Old Boys Football Club. I cannot recall any boarders joining at that time; I imagine that once they finished school they couldn't wait to get away.

That was fifty years ago and I have been helping to keep the Brotherly Society going ever since.

Sadly Lennie Houghton died in 2006. I always considered that Lennie was one of the best footballers ever to play for the school and the Old Boys. He, like me, was from the Dingle and we often travelled to the school on the No.80 bus with Bobby Roberts, Brian O'Hara, Billy Hatton, Stuart Callaghan and Arthur (Haggis) Haygarth. Fond memories.

Ernie Foulder (1952-1957)
Now living in Liverpool.

BRENTON WILLIAMS' MEMORIES

I left school in 1959 and went to work for Danny Ross at the Dunlop Rubber Company in Water Street, Liverpool. Danny allowed me time off for day release and I went and studied for my 'O' levels and after that for an H.N.C. in Business at Liverpool Polytechnic. I left Dunlops and started my own business, which I ran for 10 years. During that time I passed the Institute of Purchasing and Supply examinations, gained exemption from several parts of a degree at Manchester University, and was awarded a Masters degree. Meanwhile, after selling my business, I started teaching at Chester College, then went as a senior lecturer at East Berkshire College, and eventually ended up as the Head of Department of Business Studies at a College in London, on the way I collected another Masters degree in education from Brunel University. I got the education bug a little late, but I always thanked Danny Ross for pushing me along and believing in me after I left school, he is sadly missed, a great character.

⛪

I remember the contest the masters had, on who could slipper the hardest. They used to brag about having the 'perfect' pump/shoe. Mr. Sephton, the music master, used to brag that he had the biggest slipper; it felt like a size 18. He used to flex it before applying it to your bent-over bottom in the dormitory.

⛪

I was in the school Army Cadets and remember 0.303 shooting at Altcar and 0.22 shooting at the army barracks on Allerton Road. Funny how things work out, I am presently a member of the Altcar Clay Pigeon Club and shoot there once a week.

Brenton Williams (1955 – 1959)
Now living in Liverpool

ERIC WOODBINE'S MEMORIES

I started as a boarder at the Blue Coat School in the Autumn term of 1953 and left hotfooted after G.C.E.s in 1959. I returned for the Prize Day the following Spring and, incidentally, learned a lesson which has stayed with me all my life - don't gamble. Anyway, I became an articled pupil with the Architect's Department of Bexley Borough Council until three years later, when I decided that I had insufficient talent. I then served 12 years as an officer in The Loyal Regiment (latterly The Queen's Lancashire Regiment). On my resignation I joined I.C.I. for a similar period and then had a small business in Dorset, again for 12 years. I retired early in 2000 and now live in France.

I joined the Blue Coat School at the age of 11 in the Autumn term of 1953 and was put into the Shirley House dormitory; the one allocated for the youngest boarders. The dormitory was on the second floor, i.e. the top floor of the building, and it was approximately 30 ft. above ground level to the external window ledge. This ledge was about 30 inches wide and ran all round the external walls of the dormitory. In my day, there was an initiation ceremony which all 'new dykes' were obliged to carry out.

The initiation involved going out onto the window ledge and moving around from window to window until the other inmates were satisfied and opened one of them to allow you to return to the dormitory and thereby, your bed. If this was achieved without refusal or tears beforehand, you became one of the group.

After several abortive efforts a window was eventually opened and I was permitted to return. I was relieved to be accepted.

The following story still embarrasses me to this day, to which my only defence is that I was very young at the time and perhaps naïve. Well, I was given a diary for my birthday, which is not a lot of inspiration to a 14-year-old but can be used to record 'things'. I recorded my frequent sallies out of school at night time which were contrary to the rules, and I'm sure most of the staff were not aware of what went on. One time, three of us even went down to Liverpool city centre for reasons now quite beyond me in terms of something that was worth doing. Given that, in those days, according to Mr. Crebbin who taught English; 'Coppers go around in pairs like policemen in Scotland Road.' it was positively hazardous.

Well eventually, my diary became lost somewhere in the school which was soon followed by a call to Mr. Watcyn's study. This was such an unusual event that it always struck fear into the very fibre of little boys and I was no exception. After knocking timidly and bade 'Come in Woodbine,' I entered to see my diary in front of him on the desk. I am now reminded of the famous English Civil War painting, *And When Did You Last See Your Father?* O.K., the room was empty apart from the headmaster, but the scene was similar. Sad to relate, Mr. Watcyn had broken my simplistic code and deduced who I had been with and when! We were all gated for varying periods and I was not allowed to forget it for quite some time.

Gating at the Blue Coat was as bad a punishment as possible; the cane was infinitely preferable given that the pain was short-lived. We were only allowed out for two hours on a Sunday afternoon anyway, but it did seem like freedom, if only for a limited time. As I grew older, pupils were allowed to go out on a Saturday morning to, say, Penny Lane to buy something useless like a bottle of ink. Since the object of the exercise was connected with school-like activities, permission was never refused by the housemaster. In reality, I hotfooted it to the other side of Sefton Park to visit the girl with whom I had fallen madly in love. She was the sister of a day-dyke, who for some incredible reason, came regularly to Sunday chapel with his parents and sister. Being very much junior to me, being a prefect and all, I was able to lean on him to gain an introduction. As an aside, unlike today any term using the word 'dyke' was actually quite innocent.

One of my friends, Roger Moore, showed a remarkable talent in learning to play the pianoforte under the tutelage of Dr. F.W. Dickerson. Within a couple of years he had graduated to the chapel organ and was even allowed to play occasionally in the Shirley Hall. His ability was such that he was allowed to play in chapel in the event of the rare absence of 'Fishy'.

We had communion each month on a weekday before breakfast - not the most popular of activities and one which was not given to moments of light relief. One morning, Roger was cajoled, nay challenged, into playing a piece of music of our choice, but at his tempo and means of extemporisation.

We chose the then popular Lonnie Donegan song, *Tom Dooley*. An air of expectancy spread amongst the congregation after we started taking communion with the Parish Priest officiating (Mr. Watcyn was only a lay preacher, I believe, and not able to give communion). As the boys went to the altar rail and then sat down in the front row of benches, out came the unmistakable tune of *Tom Dooley*, played quietly and reverently, with timing appropriate to the occasion. More sniggers! As we cascaded out of chapel in a race to the dining room, we were ultimately joined by the headmaster who walked up to Roger and said; 'Moore, was that *Tom Dooley* you were playing in chapel this morning?' To this, Roger replied, 'No Sir, it was a religious aria.' You could have heard a pin drop as promise of retribution was anticipated, but no, the headmaster turned on his heel and glided away as only he could.

As an add-on to this, I should explain that, by the time I was 15, attendance at communion comprised 100% boarders. Those who had never been baptised, (and I knew of several) were baptised the week before the Bishop visited to hold the annual confirmation service. All those baptised had two members of staff each as godparents - I believe one or two of the female staff were also 'volunteers'.

⇧

I remember one boy who had failed to learn the route Magellan had taken on his circumnavigation. He was taught by the simple expedient of having his nose follow the route round the blackboard pausing only to reinforce the ports of call!

⇧

Further to Ray's recollection, Mr. Davies (Taffy) was a living-in master who taught physics. He was built like a scrum half and I knew of no one prepared to argue with him; one word was enough to control the unruly but I believe that he also had a heart of gold. One Sunday, we queued for tea outside the dining room anticipating the normal plated salad when Mr. Davies arrived looking very formal with 'Miss' Byers in tow, she being in charge of the catering department. His words have stayed with me to this day: 'Someone has stolen a hard boiled egg and if the thief doesn't own up it is more than likely that there will be no tea at all.' We were left to reflect for a while and to do a little group interrogation. No one ever 'sneaked' but woe betide anyone ultimately found guilty after the rest of us had suffered some penalty. Fortunately, one Willy Jones owned up and all was put to rights. I'm not sure what his punishment was but I don't think he was allowed a second egg!

༄

Sunday mornings, as part of the preparation prior to the slow march into chapel, was the ritual anointing of heads with brilliantine taken with a spoon from a china dish held by a prefect. This fluid had the lubricating value of WD40 insomuch as it 'ran' if applied liberally. One boy whose name I will not mention, some few seconds after being anointed, was seen to have a trickle of dirty brilliantine meandering down his forehead. Some time later, he ended up in the Sanatorium with scabies!

I recall that he refused to bathe one night after he was 'clear.' We all knew the risk of such skin conditions and we frog-marched him to the bathroom and he was scrubbed with the red carbolic soap Frank Irwin has mentioned previously. He cleaned up his act forthwith.

As an aside, when I was at primary school, the 'nit nurse' would visit periodically to scan our heads. In all the time I was at the Blue Coat, with the exception of the event just related, I do not remember a single case of what were known communal problems of the day. Incidentally, if the inside of a cast iron bath is wetted then coated with carbolic soap it can provide an enormous amount of fun for little boys sliding up and down on their seats.

༄

In the north yard, separating the tarmac from the grassed area was a strip of 'gardens'. They were as scarce as I understand allotments to be these days amongst the green brigade. These gardens, or rockeries really, ran to about 20 in number, and ownership was transferred formally in front of witnesses, so as to avoid ownership arguments. Each rockery was planted with a number of plants, which tended to suffer from a lack of water caused by out and out theft, as they moved around without a chance of taking root properly. Even the stones were mobile. I believe my hatred for the act of gardening developed there.

🛡

There were no hardened criminals amongst my compatriots but, occasionally, a scheme of doubtful provenance would develop. I don't think that it was the fault of 'Hulph', possibly Mr. Mace, but someone taught my class something about silver mining in Bolivia. 'Where's that?' you may ask. Well, it's very high up in the Andes as a matter of fact. In the Potosi silver mines, 'coca' leaf chewing Indians mine silver in extremely disadvantageous conditions. 'What is 'coca' and why do they chew it?' You may well ask. Well, the 'coca' leaf is the source of - yes you've guessed, 'coke' - not Coca Cola! Anyway, when you're cold and hungry and very high up (altitude I mean) it's very soothing. Where is the Blue Coat in all this? Well, all the old school cutlery was stamped 'Potosi Silver'. A certain group thought that they had struck it rich and decided to market the stuff. A delegation was despatched to a pawn shop in downtown Liverpool (and very downtown I mean) with a view to gaining the means of financing nocturnal expeditions - nothing really crooked! The outcome of the offer of the samples, along with a guarantee of 'many more available', was a refusal!

The exact words used by the shopkeeper were not recorded.

🛡

Smoking was a minority activity at the Blue Coat School. Even Woodbines were expensive although it was possible buy them, or Players Weights, in packets of five in Penny Lane.

Such purchases tended to be of a joint nature (no pun intended) since none of us had much money. It was not uncommon to see five or so of us, gently pulling in turns at a fag. It was a shame really, since I for one was not to kick the habit before moving to France in 2000! I once got hold of a cigar which I was not prepared to share. I duly unrolled it, breaking down the outer leaves (originally, so carefully selected that they be easily rolled on a naked Cuban lady's thigh - well, that's what I believed at the time!) to mix with the inside dross element. This was duly rolled into a cigarette shape. This was smoked at about midnight upon a number of occasions in order to avoid being caught by Anthony Gihon who was the dormitory prefect. Gihon had a Japanese officer's sword at school....that's another story!

However, can you imagine the satisfaction to be felt the following morning after six hours sleep to know that one had got away with it yet again?

⇑

Fagging was a minor activity at the Blue Coat. Rarely demanded as a service by *de praefectis*, but more normally offered by some supine creature in awe of his dormitory master. Well I can tell you, the shine wore off quickly. They were a bunch of collaborators - well, before my day they were!

Overt bullying was a rarity, which to some, may come as a surprise. It happened occasionally, but vigilantes existed who would come to the rescue of the sufferer. Two lads of my close acquaintance provided this service and no one ignored them. One lad was a sadistic individual until one worm turned with a hefty punch to his nose. After that he suffered from a condition whereby, if a nosebleed started, he was out of circulation for an hour or so.

⇑

Latin lessons were popular amongst a select group. It was the practice of our artful teachers to forecast likely G.C.E. questions as a hint for us to swot.

On one pre-G.C.E. test, two acquaintances got hold of a copy of the exam paper. Can you imagine their consternation when taken to task for quoting verbatim certain sentences which had been removed from the original text? It was possible to come to grief even with such assistance from the staff. I had 'bulled up' so much on a forecast experiment involving Fletcher's Trolley and coefficients of friction that I quoted it anyway, simply because Fletcher's Trolley got a mention, albeit for a different question - that's what Taffy Davies told me anyway. I always wondered how Taffy accounted for the really expensive elements used in his lessons, e.g. mercury. If one looked carefully in the joints in the physics laboratory benches, tiny drops of mercury were to be found and teased out with a pin head. Once collected in quantity, it was used to create a surface on clean pennies to make them look like silver. The motive was to con someone to accept such a penny as a half crown: dream on as they say. It is of interest to note, however, that the symptoms of mercuric poisoning are the same as a prolonged over-indulgence of alcohol!!! Ex-pupils given to such daft activities should not worry since one would have needed to absorb mercury through the lungs in the form of an aerosol spray.

⇑

The most meticulous of staff occasionally had an emergency on their hands. One lad in my class was an habitual hydrogen sulphide sniffer, for a reason best known only to himself. One day, in the middle of the throes of a chemistry experiment, there was loud thud as the individual concerned hit the ground, out for the count. He recovered, but the fume cupboard became strictly out of bounds without the careful supervision of Mr. Unwin.

⇑

I recall the ceremonies which were a feature of school life. Mrs. Piperno (a Polish refugee I believe) was responsible for the wardrobe of grey suits, which we were all fitted up with on entry to the school - some fairly indifferently as I recall. If you were well in with her, you could 'trade up' as natural development ever increased the gap between bottom of trousers and shoes. She also kept the limited number of the old-style school uniforms. I recall wearing one for the day of the dedication of the bi-centenary gates.

Along with the mace and that collar I felt a bit of a fool - not aided by my friends may I say! It was in Mrs. Piperno's workroom one day that I read the headlines in her copy of the Daily Mirror to the effect that Ruth Ellis had been executed. I saw her photo and decided then and there that she must have been innocent anyway with a face like that; what a waste.

Chapel was at the centre of life and not that popular really. Some would smuggle comics or books in to read, but it was a hazardous occupation. Some dozed off, inevitably to be nudged in the ribs, since it was only possible during Mr. Watcyn's sermons, and to be seen from up on high was a hanging offence. The chapel was one of the most beautiful I have ever seen, and a fitting place for worship. We spent quite a time in there, Sunday mornings and evenings. The scratchy grey suits were the norm for the morning service and normal school uniform for the evenings. I do recall that Dr. F.W. Dickerson wrote the music for the 121st. Psalm, Levavi oculos, 'I will lift up mine eyes unto the hills: from whence cometh my help'. It was a beautiful tune and, sad to say, the music is probably not in the public domain.

⛫

Billy Graham came to the U.K. one year and we had a visit from one of his disciples, one Hilding Halverson, who sang to us in the chapel. Was this the occasion when Ray Livingston thought we were expecting negro spirituals? Anyway, great religious meetings were held allied to Billy Graham. 'Slats' Slater organised some trustees to go and it was quite a powerful moving occasion. After some really powerful preaching, we were all exhorted to come forward and be saved. I went, along with some of my companions, and to this day I don't know why: 'cos. it wasn't C.of E. was it?

⛫

As Frank has mentioned earlier, Remembrance Sunday was a big affair when the tiers of benches were erected in The Shirley Hall. I actually liked the ceremony, since all the hymns and readings had a certain quality that even the most irreverent could not mock. I suppose the 1950s were still too close to the causes of it all. It is a fact that the army was never out of combat after the Second World War, until 1968!

I may be getting mixed up but I think that it was the occasion upon which two boys were selected to recite a certain passage which had been memorised. Each boy received a present from Sir Alan Tod but I never got to learn what it might have been!

Packing up at the end of term to go home invariably meant a riot in every dormitory which usually went uncontrolled for ages. Pillow fighting and so on until exhaustion set in. Those of us travelling some distance the following morning set off by bus or taxi in very high spirits. I went by coach from Edge Lane Coach Station to London and then on to Kent. It was on one journey that I sat next to an aged Welshman and badgered him into teaching me the correct pronunciation of Llanfair PG. I recall it to this day, but a Welshman would probably laugh at my efforts. On another occasion, I struck up conversation with a charming couple Mr. and Mrs. Moore, people of my parents' age who had just lost their daughter (an only child). She, in particular, was a very sad soul. There was a common attachment there immediately, and they wrote to my parents to ask their permission to visit me at school most Sunday evenings, which they did thereafter. I think my mother was quite envious since a total stranger had a degree of access afforded to their son which they could not have. What lovely people they were.

⇧

As I mentioned before, some of us had a rockery in the north play area. From time to time, black-fly infestation would seem to be causing a problem. Having learned from my parents that nicotine would at least deter if not kill them, I decided to get some. I approached Mr. Perry one day by the staff room, and explained my problem and my need for all the 'fag ends' in the staffs' ashtrays. I suppose I could imagine Mr. Perry emptying them for my benefit at the time, but he simply said 'No.' He then took out his cigarettes, crumpled four of them into the jam jar I had brought and supervised me putting water into the jar from the staff room kettle! What a gesture, albeit ensuring that the cigarettes were not used by me for any other reason!

Eric Woodbine (1953-1959)
Now living in France.

JOHN HOWARTH'S MEMORIES

I was a boarder at the school from 1952 to 1957 in the secondary modern stream. I left at the age of 15 to join the army - boys' service. I served 15 years in all, including three years as a boy soldier in the Royal Engineers. I then went to Bible College and worked for The Royal Sailors' Rests for a further 15 years. (This is a mission to the Royal Navy). I ran clubs / homes etc. in Portsmouth, Faslane submarine base in Scotland, and also in Yeovilton, Somerset. The rest of my time I spent with 'Open Air Campaigners' a mission that majors on street preaching with sketch board and paints. The spin off for this is enormous in schools, prisons and churches, and is now labelled as 'OAC Ministries'. I am now retired and living close to my daughter and family and still enjoying myself. For my sins (ha! ha!) I am known as a 'Christian' Rolf Harris.

🛈

I remember when Eric Woodbine and possibly Alan Harrison and Simpson were caught crawling along the ledge from window to window outside the top dormitory, they were caned on the spot by Mr. Crebbin I believe - though mercifully they were allowed to put their trousers on first! (No fear of heights in those days.)

🛈

We would occasionally pick up the grating for the under floor heating, crawl along them and get out of what was then the locked, during the evenings, grammar side of the school. We were then free to nip over the wall of the graveyard and go out and buy some chips. We would get back by the same route. (at a recent visit to the school, I noticed that these gratings are now covered in with metal plates.) I believe Alan Harrison once picked up a grating near to the kitchen, and a lady in there saw his head appear from the floor and dropped the tray that she was carrying to the staff dining room. I believe he got away with only a slippering from Mr. J. L. Davies for that one! Mr. Nigel Baker-Bates was having nothing to do with crawling along the under floor heating system to get out. He was quite a tall lad, so we gave him our order for chips and out he went through the front door. Guess who opened the door for him on his return, complete with chips? Mr. J. L. Davies! Nigel would not sneak on us by telling who he was getting the chips for, so to the best of my memory he was sent to the office/study where the board of education was applied to the seat of his learning.

I cannot remember the name of a Grammar School lad who was caught with a bottle of beer either in or under his bed, but Mr. Watcyn pulled it out from under his cloak and with great dramatic effect asked him, 'Why are you drinking beer instead of lemonade, boy?' To which he replied, 'I prefer beer!' Mr. Watcyn then roared at him 'Go to my study immediately.'

Not everything was awful but I was glad to leave the school and join the army at 15 - I was free from all this - and I got paid at the end of the week! I have had a charmed, very happy or blessed life ever since, but it is amazing what an influence my school days had on me.

John Howarth (1952-1957)
Now living in Preston.

TONY SALMON'S MEMORIES

THE BUMPS

It was an unofficial tradition at the Blue Coat School that any boy with a birthday was 'bumped' by his classmates. This was usually done before morning registration when we were unsupervised in our form rooms. Officially, this ceremony was banned, but I am sure that most teachers were aware that it took place.

My 12th birthday was on Monday 8th November 1971, and I remember the weather was particularly wet. Having alighted from the bus at 8.25 am, I hung around Peg Leg's corridor, making my way very slowly to Room 7 in the hope that a prefect or even BD (our form master, Brian Davies) would be there before me. At 8.44 am I entered the room, only to be seized by nearly thirty other boys and thrown up to the ceiling to a loud chorus of 'One... two... three... etc'. My fear of being dropped was unfounded, but after the final 'bump' I realised I was being carried to the far side of the classroom. The window was open and I was thrown out! As I went into free-fall towards the ground, someone held on to the leg of my trousers, just long enough for them to part company with my waist.

I landed with a splash in a deep puddle on the grass, just as the registration bell rang. It was too high to climb back in, so I hastily pulled my trousers up and ran across the West Front to the door at the far side of the school.

As I re-entered the form room, soaked to the skin, everyone was sitting quietly at their desks as the form prefect collected the dinner money, and no one reacted as I squelched my way to my seat, though I am sure I heard the odd suppressed snigger!

TIES AND ENTRANCES

There were two school rules that were enforced quite keenly, especially by newly-promoted prefects. One was that (except in extremely hot weather) our school ties had to be worn at all times in school and on our journeys to and from our homes. Another was that boys who were not in the Sixth Form were not allowed to enter or leave the building by the main front entrance. Naturally, I felt it my duty to flout these two rules whenever possible.

In my pre-Sixth Form days I regularly travelled to school tie-less and entered through the main front door, only attaching the tie to my neck in my form room just before the registration bell rang.

One morning, as I stepped boldly through the door into the vestibule below the clock tower, the headmaster, Mr. Arnold-Craft, appeared on his way out! It is amazing how quickly one's brain works during a critical situation such as this. I clasped my hand to my throat, concealing the open shirt, and launched into a fit of coughing. The headmaster looked at me and asked, 'Are you all right, boy?' I croaked something incomprehensible to which he replied, 'Well, don't just stand there - get a drink of water!'

I dived through the doors into the corridor, and stopped to recover from the shock. Then I looked back and there he was, watching me through the glass, shaking his head in despair.

Tony Salmon (1971-1977)
Now living in Dewsbury.

CHAPTER 5
GENERAL MEMORIES

Mr. G.G. WATCYN, HEADMASTER 1945 – 1968

After 23 years of being headmaster at the Blue Coat School and having been resident in the school house, Mr. G.G. Watcyn retired in August 1968 and he, his wife and daughter went to live at No.79 Menlove Avenue in Allerton, Liverpool.

On 16th March 1971 (Tuesday) he left home at about 10.45 a.m. and drove along Menlove Avenue to pick up an uncle in Booker Avenue, and from there to take him to Sefton General Hospital.

At about 11.30 a.m. Mrs. Watcyn received a telephone call from the uncle alerting her to the fact that Mr. Watcyn had not turned up. She then rang the police and was told that he had been involved in a motoring accident at the junction of Mather Avenue and Booker Avenue (nowadays there are traffic lights there, but there were none in those days) and had been taken to Sefton General Hospital.

The circumstances surrounding the accident were apparently that Mr. Watcyn's car had been struck by a coach that was carrying five school children and their teacher. It was presumed that he had failed to take sufficient account of his situation and had pulled out into the path of the oncoming coach.

After a whole week of suffering, Mr. Watcyn died in Sefton General Hospital on 23rd March. This, however, was not the end of the tragedy, nor was it even the worst of it as he himself would have said. His 27-year-old daughter Daphne took it extremely badly, and on or about 20th April she threw herself from a Mersey ferryboat. Her body was found near New Brighton pier on 21st April.

Ray Livingston (1955-1959)
Now living in York

MORE ON HEADMASTERS

Following the comments passed about the severity of our headmaster, I remember an incident that deserves mention. I recall one day whilst at a loose end and feeling rather bored, I contrived to tie a stone on a piece of string to see how fast I could spin it around my head. Despite my prowess as a boy scout, my knots left something to be desired and so the stone decided to become a free spirit and wow! a perfect shot straight through a dormitory window.

As has been mentioned elsewhere within this book, the failure of miscreants owning up to any trouble would result in the whole school being punished.

Not wanting to incur the wrath of my mates I duly owned up and was instructed to report to the headmaster after morning assembly the following day. This I duly complied with only to be told by the headmaster 'I am busy, come back tomorrow.' Now not being slow on the uptake, I thought there was an opportunity here to somehow lessen the forthcoming caning that was in the offing. The next day I reported at exactly the same time and yes, he was busy again. Now this was repeated again until to my delight I was told that my persistence of reporting for punishment was commendable and I got off scot-free, so there you go, not such a bad old headmaster after all or maybe I was one step of him.

Dave Kennedy (1948-1955)
Now living in Wirral

STAFF

Apart from 'Tan Tan', who was a dangerous little man, I have never seen or heard of any physical excess being visited upon anyone: of course, the odd clout or the slipper, but nothing serious. Members of staff were generally well thought of, but, I suppose, if someone felt they were a target they would make themselves scarce; difficult, however, in a boarding school. One member of staff kept a knot tied in his gown with which he would take a swipe at an offender. Another used verbal abuse e.g. 'Don't scratch yer 'ed man, you'll get splinters!'

Some members of the staff were extremely popular, especially in 4G where curriculum choices were made, e.g. history or scripture: art or Latin: physics with chemistry with handicrafts or 'and'. I certainly chose history and Mr. Edwards to avoid the continual detention and lines which went hand in hand with scripture! Mr. Edward's legendary accuracy with chalk had to be seen to be believed! Mr. Perry got about a half of the class which bore him great credit! since art with 'Scogs' was great fun. Geography was a choice against something but I don't remember what.

Returning to 'Tan Tan'; although I had passed the 13+, I was not allowed to learn French because of the difficulty in catching up (I have regretted this ever since given a later involvement in French West Africa and living in France as I now do).

I was obliged to sit in with the class and do some preparation and was occasionally monitored by 'Tan Tan'. He had a 'down' on one Godfrey Rawes, whose life he made a misery. The violence meted out to him would be actionable today.

All in all, these minor recollections merely reinforce in my mind that I never was hit, caned or otherwise punished unless I deserved it. I would go further and attribute much of my personal development to my time at the Blue Coat. Rose tinted glasses? I can honestly say not. When I look at today's system I'm truly sorry for the staff; the political correctness today coupled with discipline based upon, at best, some inured personal quality in the teacher, is a recipe for the poor standards of behaviour I perceive today.

Eric Woodbine (1953-1959)
Now living in France.

THE RAFFLE

One Saturday, whilst the boarders still had sweets in their pockets, one bright boy decided to hold a raffle. The entry fee was 2 sweets, as was the fee for almost all the similar activities carried out nefariously and out of the gaze of the school masters. There was a very good response as most of the smaller boys had to take part, probably fearing repercussions if they failed to do so. Anyway, one day they would be bigger and run their own scams.

All the tickets were sold and the time arrived for the grand draw. The participants gathered round in a spirit of expectancy. The boy running the raffle held the box containing all the tickets over his head and invited anybody present to select one (not really a ticket, sheets of paper were ripped up into small pieces and the numbers were applied manually) so that the winner could be determined.

The selected piece of paper was withdrawn from the box and the number was shouted out 'Number 27'. Who was the winner? It was the friend and assistant of the boy running the raffle, he had the lucky ticket bearing the number 27!

Well, chaos and uproar followed. One boy suggested that the whole thing was in fact a 'fiddle'. How is it that the winner is a close friend of the boy running the operation some thought?

A voice shouted out over the general hubbub, 'I want to check the tickets in that box.' At that the boy running the raffle fled along the corridor past all the classrooms, taking the box with him. Luckily he was a good runner and managed to leave his pursuers behind. At the dark side of the school to the east side, now known as Peg Leg's corridor, he hid himself away and watched the pack go past and into the area by the boiler house and back into the school through the door opposite the chapel.

Retracing his steps, he managed to get to the toilets by the playground unseen; there he flushed all the other tickets, also numbered 27, down the toilet pan. Suspected but unproven, he never dared to run another such raffle; perhaps the nasty taste left in his mouth spoiled the taste of the ill gotten gains, the sweets.

Frank Irwin (1950-1957)
Now living in Wirral

RHYTHM OF LIFE

As a young lad largely separated from the rest of society, it was some time before the desire to break out overcame the inbuilt fear of punishment. I had numerous partners in crime on many occasions over several years.

However, one evening was quite interesting in that a certain confrontation occurred which resulted in no consequences - silence in fact! In Penny Lane, there was an off-licence which we would often pass during our nocturnal expeditions. One evening, as we were by the doorway, out came Mr. Perry, 'Scogs' Scarland, and, I think, Jimmy Tait. All carried brown paper bags! I think it's true to say that total silence was observed by all present but we arrived back at school in half the time they took!

THE PEEP SHOW

I eventually graduated to the second dormitory on the top floor, was it Bingham? No matter, each evening we all skulked down to the middle floor to the bathroom to wash and clean our teeth. En route, descending the stairs, I happened to look out of the window towards the backs of the houses across the tennis courts.

There, to my utter astonishment, was a young lady cavorting on her bed in front of a large picture window, 'necked as a jaybird' as they say. Now I 'grew up' with her from then on; you might say we developed together so to speak. She eventually became the object of every grubby little boy's attention with her penchant for nude display. In a later, sterner phase of life when I became a prefect it became my responsibility to stop all this furtive observation. I temporarily confiscated a pair of binoculars once, not for my use of course. In any event, she disappeared shortly after. The sequel of the story unfolded in February 1960 when I was returning south on a coach after attending Speech Day. By chance, I sat next to a young lady who was the neighbour of the aforementioned young lady (on reflection, I can't believe that she could have been so Machiavellian as to hide her identity). In the course of conversation, we swapped statistics (as you do) and she told me where she lived, or, more accurately next door to where the other girl lived. A malicious sense of satisfaction was then gained from giving her the racy details and a caution to her neighbour. I was never to discover whether our little nymph knew all along that she had such avid admirers.

Eric Woodbine (1953-1959)
Now living in France.

AN ANONYMOUS (PERHAPS TO BE FORGOTTEN) MEMORY

It was reported that, feeling hungry one afternoon, a couple of boys entered the chapel just before the harvest festival when the place was full of goodies and had a feast of bread and wine, advising everybody later, that the communion wine stored in the vestry was called *Vino Sacro*. Being too young at the time to know about such things, the alcohol level was not checked.

FINAL MEMORY OF A BULLY

A number of mentions have been made within the book about a fellow classmate of mine, Alec Pearce, Self appointed 'cock' of the school and general bully. He is the boy who reportedly was given, in due course, a little of his own medicine by both Stan and Billy.

My recollections were that although a grammar school boy he was always a lot closer to the bottom of the class than the top. He didn't bother me with his bullying but when short tests were held in the classroom and we swapped papers to mark each others, he had the habit of amending answers to lower the marks of the boy whose paper he was marking.

Although bullies generally feared pain and reprisals, this was not the case with Pearce. I well remember whenever he was caned on his hands or in this particular case on his rear in front of all the boarders in Shirley Hall, he never flinched, not even a little bit. In fact after the punishment was completed, he was asked to prove that he had nothing down his trousers that would minimise his pain.

Another memory which annoyed me greatly was when we were both selected to take part in one particular year's annual school play, *Everyman*. I was given the part of 'Five Wits' and Pearce was given the major role, 'Everyman'. Unfortunately, despite many rehearsals he failed to learn his lines with the result that the play was cancelled, much to the annoyance of the rest of the cast.

Frank Irwin (1950-1957)
Now living in Wirral

CHAPTER 6
ARMY CADETS & BOY SCOUTS

BLUE COAT SCHOOL ARMY CADETS, THE COUNTESS OF SEFTON'S OWN REGIMENT, THE ROYAL ARTILLERY.

In 1950, as seemed to be common practice amongst the boys, I left the scouts and joined the Army Cadet Force. In those days we paraded at 287 barracks, which if my memory serves me correctly, was The Countess of Sefton's Own Regiment, The Royal Artillery.

I remember marching to the barracks, with lights, to allow traffic to see us rather than mow us down. At weekends we would often attend carnivals along with the Territorial Army, looking to impress and chat up the local girls in the morris dance troupes.

Later Mr. Watcyn changed the Royal Artillery shoulder flashes to 'Blue Coat School A.C.F.' That cramped our style a little, although I later learned that some of the old flashes were kept and used once boys attained a 'stripe'.

My first two-week camp was on Walney Island, Barrow in Furness, and my second was in Tenby, in South Wales. That was the first time we got to use our Lea Enfield .303 rifles in earnest, firing live ammunition on the range, located close to one end of the Tenby Golf Club.

When we used rifles back at school, it was without ammunition, and we used to crawl around the air raid shelters on the Western Front. I can imagine us trying to do that today! The police Armed Response Unit would be round in a flash and have the place surrounded.

My best remembered memory was when we formed a 'Guard of Honour' for the Commanding Officer of the U.S.A.A.F. at his base at Burtonwood (an army base camp during WWII).

Our webbing was normally 'blancoed', a buff colour, but for this job we had to scrub all the buff blanco off and apply the white version. Once the job was over we had to reverse the process and redo it in buff; what a pain!

Only ten of us formed the guard that day as the cadets only owned ten rifles! But what a day to remember! As a consequence, we were invited back to the base for a day's visit which included a feast in the dining hall. After the school food that we were used to, we thought we were in heaven.

Kenneth Hughes (1945–1953)
Now living in France

THE LUGER INCIDENT

The Blue Coat School Army Cadet Force (A.C.F.) was a thriving institution. It was normal for boys to join the Scout Troop (31st Wavertree) in their early days, and most thereafter left the scouts to join the Army Cadets because of the range of interesting things that were involved.

During school holidays, cadets were able to choose from a list of activities in which they were able to participate, to be held at army camps throughout the country. For example, cadets were able to achieve their 'Crossed Swords', the badge for qualified Physical Training Instructor (P.T.I.). Also available was training in Wireless Telegraphy and Radio Telephony. W.T. & R.T. as they were called. One involved using the radio to communicate in Morse Code and the other by direct speech communication.

Other well supported courses were in R.E.M.E. (Royal Electrical & Mechanical Engineers), R.A.M.C. (Royal Army Medical Corps) and M.T. (Mechanical Transport). I also remember and attended a course of driving instruction in 15 cwt. Jeeps left over from the war. It was held at a 'no longer used' army camp in Bluebell Lane, Huyton, near Liverpool. There we learned how to 'crash' a gearbox, how to stop a vehicle by running into a wall and how to get rid of a passenger as you turned a corner when unable to apply the brakes. All good fun as you can imagine.

Nearer home, on alternate Saturdays in the summer term, we would travel to Altcar shooting ranges, near Hightown, complete with our Lea Enfield rifles to shoot real live 0.303 bullets at undefended targets.

The insignia that we wore varied. Shoulder flashes stated either 'Blue Coat School A.C.F.' or 'Royal Artillery'. At that time there were a lot of National Service soldiers around and obviously, when in uniform we would come across them as we travelled on courses or to Altcar ranges. It was therefore preferred to look 'dead hard' when such mingling occurred, and so once a cadet achieved the rank of Lance Bombadier (Lance Jack) the Blue Coat School A.C.F. flashes would be replaced by Royal Artillery. That way, 'National Service' men were never really sure if we were regular soldiers or not. That always made us feel really good, particularly when some of them smartened up their appearance and demeanour when in our presence.

Anyway, one day we were at Altcar with our 'Shooting Officer' Major Carr, a 'Bisley 100' man from The Liverpool Scottish Regiment. (A 'Bisley 100' man was a contestant at Bisley who had scored 100 out of 100 in competition). At the end of the day, before we returned to school on the Southport to Liverpool train, Major Carr took us all to a handgun range and proceeded to show us one of his war souvenirs, a German Luger pistol with a hairspring trigger. The handgun range was rather like a bunker on a golf course with a fairly high back, the kind that only Tiger Woods could get a ball out of. Major Carr demonstrated the workings of the gun and allowed some of us to fire one round each into the bunker.

Each cadet routinely pointed the gun down after he had taken his shot and passed it carefully back to the Major. Well, not Tommy Hudson! After his shot he held the gun level and turned round to face us all with a big grin on his face and his finger still on the trigger. Major Carr nearly had a fit; he shouted to us all 'Down!' He need not have worried; we were all buried below the level of the grass before he finished his warning. The Major dealt with the incident without panic, I think, because we had all scarpered at 100 m.p.h. to the Red Rose pub as soon as we heard the command 'Put that ****ing gun down.'

The Red Rose was the haunt, of the regular soldiers and the Territorial Army men at Altcar. We were not allowed in, but a friendly barmaid at the place would serve us at the rear door with a glass or two of cider between all of us: it didn't go far!

Major Carr never brought the Luger to show us again; I think he was so shaken by the event that he taught us how to fire with 'pop guns' after that. Those days out made us feel like men, in our uniforms with stripes on our arms, carrying real rifles and firing real bullets. Surprisingly enough we never actually killed anyone, but that day Tommy came very close to it.

Frank Irwin (1950-1957)
Now living in Wirral

ARMY TRAINING DURING HOLIDAYS

Going back to Ray's recollection of the new P.T. master Mr. Weedall solving the upper arm muscular problem, whereby boys had to box and attempt to knock the stuffing out of each other, and Spike's comment about leaving school to join the army without ever noticing the difference, they were similar to my experience at Oswestry army camp, where I gained my 'Cross Swords'. (P.T. Instructor's qualification).

There, amongst other things, we were taught how to box and the method was as cruel as school punishments. After lessons in the art of self defence (we were taught to 'block' and 'parry'), we were paired off with other cadets. I was paired with this huge guy who looked and fought like a gorilla!

Then I was told that I would be attacked by this animal, and all that I was allowed to do was to defend myself using the tactics that I had just been taught. Well! This giant set about me and proved to me that blocking and parrying was not going to do me any good at all, he 'whupped' me good and proper, as they say.

Next came my turn; I was told to get my revenge and hit him as much as I could because he was not allowed to hit me back. That made no difference whatsoever; he was so big and strong that I did more harm to myself attempting to hit him, than I managed to inflict upon him with my attacks. So from school to the army, where is the difference?

In another camp, we were housed in a 'spider block', so called because the billets were like the legs of a spider all connecting at the centre like the insect's body. When we were being accommodated, three posh lads, from some posh school (Blue Coat was supposed to be a posh school but this lot were really posh) kept themselves together, and as there were too many cadets to fit into one spider the three posh lads billeted in another block on their own.

Throughout the course, the posh lads continually made it known that they were superior to us. They were real pains in the proverbial. Revenge was planned. A gang assembled and bought from the N.A.A.F.I. six of those plastic sachets of petrol, at that time used to fill petrol based cigarette lighters.

This particular course was held in the winter and the method of heating those old army billets was a cast iron, coke fuelled stove in the centre of the room, with a long chimney stack going through the roof to outside.

One of the Blue Coat contingent climbed onto the roof and started dropping the petrol canisters down the chimney stack whilst the rest looked through the window to see the effect. It was devastating! Each 'bomb' went off with a large 'phutt' and the stove started to glow red hot.

The posh lads didn't know what to do. They did try to leave via the door but somebody prevented that by leaning on it. The bombs continued to fall and the stove was now bright red. It was a good job the guy on the roof only had six bombs, because he was totally unaware of what was going on inside and if he had been able to continue, the place could have been destroyed.

Hoping there would be retaliation, a group of us wired our billet door handle to a light switch. In those days switches were easy to wire, they were not as safe as today and the terminals could easily be exposed by unscrewing the domed switch cover. We put wires from the terminals through the keyhole and thereby under the outside handle, hoping that when the return attack came the lads would receive electric shocks. It was us, however, that got all the shocks whilst attempting to do the job. The posh cadets, lacking in bravery, failed to appear and for the rest of the week they were rather meek and mild and no further trouble whatsoever.

We all realise now just how stupid that was, but unfortunately that's the sort of thing we used to do at that time.

Frank Irwin (1950-1957)
Now living in Wirral

ARMY CADET THOUGHTS

Joining the school's Army Cadets stands out as a momentous occasion in my life at school, for until this moment, although I could not be dubbed a 'cubbo', my general appearance left a bit to be desired. The issue of army uniform was the licence to consider myself a man and I was I going to lavish loving care on the same. Many an hour was spent on ironing my trousers and my tunic with the aid of an iron borrowed from the good Mrs. Piperno. Boots came under a special category, who could achieve the best shine? We all had our own secret formula how to achieve the mirror shine, spit & polish, boning with hot spoons, etc.

However, purely by chance I came upon the secret of the perfect solution to the problem, it was passed on to me by a friend of the family; 'Straw Hat Dye' obtained from any high street shop. All one had to do was to purchase a bottle of the same and proceed to float the liquid over the toecap of the boot and within seconds this would dry to a finish you could literally see your face in, but alas there was a hidden flaw in this perfect finish; it was only good for fine weather. If it rained while on parade, that was the end of the shine and you were on 'jankers'.

Another ploy was to place lead weights in your trousers just above the gaiters so as to achieve the perfect hang of the same. Again this was fine so long as you were not overzealous with the weights so risking the same falling out whilst marching.

Most notable to me was the fortnight's camp in Yorkshire. As I recall, base camp was in Sedbergh and over the fortnight we were to make our way from there to Barnard Castle, a distance, if my memory serves me correctly, of some 70 miles. During this fortnight various tasks were set, i.e. map reading, mock attacks on enemy positions entailing the throwing of 'Thunder Flashes' (great fun), fending for oneself for a day (shades of S.A.S. in our minds). Unfortunately, this did not give us license to raid the farmers' chicken coops for eggs, for which we finished up on a charge for alienating the local community.

At some stage a rumour was put about that the R.S.M. (it must be said that he was the organiser of this annual camp) was a member of the I.R.A.

He was a lucky man that some gullible cadet did not rap him on the head with a Royal Enfield rifle butt.

Dave Kennedy (1948-1955)
Now living in Wirral

UNWELCOME JOBS AT ALTCAR

No.1 THE BUTTS

When we used to go to Altcar shooting range, there were two jobs that we didn't want to be assigned to. The first was working in the 'butts', the second was the lookout, on the north shore. Being delegated to cover these jobs meant that you didn't get to fire anything on the range that day.

Working in the 'butts' involved four cadets sitting under the targets, behind a concrete defence wall 200 yards away from the action. Each was allocated an individual target. When a shot was fired at your particular target, you had to indicate with a paddle, whether the shot had hit the bulls-eye, the inner ring, between inner and outer, the outer ring, or in fact missed altogether. Each location had a particular action of the paddle to indicate to the shooter which part of the target he had hit. A complete miss was indicated by a red flag being waved sideways repeatedly. After indicating the location of the shot, we had to haul down the target and patch it up then haul it back into position ready for the next shot. In the event of an emergency occurring, we were issued with a shared field telephone, connecting us to Major Carr our Shooting Officer.

One particular day in the butts it was extremely hot; there was no ventilation below ground level and we had not been given anything to drink (Quite normal treatment of Blue Coat boys in those days). Major Carr was as usual in charge of operations at the firing line, but as was normal he did not shoot; that was the privilege of the cadets on a Saturday morning. After getting rather tired of hauling targets up and down in the sweltering heat, we in the butts came to a unanimous decision; all shots would be signalled as washouts! Waving the red flag side to side from a prone position was easy and obviated the need to move the target at all.

That saved our thirst from getting worse and conserved our energy somewhat. However, after signalling a number of consecutive washouts, the field telephone rang to disturb our peace. It was Major Carr who asked 'What the hell is going on? I have just scored two consecutive bulls eyes and I can see them through my telescope.' So it was back to work with a vengeance.

No.2 THE NORTH LOOKOUT

One day I had been assigned to man the north lookout, a small isolated location on top of the sand dunes, with only a small hut as a shelter in case of rain and a telephone to be used in case of emergency. The job was to ensure that nobody walked or strayed into the line of fire of the ranges. It was a lonely and unpleasant job.

The normal practice was for each set of cadets or regular army units to delegate a man to this place, but with orders that if somebody else was already there, to return to unit after ensuring that the lookout would be maintained sufficiently long enough for your needs. This particular day, whilst on my own, I saw a young cadet approaching and from his appearance deduced that he was a new recruit. In fact he had his gaiters on back to front, the straps pointed forward. My brain quickly snapped into action; I was a bombardier! I had two stripes on my arm! 'Good morning gunner,' I said, 'I presume you have been sent here to relieve me?' Before he could answer, I ran through his duties quickly, wished him good luck and left him there so that I could enjoy some .303 range work. New kids have to learn.

Frank Irwin (1950-1957)
Now living in Wirral

MAJOR CARR

One evening at the end of a visit to the 0.22 rifle range at 287 barracks, Major Carr decided in his wisdom to demonstrate his prowess at this calibre, having already done so at Altcar with the larger 0.303 bore on previous occasions. You will remember from an earlier piece that he was a 'Bisley 100' man.

The range for 0.22 at 287 barracks was 25 yards in length, the targets were buff in colour and 6" square in size. The butts consisted of a raised section, approximately 3ft. high and filled with sand. Because of the proximity, no attendants were required in these particular butts, indeed for that reason, no space was allocated for this function.

The targets were clipped to purpose-made supports in front of the sand, so that when a shot was fired its strike could be seen and the bullet would end up harmlessly in the sand behind.

Major Carr firstly placed a number of matches into the sand in a vertical orientation with the sulphur head upwards. He retired to the shooting end and fired a shot which hit one of the match heads causing it to flare up immediately. He repeated this exercise with each match in turn, never failing to achieve his objective.

His second trick was to place a target sideways on so that only the edge was visible to him: his object being to fire a round that would completely split the target card into two pieces. His first shot hit the target but it failed to part into two pieces as planned. What he did at that stage was amazing enough, the round had hit the leading edge and had left the target about half way down its length. Not satisfied, Major Carr inspected the target, then looked carefully at the set up and adjusted the target holding device slightly. He then affixed a fresh target and retired to make his second attempt.

This time the target fell into two equal portions. When held together after the shot, there was a space between the two sections, the width of which matched the calibre of the 0.22 round. He was an amazing shot and we were very lucky to have him as our shooting officer.

Frank Irwin (1950-1957)
Now living in Wirral

SUMMER CAMPS

Army Cadet summer camps often provided good entertainment as well as interesting outings to learn about conducting warfare and avoiding getting yourself killed or maimed by the enemy.

A typical camp would be for a fortnight's duration and shelter from the elements was provided within bivouacs, sleeping two cadets each. The immediate officer in charge was Captain Tait.

The main difference between a bivouac and a tent was that unlike tents, bivouacs did not have a fly sheet to lace up when you went to sleep after a hard days graft; there was just an open end. That meant that when you pitched the bivouac, it had to be situated such that the wind could not blow into it. If you failed to do so, you could get soaked to the skin without any means of drying out the next day. Of course, sometimes the wind direction changed in the night and you got soaked anyway.

On one particular camp, we got so wet that we had to move into the local village school to dry out. We slept in the Domestic Science Laboratory (girls' cookery classroom) and used the ovens to dry out our clothing. Unfortunately, some also dried out their gaiters and the leather straps became too brittle and snapped off!

I remember when in charge of the Light Machine Gun (L.M.G. also called a Bren Gun) we were all waiting in a field somewhere for the officers, including Major Carr, to arrive to set the exercise for the day and some of us wondered what a piece of 'bulleted blank' would do if fired from a rifle. A 'bulleted blank' round was a bullet with a moulded wooden end, identical in shape to a proper bullet and coloured pale blue. For the Bren Gun to fire on automatic, these rounds had to be used to allow the build up of gasses behind the fired shot to reset the automatic loading mechanism. To prevent the wooden end from causing damage, the flame eliminator on the muzzle of the gun was partitioned off with steel to cause the wood to splinter and thereby not to leave the end as a bullet would. However, as the wooden end was identical in shape to a proper bullet, it could be fired from a rifle: we are talking 0.303 here.

I therefore removed a round of bulleted blank from my magazine for another cadet to fire from his rifle and he aimed it at a nearby tree and duly fired. All it did was to vanish into the tree and frighten a few of the local farmer's cattle. The problem was that our senior cadet James Lyon, sporting a rank called 'under officer' wasn't, as Queen Victoria made famous, amused. He wanted to know who had fired the round. Naturally it wasn't one of us, was it?

He therefore decided to have a smell of all the rifle barrels and soon discovered the one that belonged to the culprit because it reeked of cordite.

He called for one of the 'Territorial Army' soldiers (T.A.) from the Liverpool Scottish Regiment, which was sharing manoeuvres with us, to come and also smell the barrel to be a witness when our officers arrived. He duly arrived at the scene of the incident, bent down to smell the rifle and declared 'I cannot smell anything, young man.' The 'under officer' was fuming but he had no authority over the army man, so he just had to wait until the officers arrived before dropping us in the proverbial.

Whilst waiting, the T.A. man advised, 'Clean that bloody barrel quickly before everybody gets here or we are all for jankers.' We duly obliged and when the officers arrived all was well, and the 'under officer' was not the flavour of the month for his false report into our behaviour.

Another day we arrived at Warcop tank range. There we sat in tanks as they drove across the ranges firing shots at targets away in the distance. Unfortunately, we were not considered old enough to fire live rounds ourselves, otherwise rest assured, we would have enjoyed ourselves even more.

Whilst moving between locations, usually 20 miles apart, we would march in casual order until we arrived at the outskirts of a village. At that point we would get into formation and march at attention through the place to admiring glances from the ladies as in those days it was a rare sight for them to see anybody from outside their communities. When marching with the Liverpool Scottish regiment, we would march to the accompaniment of the bagpipes.

Twice during the course of each camp, it was normal for dances to be arranged in local villages, the venues being always the village hall. In order to be able to take part in such events fully, we were taught a number of dances, they being, Waltz, Quickstep, Military-Two-Step, Veleta, Gay Gordons (Gay had a different meaning then) and the St. Bernard Waltz. We were also taught the correct manner in which to invite a young lady to dance.

'Please may I have the pleasure of the next dance?' Not quite like our after school days when the request for a dance went like this. 'Hey girl, you dancing?' 'You asking?' 'I'm asking,' 'I'm dancing.' Thus, with all our new attributes we were able to ask a lady to dance, we were able to perform that dance, after a fashion, and despite our army boots we were generally able to avoid kicking any female shins or stepping on any delicate ankles and feet whilst doing so. What little gentlemen we had become.

On another occasion when we were actually camping under canvas, we had been on manoeuvres with blank ammunition (You know - it goes with a big bang but only hurts anybody within a six-foot range - I think?) and we were standing on parade with an open log fire to the rear of us, waiting for the order to unload. This procedure involved emptying out the magazine of the rifle and passing all unused ammunition to an N.C.O. for return to the magazine at the camp.

One cadet failed to hand over all his unused stock and kept one round. It was soon discovered that one round was missing, but rather than own up he threw it away, and unfortunately it landed in the open fire and went off with a loud bang. His movements had been seen and he was duly reprimanded. Now in those days the army had problems of what to do with such stupid cadets, as their authority was extremely limited. It was decided to erect a small tent to be called the 'Glasshouse' (In the regular army the Glasshouse was where errant soldiers were brought to heel) and to place the cadet in it. We were then to guard it in shifts, with each guard told to frighten the wits out of this cadet, to ensure that what he did never happened again. Well, the things he was told varied from six strokes of the cane to being hanged at Walton Jail. The poor boy was in tears but we did realise the danger and severity of his actions, so we played our part to the full.

Strangely enough, in those days the I.R.A. was known to be attacking army camp sites, so when we went on guard duty we were issued with pickaxe handles in order to fend off any such attacks and with which to kill any who approached after our request 'Who goes there?' had been issued. Yes man, we were tough in those days.

Frank Irwin (1950-1957)
Now living in Wirral

ERIC REMEMBERS

Previous mention has been made of 'blank' ammunition used for simulation of the real thing. Blanks were different from 'drill' rounds, in that the business end of the blank was crimped so that it would burst open on firing, whereas the 'drill' had a normal bullet head at the end. However, the drill round had no propellant inside, indeed, it had a red stripe down the side to denote it as inert. As previously mentioned by another writer, there was another 'blank' which did contain propellant which was designed for use with the L.M.G. or 'Bren Gun'. The head of this round is made of wood so as to break up on firing. Confused? Read on! The inert drill rounds were used in all sorts of weapon training activities, not least of all practicing aiming and firing in the prone position without losing control of the rifle; no mean feat for a little boy of 14! Whilst this was going on, an N.C.O. would lie at the opposite end of the rifle using a disc against his eye to judge whether the cadet's aim was good, and the cadet would squeeze the trigger to confirm the sequence of aiming and firing. In later years, I was to run through this drill to teach the new recruits to aim properly. Can you imagine my consternation on one occasion on discovering a round with a blue wooden head, in with the drill rounds!!!

The Blue Coat had an Army Cadet Force unit commanded in my time by a member of the staff, Captain Tait. The school could not provide the necessary adult input with one officer and so we relied upon other people not previously connected with the school. Fortunately, the A.C.F. is blessed with an incredible number of people willing to give up their free time for the benefit of the young men or 'cadets' as part of the management team, be they officer or N.C.O.

Such a man was Lt. Walker, with whom I struck up a very positive relationship because of my interest in shooting or, more properly, marksmanship. He eventually suffered from a very serious illness (I believe that he had a heart attack, in part due to the fact that he was very much overweight) which hospitalised him. It is to my personal discredit that I failed to visit him in hospital despite the fact that I knew he was asking for me.

He obviously thought a lot of our unit because he requested that a number of us of should carry his coffin prior to the burial. He had a good sense of humour, and will not mind me relating the fact that as six 15 or 16-year-old boys staggered under the burden of carrying the coffin down the steps, his body slid forward with such a positive shift in the centre of gravity that we nearly dropped the thing. It did cause some sniggering but not in a disrespectful manner, if that's possible.

Another of the stalwarts dedicated to the A.C.F. was Major Carr of The Liverpool Scottish regiment. He was usually involved with the annual inspection of our unit, but after the departure of our commanding officer Captain 'Jimmy' Tait, he assumed command. Some ten years later, when as a captain in the Regular Army I was posted to Lancashire and I met up with him again, he was still serving the A.C.F. and as dedicated as ever.

Eric Woodbine (1953-1959)
Now living in France.

SCOUTING FOR BOYS, 31st WAVERTREE

Thinking back to annual scout camp and my scouting days at school, circumstances at the time meant that I suffered the disappointment of missing these camps due to lack of funds; if I remember correctly each scout was required to pay 7/6d (37.5p) to attend the same. Now as we all know how strict our headmaster was, it came as quite a surprise when one day he came across to me during dinner time. I could see I was the focus of his attention and of course my immediate thoughts were 'What I have I done wrong to warrant a personal visit during dinner?'

However, my fears disappeared as he dropped what was the answer to my dreams, 'How would you like to attend annual camp free of charge?' Wow, all my birthdays had come at once; he truly was the genie in the bottle after all.

As can be imagined, I was full of myself going away to camp at last. However, as events unfolded things did not turn out to be so rosy. Firstly, I received a good ear bashing from my mum for accepting charity, something that to her, a fiercely proud and independent person, was something one just did not do. Secondly, most of the time at camp was spent confined under canvas due to a violent stomach upset, which the local doctor was at a loss to alleviate. What little time I enjoyed outside of the tent was spent in dashing to the nearest latrine.

Dave Kennedy (1948-1955)
Now living in Wirral

I well remember one occasion whilst camping with the school scouts; if I remember correctly this particular camp was in Llanfairfechan, in North Wales. It was the practice of Mr. Gibson, the scoutmaster, to hold a daily inspection of each patrol's area, defined as space in close proximity to the patrol tent, where all the members slept together. Points were awarded for tidiness and deducted for any intrusive object that detracted from clean and healthy camping out.

Our patrol, The Lions, had discovered a tree, hidden away, that contained either plums or damsons, we didn't really know the difference in those days, but they were purple in colour and tasted very nice. Naturally the other patrol, The Peewits, asked us to let them in on our little secret, but Lions being Lions, we refused and continued to supplement our daily diet alone. A few days later, whilst all standing to attention outside our tents awaiting inspection, Mr. Gibson looked at the Peewit's area, adjacent to ours and declared it extremely clean. Whilst on his way to our area, also in pristine condition, the Peewits, now in a position behind Mr. Gibson, all turned round and bombarded our area with plum and damson stones, causing a loss of many points. The sods had discovered our tree and wreaked their revenge.

Another camp we used to go to was Tawd Vale, near Ormskirk. There we used to be able to swim in a roped off section of an old flooded quarry and we did our shopping for sweets and confectionery in a wooden shed called 'The Providence Store', nicknamed the 'Provvo'.

Girl Guides also used to spend camping holidays there but in a separate section that was 'out of bounds' to the Boy Scouts.

Frank Irwin (1950-1957)
Now living in Wirral

'Once a scout, always a scout' the saying goes, but I can go one better than that – 'Twice a scout, always a scout!' This is because I joined 31st Wavertree twice and (to my shame) only stayed for about two weeks each time. I now wonder why this was, and I think the answer is that I found the tasks uninspiring at that particular stage of my development. Taking knots as the example, I now find them fascinating and useful, but back then they just seemed a pointless chore. The second time I joined was recognition on my part that I had not given it a proper chance the first time round, but I found that my reaction was unchanged and left all over again. In view of this I suppose I could be accused of being a lazy child, but I think a more just adjective to apply would be 'independent'; I simply preferred to use my free time for my own pursuits. Things might have been different if some kind of outing had coincided with my arrival(s) as it was always a huge pleasure to break out of prison, as it were.

Ray Livingston (1955-1959)
Now living in York

In 1948 I joined the school scout troop, 31st Wavertree, and was put into the 'Cuckoo Patrol'. I well remember the camps that I went to, Bryn-Bac and Red Wharf Bay on the isle of Anglesey, sitting around the camp fire in the evenings singing the old songs like: 'Boomalakka, Chingalakka who are we, we are the 31st Wavertree' and always finishing up with 'Taps', 'Day is done, gone the sun, from the sea to the hills to the sky, God is nigh.' Remember?

One of the skills of a Boy Scout was to be able to use a hand axe! Well, after cutting my leg with one whilst attempting to chop firewood, I was banned from ever using one again. I still have the scar to this day.

Kenneth Hughes. (1945–1953)
Now living in France

BOB-A-JOB

Annually, during the Easter holiday if my memory serves me correctly, Boy Scouts nationally were involved in fund raising activities on a grand scale. The idea was for all involved to carry out work for members of the public, for which task they would be paid a 'bob' – a shilling. The resultant funds raised were to assist in subsidising both the national movement and also the local troop to which you belonged.

Every Wolf Cub and Boy Scout would be issued with an official card, showing the official logo of the organisation, and a table into which to enter the work carried out, the date it was done and the amount of money paid for that work. This activity has now ceased owing to the danger of allowing minors to knock on the doors of strangers and the resultant risks involved.

In those days though, this activity was helpful to both parties, the Boy Scout movement made money and members of the public got small jobs carried out for them cheerfully, willingly and hopefully efficiently.

Mostly, the whole thing was carried out in the manner in which it was envisaged, but occasionally boys were involved in gardening all day for just a shilling! Those miserable people were remembered and were not visited the following year.

On a lighter note, one scout, having knocked on a door was met by a middle-aged man who, in response to 'Good morning, bob-a job sir, have you any jobs you would like me to do for you?' said, 'O.K. son, will you paint my porch? It is round the back and there is a tin of brown paint there too.' 'Righty-ho,' said the scout, 'consider it done.'

Two hours later the scout knocked on the front door and said. 'The job is finished sir; will you please make a note on my card of the work done, and how much you are paying me for it?'

'Yes alright.' said the man. 'By the way' said the scout, 'it wasn't a Porsche, it was an Aston Martin: but I painted it anyway.'

Frank Irwin (1950-1957)
Now living in Wirral

CHAPTER 7
TEACHERS

TAN TAN

In the 'senior' dormitory, boys slept in single cubicles to give some degree of privacy. It was also a privilege bestowed on the residents that first thing in the morning the duty master would enter the room once only, just to ensure that everybody was awake. Rather than keep annoying boys, as happened in the other dormitories, by coming in shouting obscenities every five minutes, and dumping boys into baths of cold water, seniors were left to get up in their own time, with the warning that if anybody was ever late for breakfast, the privilege would be removed.

The self regulation worked a treat and nobody dared ever let down their dormitory mates, everything was working well, until Mr. Rowlands, the little moustached dictator, (nicknamed 'Tin Tin' but as he was the French teacher, pronounced 'Tan Tan') decided to live in the school and to take up his rostered duties as duty master.

For some reason best known to himself (or maybe other teachers who also hated his guts, had not informed him), he decided to make a second visit and discovered that we were all still in bed. His idea of dealing with the problem was to walk straight into the cubicle of the head boy and to tip his bed over so that he fell onto the floor. (Make an example of the head and the rest will follow!)

I may be wrong, but I think at that time the head boy's name was Barry Tudor. Anyway, he picked himself up off the floor, then he picked up 'Tan Tan', dragged him down the dormitory in front of the rest of us, and proceeded to throw him out through the door. We were never bothered again, but we were always on time for breakfast. Sometimes privileges bestowed are a better remedy than the threat of punishment.

Frank Irwin (1950–1957)
Now living in Wirral

Mr. J.E. SEPHTON

Continuing the topic of war-damaged teachers: In about 1956, Mr. J.E. Sephton joined the school and soon established a large choir unconnected with the chapel choir (which of course avoided any possible clash with Dr. Dickerson). I was in both choirs and that is why I remember all this. It was Mr. Sephton's choir that took part in the B.B.C. radio programme fifty years ago (1957) when Liverpool was celebrating its 750th anniversary and a broadcasting unit visited the school, including an 'Auntie' pianist who may even have been Violet Carson, later so famous for playing the part of Ena Sharples in Coronation Street. We sang Shakespeare's *Full Fathom Five*, from *The Tempest*, and Mr. Watcyn and the head boy, Peter Farrell, were both interviewed. Perhaps the tape still lies in the vaults at Broadcasting House, who knows?

Mr. Sephton was a stickler for discipline and other Old Blues may, like me, have recollections of his somewhat sadistic mass-punishment of we boarders by assembling us in the common room and making us stand absolutely motionless for twenty minutes instead of going on our Sunday walk. Pity help any boy who made any perceptible move, for he would have been harshly punished later on his own account. Even back then I remember thinking 'This must be physically very bad for us!', but one felt powerless in that stern 1950s regime.

The point I am coming to is that Mr. Sephton had been the pilot of a Lancaster bomber in the war and had therefore been through hell. In his friendlier moments, we would urge him to tell us stories from those days, but he never would. Now I understand, but back then I was rather puzzled and somewhat frustrated.

He loved Russian music and tried very hard to get us to like *Prince Igor*, *The Sorcerer's Apprentice*, etc, but with only partial success. Pity he never tried Beethoven, which might have worked on me even at that age.

Ray Livingston (1955-1959)
Now living in York

MR. PERRY

Lest readers of this book are left with the impression that Mr. Perry went about his business in this world with two little horns sticking out of his forehead, I would like to record that he had a kindly nature and evidently only 'bit' when life's stresses got the better of him, viz. the time when he struck me for whistling in the corridor, described elsewhere.

For example, Eric Winterbottom and I were keen on astronomy and, on learning that Mr. Perry owned a pair of decent binoculars, we plucked up sufficient courage to knock on the door of his room one dark evening and request to be allowed to borrow them for half an hour or so in order to do some star-gazing on the tennis courts. He did so, so willingly that we were encouraged to repeat the exercise on a few subsequent occasions (for those who like to know these things, the binoculars were 8 x 30 by Carl Zeiss).

Perhaps we all remember a moment in our lives when we find ourselves being treated as something like an adult for the first time. One sunny evening in the late spring of 1959, Mr. Perry politely summoned all the boys who were going to be 'promoted' from Stythe dormitory to Tinne dormitory if they returned the following term, and gathered them around him for a cheery team photograph. (See page 288) It was a distinctive, good-natured occasion and you sensed that you had reached a more mature phase of your life and could soon look forward to better times, although of course I did not return after the summer because I found a job in the meantime. The photograph appeared in the autumn 1959 issue of *The Squirrel* unseen by me, but it gave me enormous pleasure when I did see it for the first time some thirty years later.

Think of all those watches he fixed too! R.I.P. Mr. Perry.

Ray Livingston (1955-1959)
Now living in York

MORE ON MR. PERRY

My memories of Mr. Perry were on days when he either stood in for a class, due to the absence of a teacher, or the weather interfering with outdoor sports. During these classes he needed no encouragement to show off his artistic skills on the blackboard. Although he was quite good at demonstrating these skills (which of course we encouraged - a lesson doing nothing was more pleasure than feeding our brains with boring facts), the only trouble was he seemed to be suffering from compulsive disorder syndrome as all he ever seemed to draw was an African warrior in full war paint. Now, three is good, but every time he stood in we would get this same warrior.

My other recollection was being collared by him to perform what some would think an imposition: this entailed that on the days that he was on 'live in' duty, I was to go to his room well before he retired for the night and switch on his hot water bottle. Now the technology at the time did not include electric blankets for 'live in' teachers, so how come a hot water bottle needed switching on, you may ask? Well the gadget was quite ingenious if not outright dangerous; it consisted of a biscuit tin with a light socket attached to its interior. This I had to place inside the bed and plug the lead into the light socket on the ceiling. This duty turned out to be quite profitable, as he would reward me with a sixpence now and again.

Dave Kennedy (1948-1955)
Now living in Wirral

BRIAN PERRY (THE OBITUARY)

Recently I came across the September 1975 edition of the magazine of Fulneck School, where, if you remember, Brian Perry went after the teaching of Latin at the Blue Coat School was discontinued. Here is the tribute published therein.

Nobody who taught at Fulneck during the past fifteen years could have failed to be influenced by Brian Perry; nobody could have failed to like and admire Brian.

To his colleagues on the staff, he was an elder statesman, a wise counsellor, whose greatest wisdom was that he gave his opinion only when asked it. At countless staff meetings Brian was the one whose keen mind and gentle persuasive tongue solved problems which, otherwise, would have remained unsolved.

To the boys of Fulneck School, Brian was an avuncular friend. Every boy who approached him for help received kindness, for his gentleness and generosity were boundless. He turned away nobody: there were, at times, boys in whom Brian was the only person to retain any trust. No matter how often his trust was abused, it never faltered.

As a Latin teacher, Brian was a perfectionist. Room 4 was a fortress of classical civilisation, through which no barbarian breath was permitted to blow. Unable to find a Latin course to his liking, Brian produced his own, not for the benefit of a publisher, least of all for the benefit of his own pocket, uniquely for the boys whom he taught.

Latin has vanished now, a few months after Brian's untimely departure, but the hundreds of Fulneck boys who were fortunate to be taught by Brian will carry the mark of their Latin lessons throughout their lives.

There were so many ways in which Brian excelled that it is difficult to be specific: outstanding craftsman, an entertaining raconteur, a shrewd card player, above all the finest speaker I have ever heard.

Brian's dog was called 'Caesar', but Brian was no Caesar himself - a Brutus possibly, certainly one to whom the closing tribute to Brutus may ideally be addressed:

'His life was gentle, and the elements
So mix'd in him that Nature might stand up
And say to all the world, 'This was a man'.

Frank Hulford (Teacher 1956-1966)
Now living in Leicester.

DELVANTÉ

'Delvanté' was, in fact, Derek Jones, who was one of the school's form masters for a time and taught English, plus a few other subjects.

One day at the start of a new term, January 1956, Mr. Watcyn gathered all the boarders together to inform us that one particular boy and a certain schoolteacher would not be returning to school again for the forthcoming term. Allegations had been made.

One pupil goes on to say, 'Derek Jones was actually a very entertaining teacher, and was popular with most of the lads. He would often perform impromptu magic tricks in front of a class, or have us laughing at some of his theatrical stories from his other profession. He was also a member of the exclusive "Magic Circle".'

It was confirmed by another that he had been seen performing astonishing tricks with candle-greased playing cards during lessons. Showing fantastic dexterity, he would shoot the whole pack along the length of his arm and gather them up again in a flash. If you blinked you missed it. He really was a top-drawer conjuror and it's a shame that he had to leave when he did.

One pupil reports, 'In my early days at the school he was our music master and I have this ridiculous memory of him giving us a lesson in the Shirley Hall and getting us to sing the Irving Berlin song *Winter Wonderland*, whose lyrics are far removed from anything that little boys would ever choose to sing.'

The same pupil goes on to say, 'In a strange sequel, I encountered him one last time a year or two after I left the Blue Coat. I was calling at Rupert Road Secondary Modern School in Huyton one morning c1962, because I wanted to enrol for a certain night school class there, and he was present in the staff room. He recognised me but turned away. I was later informed that he went to Skerry's College in the immediate post Blue Coat period.'

Mr. Jones was the teacher who helped me to repair the damaged school mace, mentioned elsewhere in this booklet. He tried to keep me out of trouble over this episode, but the mace had to be repaired so unfortunately his assistance was ultimately to no avail.

On at least one occasion, he took six of us boarders out to a local theatre during the evening to see a magician's show, at his own expense. The show was held at a local theatre in Liverpool and involved one of his friends in the Magic Circle. As well as performing all the usual tricks of the day, the highlight of one performance was making a motor car disappear from the stage whilst in full view of the audience.

In 1966 it was agreed that magic in general would be better served if the Liverpool Magic Circle and the Mahatma Circle of Magicians were united. The two societies therefore amalgamated on 1st January 1967, assuming the new name of the Mahatma Magic Circle. For the first year there were joint presidents, one of those presidents was Mr. Derek Jones.

Frank Irwin (1950-1957)
Now living in Wirral

DICKERSON ('FISHY')

One lesson at school which was universally hated in my form was music with Dr. F.W. Dickerson or 'Fishy' as he was known. *'On wings of song I'll bear thee, enchanted realms to see..... and on the lake reposes a balmy lotus flower!'* How I hated that soppy song! Poor old Fishy was quite deaf and it was, I believe, the frustration that this must have caused that made him a little bad tempered and thus a target for some fairly unpleasant attention from us all. A visit to the headmaster was a frequent result of our music lessons for some miscreant since poor old Fishy had no other sanction he could apply being beyond, I believe, some 70 years old.

A friend, we'll just use his Christian name, Roger, put us up to a really wicked ruse. I say wicked because that's often what young boys in a school environment can be. Well, he got us all to sing silently (mime) at a signal from him and resume normal volume at a second signal. Fishy wore one of the first generation electronic hearing aids, which were bulky, and which he kept in the top pocket of his jacket, with a cord connected to a plastic earpiece.

The poor old chap suddenly banged his battery, and then turned the volume up, only to suffer the inevitable consequence, which we could not imagine, after the resumption of normal singing volume. I started pianoforte lessons with a pal, Doc Libby, under Dr. Dickerson's tutelage and was soon thumping out scales with excruciating slowness and lack of rhythm. I got the sack eventually for fighting!

Eric Woodbine (1953-1959)
Now living in France.

WHY WAS 'FISHY', 'FISHY'?

I think I may have the answer (or, at least, I have always assumed that my theory is convincing and probably the correct explanation).

One evening in the autumn of 1955, he took all the boarders for a singing practice in the Shirley Hall. I recall that we boys occupied the left-hand-side of the hall and he had his piano (a grand, I recall) at the front. Even at that age (I was 11), I formed the impression that he lacked the ability to control a large bunch of unruly youngsters like us. From time to time he would grow red-faced and angry with us, and at those times he would stand up and take a couple of steps towards us, his mouth opening and closing. In this irritated state he looked just like a fish - hence, I presume, the nickname. I do not claim that the nickname stems from that particular occasion but merely offer the example to illustrate the theory.

Ray Livingston (1955-1959)
Now living in York

I was curious to know why all the girls gave Dr. Dickerson the nickname of 'Dr. Fish'. Vera and Betty told me that he was called that because, when they were back in Liverpool, he only ever came in to eat with the rest of the staff on a Friday, and what was always served for dinner every Friday? Fish. I understand that he continued this habit after the war as well.

Margaret Thompson (Formerly Bond, 1941 – 1948)
Now living in Cambridgeshire

MR. CHIPS

Despite the adverse report elsewhere in this book, most of the time Dai Davies, known as 'Taffy' then, was held in great esteem by the Blue Coat boys. He hailed from the farming community of Clynderwen in Pembrokeshire, and in his youth he was a sportsman of some renown, but overshadowed by his brother, who apparently played first class cricket for the Glamorgan County side.

Dai, the physics teacher, lived in the school and took a great interest in helping boys to develop their sporting prowess in many fields of activity.

Despite not being the school's P.T. master, he took charge of an age group as far as inter-schools football was concerned and gave dedicated tuition to any interested party after school hours in his free time. He did the same thing in the summer term with cricket and athletics coaching, and naturally became very popular. I well remember him getting a rope and fastening it round the girth of a large tree at the side of the school playing field and then getting boys to form up into a tug-of-war team, in an attitude pulling against the tree's resistance. He then proceeded to get each boy into the position whereby, according to the laws of physics, he could impart maximum weight to pull and also maximum resistance to being pulled. Despite pulling with maximum efficiency, we never did manage to dislodge the tree.

I suppose at that time, we all accepted bullying and beatings as being a normal part of school life, so it is natural that his shortcomings were largely ignored by those on the receiving end. We lived for the better moments of our schooldays.

Around that time, I was a collector of football club programmes and had a great collection from Everton, (the team I support), Liverpool and the odd local clubs that I could visit during school holidays for Everton's away matches, like Bolton Wanderers and Preston North End. I was able to visit both Everton and Liverpool in school holidays, sitting in comparative luxury in the shareholders' stand as my father had occasional access to tickets for both clubs.

Compared with the opulence that can now be experienced at Goodison Park, those conditions were actually quite spartan.

However, because of this hobby, Dai would always save for me, his and his friends' football programmes and would bring me plenty from Cardiff City, Swansea Town and also Merthyr Tydfil to add to my collection.

Another 'Old Blue' mentions that Dai stayed on at school after his retirement and acted as caretaker, walking his Labrador dogs whilst on his rounds. He became known as the 'Mr. Chips' of the school, which, given the famous 1939 film of that name, *Goodbye Mr. Chips*, starring Robert Donat, was a compliment to him.

He died whilst still living in the school, in reportedly somewhat austere conditions, without complaint.

Frank Irwin (1950 -1957)
Now living in Wirral

TWO MASTERS WHO DESERVE OUR SPECIAL GRATITUDE

In the early-to-mid-1950s, two masters took separate initiatives, both of which greatly enriched the lives of the boys.

Mr. Mugglestone the crafts master decided one day to hire a film and show it to the boys at the weekend. This must have been a success, for a fortnight later he hired another one, and before very long the school had acquired a new, deeply ingrained habit. In the course of time it became a weekly affair - a regular and much-looked-forward-to Saturday evening event. Not only did it provide an opportunity for escapism but it was often also educational. Articles elsewhere in this book describe the sort of fare we watched. Mr. Mugglestone also served as the scoutmaster, so it is possible to speculate that it was serving in that role that inspired his bright idea (fancy! - we owed all that enjoyment to Baden-Powell!).

Dave Kennedy has a less glowing testimonial for Mr. Mugglestone: 'I well remember Mr. Mugglestone, if only for the resounding clout about the head I received from him. This was the result of misbehaviour during a craft lesson; a group of us had discovered that the thin cane used to make baskets, if cut into short pieces made a passable substitute for ciggies, and by lighting one end, one could draw smoke through the same. Alas, I was caught with the cane in my mouth hence the clout; and did he catch me full square on! I can feel it to this day.'

The second master was English teacher Mr. Kenneth I. Smith. He is credited with having been the founder of the school's magazine, *The Squirrel*. Excellent quality was achieved by him and his team and it is good to know that the magazine they started is still published today. The school we remember would have been a poorer place without it.

We understand that Mr. Smith turned 80 in 2006 and that he now lives in France. May we take this opportunity to send him our grateful thanks for the marvellous job he did all those years ago and send him and his wife our warmest good wishes.

Ray Livingston (1955-59)
Now living in York.

CHAPTER 8
LEISURE TIME

THE GAMES WE USED TO PLAY

As boarders, not being able to go home to enjoy (or otherwise) evenings, we amused ourselves by playing various games. Some of these games would not be allowed now by the present sissy 'nanny' state, which believes that even playing 'conkers' is dangerous.

The games were often rough but did serve to toughen us up and, in actual fact, despite the severity with which we tackled these games and some of the rough treatment afforded to opponents during them, I don't believe it actually did anybody lasting harm.

BRITISH BULLDOGS

In the evenings boys would generally gather in the common room which was located halfway along the western half of the south corridor. It also served as a locker room, but the lockers only measured about 325mm square by a similar depth, so in actual fact, nothing much could be held in them. Mind you, our general impoverishment whilst at school and sometimes even during holidays, meant we had very little of value to keep in them anyway.

The boys present would divide up into two teams, not necessarily of similar strength and size, but more of friends together to sort out the 'other lot'. After the initial selection of friends, others would be selected alternately to ensure teams of equal numbers of players. Each team would position itself at opposite ends of the room.

Each team member would then have to stand on one leg only and fold his arms in front of himself. The object of the game was to hop towards the other team and to reach their end of the room, knocking down as many of the opposition as possible whilst remaining on your feet yourself, by nudging with the shoulder whilst staying on one leg and with arms still folded.

Anybody who either fell over, or in fact touched the floor with any part of the body other than the leg that he was standing on, was considered 'knocked down' and was not permitted to take any further part in the game. The eventual winning team was the side that had anybody still standing after all the members of the other team had been eliminated.

Naturally, when there were perhaps six members of one team left standing and only one of the other, it got rough. However, nobody ever gave up. The Bulldog spirit prevailed, and the singleton attempted to sort out the other six, despite the adverse odds.

During nice weather, this game would also be played anywhere found to be convenient. Playing fields, playgrounds; same rules but a larger arena of combat.

TWO-TON-TESSIE-ON

This game also consisted of two teams with the selection procedure as described in British Bulldogs applying again.

For this game, a table would be positioned at one end of the room: for outside play, a wall would suffice. Teams would draw lots for first choice, usually being the 'Two-Ton-On' option.

The other team would generally position its weakest or smallest player sitting on the table, with his legs apart and hanging over the front of the table. The next team-mate would stoop down and place his head in the stomach of the guy sitting on the table with his legs apart, ready to accept the head of the next member of the team. Thus a line rather like a gymnasium vaulting horse would be formed. Other people would then crawl beneath the 'horse' to help stabilise it; they were known as 'supports'.

Once the team was in position, the other team members would, in turn, run along towards the end of the 'horse' and vault high in the air, landing down on the backs of those below. They would usually be guided as to where to land by the team captain, who would assess the weak points of the human structure. Once on the backs, he would shuffle along towards the front of the 'horse' making room for the next player to land down hard again in an attempt to break the stability and thereby make the team below collapse.

The idea was for the 'vaulting team' to cause a collapse and the 'supporting team' to take all the 'vaulters' on their backs without collapsing. Once all the 'vaulters' were 'on board' the structure had to maintain its place for 10 seconds.

If the supporting side collapsed the 'vaulters' repeated the exercise. If the structure stayed in place, the roles of the teams swapped and the supporters became 'vaulters'.

INDOOR FOOTBALL

Because playing football indoors could possibly result in broken windows, a feature not much appreciated by the headmaster Mr. Watcyn, the Blue Coat boy's design team came up with the perfect solution.

Any small object was wrapped in newspaper, and further layers of stronger paper were added until a nice, small, hard parcel had been shaped, which was finally covered in brown paper and tied up with string. The result was a tough 'ball' that could be kicked around without it having properties that allowed it to be kicked into the air from off the floor. Coats would be placed at each end of the common room to serve as goal posts, and the match would be keenly competitive, with many arguments about whether or not the ball had in fact passed between the 'posts' for a goal.

OTHER GAMES

For some reason I cannot recall, we used to occasionally declare 'Beaches On' somebody. That meant everybody present had to beat up whoever was named.

'Realio', was an outside game and we also played 'All Aboard', which involved a pile of three stones, decreasing in size upwards as they were stacked on top of one another. For some reason we used to, in teams, knock the stones down. I wish I could remember all the details, but that's age for you.

TABLE TENNIS

This was enjoyed and in fact the table we used was manufactured in the school's woodwork shop, by pupils under the guidance of Mr. Hickman. He did most of the work because, unlike us, he was highly skilled, and this table was made to competition standards. Having qualified as a National Club Table Tennis Coach when in my 30s, I now realise the quality that he achieved. Using the incorrect timber or the wrong thickness affects the bounce of the ball, and this table was really of excellent quality.

TENNIS

This was played on a regular basis, but we only ever played on hard courts. There were two such courts located to the south of what was then the staff room. The staff room bay window protruded between the two courts. In fact, some of the staff were very good players. I and other boys used to watch them in action and given all the differing styles of service, chose the one we each wanted to model ourselves on.

We would play regularly but it was very difficult to be able to obtain the necessary equipment. We often had to barter for second hand stuff and many times we had to play with broken strings to our racquets and we never had the facilities with which to repair them. Balls often refused to bounce as they should because they were invariably threadbare and worn out. Despite that, quite a few players became of good standard and it became the practice occasionally for staff to play doubles matches against senior boys.

The wall to the south of the courts, a fairly high red brick affair, and also one wall within an adjacent undercover area called 'the shed' had white lines painted at the height of a tennis net. (See photograph) This proved very useful for practising shots, hitting the ball repeatedly at the wall and hopefully just above net height.

On returning in 2007 to look at the area, I noticed that the tennis courts had become the car park for the private apartments and maisonettes that have been built in the area where our dormitories used to be, but the white line could still be seen on the south wall. The feature known as 'shed' has been converted into one set of living accommodation and also a small narrow arched access way to the front doors of the various apartments.

I feel sure the school created a good set of tennis players. I always enjoyed the game, at school and also afterwards, in fact I played well into my 40s.

CIGARETTE CARDS

Boys would collect cigarette cards (given away free in packets of cigarettes in those days) and to play, would stand at an agreed distance away from a wall and throw the cards at it. The winner was the person whose card ended up nearest to the wall and he won all the other cards that had been used in the competition. The best way to achieve this was to glue two or three cards together so that they flew better through the air and dropped like at stone on contact. These cards also were the subject of collections. There would be sets of 50 of famous footballers, butterflies, motor cars and other popular items. Cards would avidly be bartered as swaps in the race to collect a full set. Full sets in good condition are worth a fortune today.

THREE CARD BRAG

This was, I think, the only card game played for cash, even though stakes were very low. This was usually played on a Sunday evening after chapel, when some boys had been lucky enough to receive some coppers from their visiting parents.

The games were generally played in the small room to the rear of the table tennis room, this room also contained a chimney, so that smokers could sit close to the fireplace and exhale up the chimney to avoid the smell from tobacco permeating throughout the room. Somebody would 'Keep douse' at the table tennis room door, but teachers became aware of the activities and would dash up and clear the table of money before 'douse' could be called. When that happened, no more was ever mentioned about it and there were no repercussions. I wonder what happened to the money taken.

The safest place to play cards was in the centre of the school field. From that distance it was possible to see masters approaching, but impossible for them to see if anybody was actually playing for money. By the time masters arrived, somebody would be calling out 'Snap!'

FOOTBALL & CRICKET

I have not mentioned much about football and cricket, because these two sports were played with full decorum. Both games were enjoyed to the full with inter-house matches (Bingham, Blundell, Graham & Shirley) and also inter-school games.

Lance Lane and the home field, (now the car park), were both used, but I am unaware of the method by which the pitches were selected for each individual match.

MARBLES

Played with glass spherical balls, bottle washers, (sometimes ball-bearings) and still probably a game played today! The favourite game was to draw a small circle in the playground, using a convenient soft stone, like limestone or chalk.

Usually played by two players, each would place three or four marbles within the circle then retire to an agreed distance and take alternate shots with a 'basher', attempting to knock the marbles out of the circle. All those that you knocked out, became yours.

ATHLETICS

Athletics was keenly competitive and in fact at the start of the annual Sports Day, a good many points had already been awarded to each house for the attainment of 'standards'.

It was, if I remember correctly, compulsory for schoolboys to enter each event. During the heats which took place earlier, a standard time or target was set, and even though only a limited number of boys were allowed to contest the final, everybody who achieved the standard or target, was awarded some house points. Thus every entrant, whatever their standard, played a useful part towards being the Champion House on the day. (The illustration shows a winner's medal awarded in 1955).

BASKETBALL

Basketball was played as inter-house matches only. It was generally played on the north playground, where a court was marked out. Size didn't matter much then as none of us were really tall enough to take advantage of our height when attacking the basket.

Frank Irwin (1950-1957)
Now living in Wirral

THE CRICKET MATCH

It was one of those balmy afternoons and it was our P.E. period. I generally liked sports, but on this occasion a cricket match had been decided upon.

Now I don't like cricket and never did. For me it is a game where 11 players are 'in' and 11 players are 'out', i.e. 'not in'.

The eleven players who are 'in' are only 'in' until the team who are 'not in', get them 'out'. Except for the last player, who is deemed to be 'not out'. At that point the team who were 'in' becomes the team that is 'not in' and the team who was 'not in' becomes the team that is 'in'. But that is only until the team that is 'not in' gets them all 'out' except of course for the last player, who again must, by definition be 'not out'.

During this skirmish, players have to attempt to score runs by running up and down a distance of a chain, which as you all know is 0.1 furlong. Each time you complete 0.1 furlongs without being deemed to be 'out', you score a run. The team that runs the most chains is called the winning team. To me this seemed stupid and is why I have never liked the game. So what should I do whilst these 22 players perform duties called being 'in', 'out' and 'not out' and running stupid distances?

I decided to explore the foliage that surrounded the school field and found myself by the dividing wall between Holy Trinity Church and the school playing field and I came upon a 'skulk' (if that is the correct collective noun) of schoolboys, in a den made from grass, twigs and branches. The den was in the base of a bush about 20 ft. high (6,096mm to modern youth) and inside it a couple of schoolboys were smoking a fag. (One always had to share!)

Not being trained in Health & Safety like today's modern schoolboys, within minutes the whole den and bush were ablaze and the fire created an effect rather like a Roman Candle! Within minutes, a Fire Engine could be heard coming down Church Road and Mr. G.G. Watcyn turned up on the school field to see just what was going on.

Anyway, it now being 4.00 p.m. and me being a dayboy I decided that not only was cricket not for me, neither was this fire. I went home and left everybody else to it. Luckily for me, that was the end of the matter.

Dave Bolt. (1951-1957)
Now living in Vancouver, BC

CHAPTER 9
TEACHERS REMEMBER

MEMORIES OF A TEACHER

Mr. Mace was the geography teacher until the summer of 1955, and then a Mrs. Hughes filled in for a term until I could start in January 1956. I stayed until the summer of 1966 when I eventually married. I have been married now for over 40 years, and we have two daughters and one granddaughter. I had to wait until I was 76 to become a grandparent!

In 1966 I moved to Merchant Taylors', Crosby as a maths teacher, and then three years later moved to a school in Oxford as deputy head. I stayed there until retirement in 1988.

THE BOARD OF PARSIMONY

The domestic side of the school was controlled financially by a body by the name of the Board of Economy. I chose to rename it, privately, the Board of Parsimony.

I was unaware of the details of the finances or the constraints under which the Board found itself, but some of the day-to-day impacts were very noticeable. I started at the school in January 1956 and arrived on the Friday afternoon before term began on the Monday so that I could settle in and find my way about. I was allocated a room off the staff corridor on the second floor. Unlike the main staff bedrooms it was unheated, but I was told by Mr. Watcyn that I could buy myself a one-bar electric fire, which I did the next morning. Unfortunately, there weren't any power points in the room: the fire had to be plugged into the light socket using a two-way adaptor.

On the day of my arrival Miss Warren (the matron) brought some food to the staff room for me, after which I set out to remind myself of the building of which I had had a conducted tour on the day of my interview several months earlier.

I wandered round the main corridors which had few lights. I found some staircases and felt around for light switches but most of them produced no response as there were no lamps in the sockets. It was a strange welcome.

The feeling of having arrived at something akin to Dotheboys Hall was increased at the first assembly, held in the chapel. Mr. Watcyn announced: 'I'd like to welcome two new members of staff: Mr. Price, who will teach mathematics, and....., and....., the new geography master.'

Saving electricity was a constant worry for Mr. Watcyn. He would phone across to Mr. Crebbin if he saw a light on at the north end of the building in the evening. At one stage Brian Farrell started to give woodwork lessons to Brian Perry and me. I successfully repaired a chest of drawers for my room, and made a pencil box and a table lamp, both of which are still in use. When Mr. Watcyn found this activity going on, he immediately stopped it because of the consumption of electricity for the lighting. It was a pity that facilities such as the woodwork room were not available for hobby classes for the boarders.

CLASS SIZES

The standard entry to the school at 11+ was 32 boys to 1G and 32 to 1M. But the boys of 2M sat the 13+ transfer exam, and each year some of them passed and joined 2G (a year behind) the following year, swelling the numbers. When I started teaching in January 1956 the smallest class amongst 2G, 3G, 4G and 5G was 36 and the largest 39. 3M and 4M were correspondingly smaller and 5M, after some boys had left at 15, was usually 20 or fewer.

That's not the end of the story however, as Mr. Watcyn would (under pressure from parents?) transfer other boys to the Grammar stream at his discretion, and there was also the occasional additional boarder. The largest class I ever taught was 4G when one year it reached a total of 43!

The problem disappeared when it was decided to create a new set of classes, 2GB etc. with a full 13+ intake, including boys from other schools.

This was dependant on more classrooms being available. When the gymnasium was built, the former gym was converted into laboratories, and the cadet force area became a series of classrooms above 1G-5G.

SIR BAGGUS'S BUNNY

When a boy named Baggus addressed a teacher he said 'Sir' at both the beginning and end of his remarks. If asked his name he would reply 'Sir, Baggus, Sir'. We referred to him amongst ourselves as Sir Baggus.

It was the day before the end of term when Baggus arrived at my door carrying a cardboard carton containing a rabbit. Could I keep it in my room until he went home the following day? I had little choice. It enjoyed chewing my carpets. It was duly collected the following afternoon. I hope it survived.

THE MAN

One summer term a new boarder arrived, Martin from central Lancashire. He was a rather undersized boy of 11 or 12 years with glasses that were always awry, and he was somewhat monosyllabic.

I was supervising a homework session and I had given him permission to go to the toilet. On his return he came to my desk and announced: 'E wants some string.' I was a little mystified. The conversation continued as follows:
'Who wants some string?'
'The man.'
'What man?'
'The man on the tennis courts.'
'But what's his name?'
Then, after a pause for thought, very hesitantly came the word 'Taffy'.
It seems that some running repairs were required on a tennis net.

A SECRET HOARD

One summer afternoon some boys were playing tennis under the supervision of a non-resident master. A ball went over the fence at the west, Grant Avenue, end. A dayboy climbed over to get the ball and in doing so came across a suitcase. He duly reported his find to the master in charge. It turned out to be full of bottles of beer, presumably stashed away by some boarder to be collected after dark. It was reported that Mr. Crebbin poured the contents down the sink.

RECORD CARDS

One year when I was form master of 1G, all form teachers were issued with blue Record Cards from the Liverpool Education Committee, one for each boy, intended to record their academic progress through the school. The cards were rather large and unwieldy.

I filled in the basic details required and, having no further instructions, put them on a shelf in the staff room. They were never referred to again. When the staff room was cleared for redecoration two or three years later we discovered my batch, which had fallen down behind the pigeon holes in which staff mail was put. Then they were just thrown away - surplus to requirements.

WAS HOME LIFE BETTER?

A small number of boys would visit me from time to time just to have a chat, usually about nothing in particular. Ron was one of these. I had bought my first car (Austin Cambridge in Tweed Grey) and at the end of a term, knowing that no arrangements had been made to pick him up, he asked me if I would take him home to Penketh. I was not allowed to meet any family member as Ron waited until I had left before ringing the bell. It was probably a couple of years later at the May half term break that I found Ron still waiting to be picked up after everyone else had gone. This time he had expected someone, but nobody arrived.

Eventually Ron asked if I would take him to an aunt's house, somewhere not very far from the school. I drove him there in my, by this time, 12-seater Land Rover. Again I was not to meet any of the family, and, since he was not expecting to get any outings during the week's break, I arranged to pick him up one day (my mother had died in 1958 and my father had remarried, so I often spent half term breaks in Liverpool or elsewhere). We went to Southport and took a boat on the lake and had some rides at the fairground. I last saw Ron when he was in the army and just about to go to Cyprus and he called at my house in Thornton. We lost touch after that.

WHO PAYS?

The O-level geography results gradually improved over the years, and A-level classes grew in size. I began to take groups on more field weeks, usually during the summer holidays. They were not expensive as we stayed in Youth Hostels and we travelled in my Land Rover and I only charged petrol costs. One boarder, A, said, however, that he could not ask his mother for more money, so I referred him to Mr. Watcyn. He adamantly refused to see Mr. Watcyn about extra funding. He was a quiet, thoughtful, very likeable boy though, with a genuine understanding of people. I think it was about the third time A and I had discussed his problem, the solution to which was escaping me, when he simply said, in a quite matter-of-fact manner without any sense of pleading 'Couldn't you pay for me?' So the matter was settled. As far as I know, A and I were the only ones to be aware of this arrangement and it was never referred to again.

SAN, SICK BAY & SENIOR WING.

At the time of my interview (mid-1955) the San. (i.e. Sanatorium) was located at the front of the school, near Mr. Watcyn's room. But then it was moved to the matron's corridor and became Sick Bay. The rooms at the front were then adapted as extra boarding space for about ten boys. The total number went up from about 120 to 130. This area was known as Senior Wing and was occupied by boys selected as 'trusties'.

It was directly under Mr. Crebbin's control, and the duty master had no responsibility in that area.

Boarding duties by the resident staff were done in return for free board and lodging, to which no particular value was assigned. In these circumstances the board and lodging were not taxable - very useful for young men who wished to build up some capital, and part of the reason why some stayed for only a few years until they had accumulated a little.

STAND-IN ORGANIST

After Mr. Sephton's departure there was an interregnum in the music department and I took on the duties of chapel organist (manuals only) for a term. Quite unexpectedly I received an honorarium of £20 at the end of it! Mr. Norman Price took over the following term.

THE STOKER

Mr. Lewis, the stoker, had been in the Merchant Navy and told me that in 1949 he was on a ship in China at the time of the famous Yangtse Incident (in which the Communist forces attacked *H.M.S. Amethyst*). High on the wall opposite the boiler house was a mirror so that the boilerman could see the smoke coming out of the chimney. Dai used to call this 'Mr. Hulford's mirror' when he used it as an example of reflection during the work on light. The heating was changed over to oil-firing, and the boiler house partly rebuilt about 1961. Even then the heating system was not very efficient. In the earlier days, though, I recall one day when the temperature in the old geography room rose to a chilly 48^0F (9^0C) by lunchtime.

TEACHERS' WAR TIME EXPERIENCES

Almost all men born before 1927 (unless too old or in a reserved occupation) will have had some experience of military service. It is something they only rarely talked about though. What I can say about my former colleagues is limited to the following.

Mr. Smith had been in the Royal Navy. Mr. Unwin had been aircrew in the R.A.F. Mr. Perry had been in the army and on D-Day was a sergeant in charge of a landing craft on the Normandy beaches. Mr. Davies was also in the army and was sent to Burma. In his cups he repeated three things only; a native woman giving birth in the toilet of a train in India; awaiting action - 'There we were, only 18, drunk every night'; and Henry, a sergeant, who was a bit of a joke as he was 'straight from training camp in England', and, presumably, tried to adhere rigidly to all the regulations in circumstances which warranted some relaxation.

For myself, I was only 17 when the war ended, and I did two years National Service after graduation and teacher training. I was trained as a teleprinter operator in the R.A.F. (hence my keyboard skills), passed the 'Procedure' test with 99% ('Only the Senior Training Officer can get 100%'), and immediately became an instructor on the twelve-week course. (It wasn't difficult to get full marks as it was a multiple-choice test and one merely had to recognise the exact sets of words which appeared in one's notebook). The three-week Instructors' Technique Course I attended was full of valuable teaching tips.

TELEPHONE COMMUNICATIONS

These days it seems almost incredible that then, considering the distances to the head's room, the office, and Mr. Crebbin's room, the staff room had no telephone. To reach the office or Mr. Watcyn's room one had to go either up the stairs and through Shirley Hall, or up the 'back' stairs via the open corridor.

The situation was even worse in the evenings and at weekends when the office was closed. Only the extensions to Mr. Crebbin's room, Miss Warren's room, and maybe the kitchen were connected. If I wanted to make a call I had to leave the premises and use the callbox on the other side of Church Road. Incoming calls were rare, and could be awkward.

I was summoned to Miss Warren's room just after eight o'clock one morning to receive a call from my father saying that my mother had died.

And one evening Dorothy, now my wife, called (for the first and only time), to be answered by Mr. Crebbin. A boy had to be sent from the north end of the building to the south end, where, fortunately, I was to be found in the staff room, and then I had to go the whole length of the building and up the stairs to receive my call and make arrangements for a meeting. Things are so different today!

TRIPS OUT

In the early sixties I bought a 12-seater Land Rover. This was useful for ferrying teams to their match venues. Intended primarily for chess teams, it also coped with football and cricket teams. It enabled A-level field studies to be done conveniently and cheaply. Weeks were spent primarily in Swaledale and Swanage. There were also more local trips in south Lancashire for soil studies and village sitings. I also arranged walking holidays in the Lake District and days out to Snowdonia or Ingleborough. For Snowdonia I recall getting up early and rousing the boys who were going, then cooking bacon and eggs for them, and myself, in a huge frying pan in the kitchen. We left before daylight. On one occasion I bought petrol in Denbigh at ten past eight. Then on to Pen-y-Pas and over the northern half of the Snowdon horseshoe via Crib Goch, and back down the 'PYG Track'. Once, when the causeway across the exit from Llyn Llydaw was flooded, it was off with boots and socks, and for the shorter boys, trousers too, in order to wade across. On other occasions we might go on to Cwm Idwal and up over the Glyders, down Bristly Ridge and up onto Tryfan before making the final descent. We would have fish and chips in Mold (or in Clitheroe from Ingleborough) on the way back to Liverpool. Such trips were open to all, and encouraged many boys to try an open air life style.

UPDATE ON SOME PAST TEACHERS

The only person I still have contact with is Mr. K.I. Smith (English). In fact my wife and I dined with him and his wife last summer when he was living in Dorset, near where we were on holiday. They both had their 80th birthdays in 2006. They moved back to France in the autumn. They had previously spent a couple of years there.

They have had about ten different addresses since retirement! From Blue Coat, Ken went to become head of English at Rock Ferry High School, and then at a comprehensive in S.E. London. After that he was deputy head in Coventry, and finally head of a school in South Gloucestershire.

John Tait moved to a Jewish school on Camden Road, N.W. London. He showed me round there once, but I later lost contact.

When Latin was removed from the Blue Coat curriculum, about 1963, Brian Perry found a similar job at Fulneck School, between Bradford and Leeds. He had a flat there, and a dog, retriever/collie, called Caesar. Never careful of his own health, he died after a heart attack in February 1975, close to his 50th birthday.

TRANSISTOR RADIOS

Mention has been made of transistor radios at the school; I don't remember any problem with them at all. I imagine they were accepted played at low volume after lights out. I do remember John Whitehead taking his with him to Snowdon so that he would not miss his favourite Saturday morning programme as we walked along the northern ridge. There had been a problem in pre-trannie days with boys trailing leads from the light sockets to power their radios. Some of these were extremely dangerous. They were accepted initially, when they were few in number, but it all became too much and they were all cleared away.

FIVE MEN IN A BOAT AND OTHER STORIES

In 1955 Mr. Perry, Mr. Jones and Mr. Smith made their first pilgrimage to Stratford-upon-Avon for a couple of days in October in order to see two of that season's Shakespeare plays. This became an annual event, coming to an end only with Brian Perry's death in 1975.

I joined them in 1959, and others who joined the party at various times were Mr. Sephton, Mr. Farrell, Mr. Norman Price, Mr. Perry's brother, and one of Mr. Smith's brothers.

In the earliest years a car was hired for the occasion, but from 1959, car ownership becoming the norm, we used our own vehicles.

Some years; 1964 may have been the first; additional holidays were planned, in May or August, to visit the Forest of Dean, Hadrian's Wall (1966), and Oxford (1973 or 1974) or to make voyages on the Thames or a canal.

During our visits to Stratford, we not only attended the theatre, but visited nearby towns (Warwick, Banbury), and other attractions (Ragley Hall, Charlecote Park), played bar billiards or dominoes in village pubs, and had picnics or pub lunches.

We generally looked for cheap accommodation. For example, on the first night of the Hadrian's Wall trip we stayed at Mrs. Waugh's establishment in Durham. We had a lively discussion as to the proper pronunciation of her name, which led, later, to us always referring to her as 'Mrs. Wow,' maybe the least likely of the suggestions.

The most adventurous occasions undoubtedly occurred when we were waterborne: on the Thames, not finding a mooring spot before darkness fell; on a canal in Cheshire, our moorings coming loose early one morning as a train of barges passed by; on the Thames, when the gear lever came completely adrift when we were in reverse; at Bunbury locks, when the narrowboat rudder got caught on the rear sill of the lock, and the lock was emptying (much enjoyed by the Sunday afternoon onlookers).

There is so much more, over so many years, but I hope the above gives some flavour of those extraordinary occasions.

Frank Hulford (Teacher 1956-1966)
Now living in Leicester.

DORMITORIES

In or around 1958, the dormitories were renamed so as not to be the same as the names of the houses used for sports.

Blundell became Earle, Bingham became Macauley, Graham became Stythe, and Shirley became Tinne (Pronounced, Tinny). I originally occupied the room outside Bingham dormitory, Brian Farrell was outside Blundell, Brian Perry outside Graham, and Dai Davies (Taffy to you!) outside Shirley. I later moved onto the staff corridor on the top floor in order to get a little more peace!

Regarding locking up at night; that was the responsibility of the duty master, but was normally carried out by the duty prefect. The prefect would approach the duty master to ask for the pass key to lock up.

BOARDING DUTIES

During my time at the school, January 1956 to July 1966, there were very few changes in the routine of boarding duties. The one major change was the advance of the boys' getting up time from 06.45 to 07.15. Mr. Crebbin, the housemaster throughout my time, although not a very sympathetic person seemed to be well organised, and was generally happy to leave all the daily chores to the other resident masters. The boarding accommodation was almost entirely at the south end of the building, but Mr. Crebbin's was at the northern end, and he was in the habit of disappearing in that direction quite early in the evening, having conducted roll call at 18.00 and supervised homework in 5G form room until 19.00.

I don't think he had been in the post very long before my arrival, and he soon introduced a few rearrangements which seemed eminently appropriate. He never formally consulted his resident colleagues, but obviously listened to our conversations around the dining table and took some things to heart.

One change was to arrange the 'promotion' of boys from one dormitory to the next purely on date of birth. Although this occasionally split some friendships, there could never be any accusation of favouritism. Secondly, the dormitories were given new names, as stated elsewhere, different from those of the houses used for school games and sports. At the same time one of the common rooms was linked to each dormitory, and one of the resident masters was given general oversight of each age group.

This gave four of us an interest and responsibility beyond just performing the routine duties. Finally, a different pattern of duties was arranged. When I arrived at the school, the duty rota looked completely haphazard, a master doing an odd day here and a couple there, and so on. The new arrangement was that Mr. Moore (who lived out) should be duty master every Monday and never be on relief duty, someone else did Tuesday, Wednesday and Thursday, and a third man Friday, Saturday and Sunday. The relief duty master, who was basically on duty while the duty master had his meals, did Monday to Thursday or Friday to Sunday. The rota ensured that you were paired, duty and relief, with a different person each time.

I will describe *relief duty* first. Breakfast was at 07.45 (in the staff dining room), half an hour earlier than the rest of the staff, after which the relief master had to take over from the duty master in the dining hall halfway through the boys' breakfast (08.00 – 08.30), and continue on duty until the start of the school day. The relief master was next on duty 16.00 – 17.00, finishing by lining up the boarders for tea (and inspecting hands for cleanliness) at 17.00, when the duty master took over. Finally, the relief master supervised homework in 2M form room 18.00 – 19.00, although the start of homework would always be delayed a little as Mr. Crebbin took roll call in Shirley Hall right on 18.00. Normally this lasted no more than a few minutes, but if he had a major issue to deal with it could take much longer. I think the relief master had additional duties at weekends, but I cannot remember exactly what they were. One perhaps was to supervise the wardrobe room while the boys were changing into their grey woollen suits ready for chapel on Sunday mornings.

Regarding the duty master's routine, in my earlier days at the Blue Coat the boys' rising time was 06.45 and I used to get up at 06.15 to give myself time to wash, shave and dress. Unfortunately the pump for the hot water system was not functioning at that hour, so I had to go downstairs (two floors) to the staff room to boil a kettle for shaving water! At 06.45 it was my practice to make sure that every boy was awake, threatening to pull off the bedclothes if necessary, but never actually doing so, so as to avoid any possible embarrassment. I would then leave it to the dormitory prefects to take over.

All the younger boys had to go down two floors to wash which resulted in the noise of a stampede down the wooden stairs and, a few minutes later, up again. Once a week one of the matrons would open each dormitory door and call out 'Sheets and pillowcases', when the beds had to be stripped for these items to be changed. One unfortunate lady was far from popular and she withdrew from each doorway as quickly as possible before the chorus of catcalls from some of the slightly older boys could make an impact. The only task the boys were expected to undertake before breakfast, apart from washing, dressing and making their beds, was to clean their shoes, so there was ample time before breakfast at 08.00. In those early days it was the custom for one boy to fetch a cup of tea from the kitchen for the duty master; I remember how pleasantly surprised I was when it happened the first time I was on duty. I have a feeling that this custom fell into disuse, maybe when rising time was moved to 07.15.

At about 07.55 the duty master would collar the nearest boy and direct him to ring the handbell, kept in the staff room, to signal breakfast time, and the boys, supervised by the prefects, would line up outside the dining room. At the duty master's signal they would enter the dining room and stand in front of the long benches set at the long tables. Grace was then said, usually by one of the younger boys who would emerge from the assembled company, obviously persuaded to 'volunteer' for this task. Occasionally I would take it upon myself to select someone, usually more senior, to say grace instead. Breakfast would then start: the doors from the servery would open and Miss Morris (usually) would wheel in a large trolley with the food for the meal. At 08.10/08.15 the relief master would appear from the staff dining room to take over.

A strange anomaly had persisted at lunch time, perhaps for many years. During my first years the boarding duty master was on duty for the dayboys as well as the boarders during the lunch period. However, eventually, sense prevailed and day duty was instituted, the rota consisting of all teachers, resident and non-resident. Thereafter, the duty master's only responsibility at this time of day was to supervise the boarders as they lined up for lunch – on the opposite side of the dining hall from the dayboys.

At the close of afternoon school there was half an hour's freedom, then tea with the other resident staff at 16.30. At 17.00 the longest period of continuous duties started with supervision of the boys' tea and lasted until 22.00. After tea there was a short respite until after roll call, when there was supervision of homework in 1M form room until 19.00. Very soon after this the bell was rung for junior supper at 19.15 (for Earle and MacAulay dormitories - otherwise Blundell and Bingham) and the long evening routines had started. The duty prefect would usually appear promptly after junior supper. Earle boys would normally go upstairs straight after supper, although according to 'the book' they were not due upstairs until 19.45. After that MacAulay were due upstairs at 20.15, senior supper was also at 20.15, Stythe (Graham) were to be upstairs by 20.45, and Tinne (Shirley) by 21.20. 'Lights Out' times were half an hour later in each case, except for Tinne when it was 22.00. 'Lights Out' was not too traumatic as, by this time, one or other of the two dormitory prefects was usually present in his cubicle.

These fairly straightforward timings were complicated by the various bath nights. Earle boys bathed on Wednesday evenings and Saturday afternoons, MacAulay boys on Monday and Friday evenings, Stythe on Tuesdays, and Tinne on Thursdays. One problem every time was the limited flow of hot water. Were there as many as 17 baths? I am not sure about this, but the flow of hot water was barely sufficient to fill more than about five at a time. Consequently one would see boys, clad in just a towel, sitting on a bath-side watching a tiny trickle of hot water coming from the tap until such a time as someone else turned theirs off. It was of some help that the Earle bathing was supervised by a matron as she made it her business to start running baths well before any of her charges arrived. Generally, though, it was amazing how little trouble bathing turned out to be, probably because of the willingness of boys to go upstairs on their bath-nights earlier than prescribed in order to get a quick and early share of the hot water.

After 22.00 no responsibilities were laid down for the duty master, and I do not remember a single occasion when my assistance was required during the night.

Frank Hulford (Teacher 1956-1966)
Now living in Leicester.

BOARDING DUTIES 2

Living on a permanent basis with 120 to 130 boys aged 8 to 18 is quite demanding, and each master had to find his own *modus vivendi* in this situation. To most it posed no problem although some were better at it than others. Here is an account of two of those who had least success.

Mr. Hugh Gibson, a man in his mid-thirties, was appointed to teach principally history and geography in the secondary modern stream. One rather odd thing about him was that he subscribed to *Hansard* – the proceedings of the House of Commons. Whether he actually read his purchases I do not know.

As far as I am aware, any problems he may have had in the classroom were nothing out of the ordinary. He was also reasonably successful as a scoutmaster. A jovial man, he was always ready to laugh, not least at himself, and, a sensitive man, he too readily became the butt of some of the less sensitive boys. One evening when I was on duty in the dining hall, supervising junior supper; he came in, ostensibly to speak to me, although it was immediately clear to me that he actually had nothing to say, but was there to escape the attentions of a small group of boys who had been pestering him as he walked along the corridor. I could see their disappointed faces as they peered through the glass panels in the door before retreating from my gaze.

On another occasion – it may have been the first of April - he disappeared for several days, leaving a message saying that he had gone to an aunt's house in Birkenhead 'for warmth and comfort'.

The only other master to have had real problems was Mr. Philip Lovatt, who succeeded Mr. Edwards in charge of history. He was in his early forties and had been a successful teacher of history and Spanish and had also held a senior role in another school before his arrival with us. He told us, his colleagues, informally, that he was looking forward to a comfortable life, with all found, and intended to stay until retirement. Unfortunately for him, it didn't turn out like that.

His sometimes formal, sometimes distant, sometimes rather sarcastic manner did not go down well with some of the boarders, and a permanent state of animosity developed. He very wisely resigned after just one year.

This was at a time when a somewhat bolshie element was present amongst the boys, and one found oneself facing something like a trade union mentality – in fact, at least once, all the boys were found to be having a 'meeting' in the games room. I don't think they ever revealed their agenda! It was at such a time that I had done something or other in the disciplinary line which displeased them. I do not now remember what it was, but on the following day I experienced an undercurrent of murmuring when I was moving amongst the boys: they were expressing their displeasure. I simply had to endure it until it subsided after a day or two.

Frank Hulford (Teacher 1956-1966)
Now living in Leicester.

A LITTLE BIT FROM PETER

It was the tradition in those early days for a class to stand up when a member of staff entered. Once when I entered, everyone stood for me. I asked them to sit down, which they all did, except one. I harangued him about good manners and the problems of deafness, until he then by way of reply stood up. He must have been nearly 7 feet tall! He had sat down, though it had not seemed so at the time.

Also, I recall an occasion when the bishop phoned the school but unfortunately got through to the kitchens. They did not believe who he was and told him off for pestering them with that posh voice and silly requests.

Peter Ling (Teacher 1961 -1995)

CHAPTER 10
AFTERTHOUGHTS

THE CLOCK TOWER

The school clock tower has been fairly messed about with in recent years. Nowadays, when you look up at the right-hand face (see photograph), you see a stream of grey plastic cables flowing over the parapet and down into the school. It was explained to me that it has something to do with the school's internet equipment.

You get a bit of a shock in the dark, too, for they have installed very bright lighting behind the clock faces and you are fairly dazzled when you try to read the time. In our day there was no back lighting at all, and I liked it that way.

The main entrance area (i.e. straddled by the boardroom and the school office) has been illuminated with purple lighting – someone's idea of progress.

Here in York we have an occasional TV programme called *Grumpy Old Men*, in which famous elderly men (or women in its sister programme) gripe about things that they hate or are annoyed by. By writing this article, I've just joined them.

One last point; if there was any truth in Bob Kelly's claim that he once ascended the clock tower via a drainpipe, then the said drainpipe must be the one that is plainly visible in this photograph of the north and west faces.

Some believe that what Bob really did was use the corner stonework like a ladder and steady himself with the drainpipe as required. A reckless fool or a hero? - You can choose.

Ray Livingston (1955-1959)
Now living in York

A VISIT TO THE SCHOOL

The last time that I was in England was around 1983 or 1984. My mother was not well and I went to see her while she was still in reasonable shape.

During that week I went to see the old school, I walked in through the front door and met, quite by chance, Dai Davies and also Mr. Rees. I hadn't been to the school since 1957 so almost 25 years had passed and so I was extremely surprised when Mr. Rees looked at me and asked 'Didn't you once play the cello?' That was quite a shock as he was correct but my playing was awful, to the extent that I gave it up after only a few months of trying to learn how to play the thing.

What I really found amazing, is what people are able to remember about you, that you yourself have forgotten.

Dave Bolt (1951-1957)
Now living in Vancouver BC

THE OLD SCHOOL TIE

While I was at the Blue Coat School I really wasn't aware of who the school's benefactors were except that occasionally we would see some dignitaries show up at Speech Day in Shirley Hall.

By the time I left the school, and, thanks to Mr. Farrell, I had a keen interest in wood and decided to start a career in the timber industry, not really knowing where that would take me. At that time there was a Timber Institute which I had visited and they arranged a job interview for me at a company called Alfred Dobell on Castle Street, near the Town Hall: they were both timber brokers and importers of softwoods and hardwoods.

At that time there was no such thing as résumés or C.V.s printed on computers, you just showed up at the appointed time. I was interviewed by an elderly gentleman (he must have been in his 60s), the only words that I can remember were 'So you are a Blue Coat boy?' and that was it. I got the job as a junior.

I didn't realize what the connection was for a few months. Apparently the two elderly gentlemen who owned the company were friends of Lord Leverhulme, who was at that time one of the school's benefactors.

I can still recall them coming into the office on many occasions with a brace of pheasants which they had bagged on Lord Leverhulme's estate in Thornton Hough on the Wirral.

Dave Bolt. (1951-1957)
Now living in Vancouver, BC

AFTERMATH

Enough has been written in this book already to show the reader that life at the Blue Coat School was not all unrelenting halcyon bliss; and we haven't even mentioned the bullying that was carried out by some of the more emotionally disturbed pupils - a topic that is perhaps best left unchronicled.

What an institution like the Blue Coat mostly deprived its boarding pupils of was privacy, and this lack would have had a greater or a lesser affect on the psyche of each boy depending on his particular personality. It so happened that I was one of those who needed a greater degree of privacy than the regime was designed to provide. Neither did the regime in the 1950s make much attempt to raise my self-esteem and make me feel a valued and respected individual (kids like me felt quite Cinderella-like on Prize Day, for example).

After I left, I overcompensated for several months and made use of any free time I had to cut myself off from the world and read books.

It was a need for peace and quiet to calm my jagged nerves and was definitely a reaction to the four years of incarceration and - as I saw it - the many indignities and privations I had been subjected to (I can imagine our poor shell-shocked masters passed through something similar and even more markedly after World War II). I was quite sociable but I had a good deal of reserve and wanted to be on my own a lot.

I have no way of judging how typical my reaction was and I merely offer this as an honest account of what happened to me.

Bound up with this problem was a second one. My family lived in a working class area and going away to school had disrupted my social contacts with young people in our locality. Moreover, when I left school I lost contact with all my Blue Coat friends. Consequently I had no social life to speak of, and it took me about two years to even begin to climb out of my shell. Meanwhile, I walked in the country every Sunday with a walking group and I also became a member of Liverpool Astronomical Society, which proves that I was no misanthrope. That I was partly to blame for the lack of local friends is evidenced by the fact that Stan had had no such problem when he left the Blue Coat long before me, but this would be explained by his more gregarious personality.

All these years later it seems sad to me that what should have been my carefree teenage years bonding with friends were so damaged by what I had gone through in my schooldays. Recent re-contact with people I was at primary school with has revealed to me that I would have been quite happy going to the local school, and moreover I would have come away with some academic attainment. On the other hand, if I had taken that path I would have missed out on all the tradition and history that Blue Coat pupil-ship entailed.

Modern research on brain development has revealed that the prefrontal cortex in the brains of teenagers has not yet finished growing, and because of this they are unable to make sense of certain situations they encounter and become confused about life as a result.

I know that this happened in my own case (as it must do for everybody to some degree, whether or not they remember it) so a few more years elapsed before I found the peace and calm that I was seeking when I first left school at the age of fifteen. (An aside:- Given this new revelation about brain development, it seems strange that politicians are inclined to go in the opposite direction and give teenagers more powers than ever before; recently I heard that there is a proposal that sixteen-year-olds should even be allowed to stand in parliamentary elections).

Therefore I am ambivalent about my Blue Coat period. On the one hand, I disapprove of boarding schools on principle if the child has the possibility of a normal home life, but on the other hand I join with the other contributors to this book in looking back with love and fondness to that distinctive period of my life. I know I will never resolve this weird dichotomy and must simply accept it as it stands.

'Men prize most highly what they win hardly' (W.H. Murray, Scottish mountaineer).

Ray Livingston (1955-1959)
Now living in York

OLD (i.e. REAL) MONEY

In this book, when we talk about the cost of purchases in our school days, we mention 1/6p., 10 bob or 2 shillings. Now this is what we call real money, not the modern decimal-style 'funny' money that is in use today. The money was denoted in Latin as 'librae', 'solidii', 'denarii', the Latin for pounds, shillings and pence, and was written down as £.s.d.

But 1d. would get you a ride on the tram to Liverpool city centre and back (called 1d. return). It would also buy an ice lolly in the corner shop. Strangely enough, '1d. barmcakes', as they were known for many years until they crept up to 1½p. (called three ha'pence), could be filled up inside with three-pence worth of beautiful golden chips, plus all the salt and vinegar you wanted; 4d. for the lot!

The system was easy to understand as there were 12 pennies in a shilling, 20 shillings in a £1-0s-0d. Therefore there were 40 tanners, 80 three-penny joeys, 240 pennies, 480 half-pennies or 960 farthings in £1.

There were coins as above: Top row L-R: A sixpenny piece (sixpence) known as a 'tanner', (2½p would be today's equivalent); a shilling, known as a 'bob' (5p); a 2 shilling piece known as a 'florin' (10p) and a half crown, known as 'half a dollar (12½p).

Bottom Row L-R: A farthing (¼d.); half penny (½d.), a penny (1d.): and old silver three-penny bit (3d.); and a later three-penny bit known as a 'three-penny joey' (also 3d.). These have no significant value in today's money. (N.B. The illustration does not show the coins in full size).

In terms of paper money, there was a 10s. note, £1. note and two types of £5 notes (fivers): a large white paper version and the new smaller one, somewhat similar to that in use today. We were never sufficiently rich to be aware of notes of larger denomination. All very simple to us budding entrepreneurs.

Frank Irwin (1950-1957)
Now living in Wirral

MR. G.G. WATCYN'S OBITUARY OF MISS MARY BYERS

Spring 1957 issue of *The Squirrel*:

It was with deep regret that the Blue Coat community heard of the sudden and unexpected death of Miss Mary Byers on Sunday, 17th February.

Miss Byers had been visiting friends in Birkenhead - as was her practice at weekends for the past 30 years - and had had a particularly happy day, and had left for school in, apparently, good health. She became ill on the way home, and was taken by ambulance to Sefton General Hospital, where she died peacefully a short time after admission. It will be recalled that she had been taken ill last June in similar circumstances, and spent a period in hospital and was discharged fit and well a few weeks later.

She was known to many generations of Old Blues, particularly to the Old Girls, for she had been a member of the House Staff for about 40 years, a life of service to the school. Until 1949 Miss Byers was in charge of the girls' wardrobes, and the way in which she turned out the girls was always a great credit to her and her work.

Miss Byers came from a well-known Maryport family, and leaves two sisters, Mrs. Blackburn and Mrs. Nixon. The funeral took place at Maryport on 20 February, and many floral tributes were sent on behalf of the school.

Those of us of the Blue Coat family feel sad that another link with the old pre-war and pre-1949 Blue Coat has been broken by her passing, and we shall miss her familiar, busy and cheerful presence.

Mary Byers, as some of us familiarly called her on occasions, was a 'good and faithful servant' and had earned the respect and affection of the governors, Ladies' Committee, staff and pupils, and it will be very difficult to replace her loyal and devoted service. The school was her home and her family, and her spirit and devotion to the school will live on.

CHAPTER 11
ALBERT BLUNDELL'S VISIT

ALBERT'S VISIT TO THE BLUE COAT SCHOOL

I knew that today would be a special day, not only for my grandad but for us all. On arrival my first thought was, what a beautiful place, so grand in its presence, not what I expected at all. In my grandad's day of 1923, when he first arrived, I'm sure that wasn't his first thought; but probably one of sorrow having to leave his family, mother, brother and two elder sisters, but also one of joy as he was joining his elder brother and sister, Leslie and Muriel, who were already attending the school. It was the chapel that was the most striking building on arrival. The chapel was a significant part of daily life at the school. He would attend Sunday Service, where the organ was played and hymns were sung. We then entered the building and Eddie met us, who would be our guide for the day. The boardroom was our first port of call, a magnificent and grand room but one which my grandad doesn't recall, but I believe it was out of bounds for pupils at that time.

We headed off next to the chapel. This was my favourite part of the tour, as the features still look original from when it was first built. Looking around the chapel, it was easy to picture the boys and girls, all in their prim uniforms, bellowing out to their hearts' content. It was here that the slow march was performed.

My grandad had a slight tear in his eye as he remembered the days of the Sunday Service; it would have been nice for the organ to have been playing. On departure from the chapel, we entered a new era of the school, the new building, only a stone's throw away but set a million light years away from where we had just come. This was our easiest access through to see the old buildings on the other side, where the dormitories and Shirley Hall were.

Our mission was to locate the position where my grandad's bed would have been. A flight of stairs loomed in front of us in our quest to find the location. We passed through a new corridor which was built on the outside of the old building; the original brickwork was still exposed, along with all its original doors and stairways. My grandad had managed to conquer the stairs and on entering the room where his dormitory would have been there was a sudden silence. I could see my grandad was a little confused as all he could see was a classroom full of artwork and it seemed he struggled in remembering the layout of the room, but wouldn't you from nearly 83 years ago!

After his rest, he managed to gain enough strength to wander to see further along the rooms. My grandad's dormitory stretched along 3-4 classrooms and it seemed hard to envisage the way it was. He had mentioned his bed was next to the toilet at the time, and according to the records the toilet is now the store room. He wandered over and tried to peer out of the enormous windows, which none of us really could and how the children would also have struggled to do.

As he sat down and gathered his thoughts he then pointed to the position where his bed would have been; it was the right-hand-side of the door leading to the toilet. He certainly would have been first in the queue for the toilet, which is what they had to do each night before they went to bed. We made our way back down the stairs to Shirley Hall. This looked as if it was still in its grand state from when it was first built, with its ornate carvings in the ceiling and flamboyant organ at the front. An original dining table stood proud on the stage, from which my grandad may have eaten one of his meals. I asked him what he would do in Shirley Hall and he said it was a sacred place and he used to sing in there. At this point he sat down and pondered. This was to be the end of my granddad's tour, but we wandered towards what used to be the service area and down the stairs. We encountered the 'spud corridor', where he had said he would meet kitchen staff.

We also visited the library which used to be the dining area, but it was hard to picture how it used to be. The day will hold a place in all our memories for a long time as a special day, Albert's Day, and we wouldn't have missed it for the world.

Shelley Blundell, August 2007.

CHAPTER 12
VIVE LA DIFFERENCE

Whilst considering an article for this book, I realised that it would also be nice to provide some illustrations for existing articles. I had written a small item about Cathedral Sunday, (the school's annual visit there, with a mace bearer and two escorts, dressed in the old powder-blue, tailed uniforms), but realised that I did not have any photographs of the Liverpool Anglican Cathedral to use. I therefore decided that as I was due to visit an aging aunt in Childwall, I would kill three birds with one stone and take some photographs of the cathedral and some more as the school is at present, and then visit my aunt.

I had also wanted to check the school for myself, as I had heard about alterations and the selling off for commercial development of the old dormitories areas. I also understood that, the 'western front' as we knew it, had been changed from the old air-raid shelters to a pleasant landscaped area.

I duly set off and arrived at the Anglican Cathedral, it seemed quite different from the times that I used to visit as a Blue Coat schoolboy. I had visited the place on other occasions but I suppose it is a sign of familiarity that since the 1960s I have visited many cathedrals in other cities throughout the country, but have not bothered to revisit those in Liverpool. Many Merseysiders are guilty of this I would guess, and that guilt extends to art gallery visits as well.

Looking up at the towering edifice, I could almost hear the strains of the *Slow March in 'D'*, Dr. Dickerson's 'dirge' as it was known by many. I could feel the towering arches as we used to proceed down the aisle towards our pews in the centre area: I could hear the strains of traditional hymns and anthems, then I realised that I was outside and there to take a photograph. As the organ strains died away, I got on with the task in hand. Driving away with the strains of, *Who would true valour see, let him come hither,* wriggling about in my head I headed for the old school.

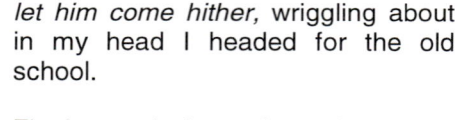

Firstly, as I drove from the south, Smithdown Road end, I arrived at the bottom of Grant Avenue, alongside the gates that I mentioned in the Mystery Mile race. From there the road goes uphill to drain the last drops of energy from the boys who are in serious contention in the race. When I reached the bend at the top, although driving, I felt tired looking at the stretch of road to be negotiated to take me to the finishing line. I was gasping for breath; my lungs were bursting as I strived to win the race. This time, I was in the lead, nobody was ahead of me. I charged along towards the finishing line, and as I reached it, things changed and I noticed a new board advertising the presence of the school. Never in our day was a school sign placed to the west. I parked my car and got out.

I noticed that the western front was in fact nicely landscaped, with some flowering cherry blossom trees here and there and the odd bluebell showing its spring colours. Although the air-raid shelters had been removed, the old school facade remained intact, and the bulge where the library used to be was still evident. I could see that my old dormitories were now changed to become commercial apartments, but I could still see my route down the drainpipe to the road below! The old playground / tennis courts had now become car parking spaces for the residents who had taken over as victims for 'Peg Leg' and the 'Old Lady.' Would they be visited like we used to be?

Along the length of the western front, the exteriors of the classrooms were still there. Secondary modern to the south and the grammar to the north. I could hear Mr. Perry teaching his Latin, Video, Vides, Videt, Videmus, Videtis, Vident. Mr. Unwin was holding forth about the properties of an atom of oxygen. Somewhere a boy was screaming as the wooden blackboard duster caught him on the side of the head, the result of an accurate shot from a teacher! The brief memory faded and I was back at the west side railings of the school.

To the north end of the building, the old shelter had gone, so I had to stop myself from playing football and from using the old slide in the winter on the playground that used to be there. I could hear the commands of the Sergeant Major as we army cadets drilled on that playground, 'Squad, right wheel' 'Squad, Halt!'

The strains of boys playing football, 'Over here Brian,' 'Ah! you missed a sitter.' From further over came the whistle of Mr. Tait as he refereed a game on the football pitch, he pulled me up for a foul as I responded 'Never was.'

Stuart Callaghan blasted a ball from defence as Dai Davies called over in his Welsh accent, 'Don't kick the ball across your own goalmouth boy!' I looked up and found that I was no longer on the football pitch! It had gone and in its place was a car park.

The old sounds died down as I realised that so many changes had taken place in this part of the school. It had been modernised and to my mind it was to the detriment of the buildings; perhaps education had been improved but the buildings, no way. The old headmaster's house still stood in its elevated location to the north east of the site, now rented out to somebody totally unconnected with the school. I could still see Daphne walking along the path, returning home from school. She stopped briefly to talk to me as I was in the sanatorium, leaning out of the window so that she could see me - then she was gone. I returned to my car and drove round to the front of the school, into Church Road.

The chapel was still there but major construction works were progressing in the area to the rear, where the boiler house used to be. The old locked gates to the tennis courts had been replaced by an electronic access system, for vehicular access to the new commercial development.

Our dormitories, as mentioned earlier could now be seen more easily. I could hear the sounds of a tennis ball being bashed against the wall in the shed area and see the handkerchief parachutes being thrown from dormitory windows. Four members of the staff were playing on the tennis courts watched by a group of scruffy boys, who acted as ball boys for the more mature, aging players.

Then I realised that 'the shed' in total didn't exist any more; only a small opening remained, the rest had been filled in to increase the accommodation area. But I could see where it used to be, arches above were only in that location, not anywhere else. Sounds returned to me, boys fighting, squealing with joy (only occasionally), and teachers remonstrating with obstructive pupils. Model aircraft being flown on control wires, engines screaming. All the usual noises of a boarding school in the 1950s.

I was brought back down to earth by the gate controller talking to me via the intercom on the electronic gates. 'What do you want?' he asked, as miraculously, the gates opened for me. I just took my photographs whilst the gates were open and left. Had I entered he may have shut the gates behind me and left me to accompany 'Peg Leg' and 'The Old Lady' who may well have been ostracised to the forecourt during the building works. I then walked round to the front of the building. The main façade remains unaltered and still looks in excellent condition: a tribute to the Blue Coat Foundation. The only faux pas to my mind is the colour and form of the cladding to be seen towards the north east end, I think it totally detracts from the original style.

Whilst taking photographs, a gentleman emerged from within and asked me what I was doing taking photographs of the school. I told Eddie, as he turned out to be, that I was an Old Blue. After a brief conversation, he invited me inside for a limited look around.

Firstly he took me along the old corridor that led to the chapel via the Music Room. This involved walking past the place where we used to be made to stand and wait outside Mr. Watcyn's study to await our fate if we had transgressed in any way. I could still hear the swish of the cane as it flew through the air on its way to inflict pain on whichever part of my body he had decided to beat that day. After the beating he would tell your parents who would, in some cases, repeat the punishment at the earliest opportunity. Quite unlike today, when parents will support their kids no matter what. Not that I agree with that; it is probably one of the major causes of disruption and lawlessness that exists today. Along the route I was somewhat disappointed to see that the décor had changed from traditional to modern. I always liked the timbered panels and the oil paintings that lined the walls.

As we neared the chapel, I again could hear the schoolboys scrambling up the spiral stairs leading to the chapel door. There I was again, just like at the cathedral, waiting at the doors, all the boys lined up in pairs waiting for the 'dirge' to strike up. Then it came, Dr. Dickerson started the music on the organ and we all commenced to slow march into chapel. I could see my mum and dad sitting just to my right. They smiled at me; (well they might, they didn't have to put up with me at home, they had packed me off to here!) marching into chapel I arrived at my pew. I looked around and everything was different.

Everybody was singing *Lead us heavenly father, lead us, o'er the world's tempestuous sea*, but the pew was no longer there! Nor was the teachers' pew across the way from the pulpit. The whole place had been refurbished and a freshly painted ceiling dome was above for those who chose to look up. Signs of newly varnished woodwork were evident. I could remember my confirmation day, when the Bishop of Liverpool came along to confirm me, along with those schoolboys who had also managed to survive a course of confirmation classes. We were told not to have 'Brylcreem' on our hair as the bishop had a dislike of getting his hands dirty. I could hear Garvey singing like a canary, next to me.

I also remembered Harvest Festival, when the chapel was full of goodies, freshly baked bread (or was it artificial?) fruit, grapes, apples and oranges, sheaves of corn and wheat, the place used to look so nice decked out in all its glory.

Now the place had little feeling: pews were there but in a different layout; its limited use seemed to remove its soul, such a shame. We spent so much time in there in our formative years, without being or becoming religious, it was a part of us. Now it felt so sad and lonely without the throngs of Old Blues who had passed through whilst making their way in life.

The stained glass altar windows remain the same as do the pulpit and the vestry door although as mentioned earlier, all have been refurbished. The organ has been similarly treated and still stands there on the marble mosaic floor, awaiting the return of Dr. Dickerson. It seems quite different without him at its helm.

The memorial to Bryan and Jonathan Blundell is still in place on the west wall, close to where their remains lie buried. Eddie and I had a chat about old times and then we left, leaving behind us the strains of Mr. Watcyn delivering yet another sermon.

Perhaps like 'Peg Leg' he returns occasionally to relive his glory days as the headmaster, rather than to remember his sad demise all those years ago došli. To us, an integral part of our educational and life's experiences.

From there we returned to the foyer and looked down the corridor to Shirley Hall. What a disappointment! Again, what had once been a hallowed hall of traditional timber panelling and old master paintings was now reduced to magnolia paintwork and blue doors!!

I could hear the clip-clop of footsteps as parents over the years travelled along this route to the services in Shirley Hall, suddenly it was Remembrance Sunday and my mum and dad were walking down to see me at the service. Once again Dr. Dickerson was at the organ preparing for yet another 'dirge' and I was waiting with trepidation to march in, dressed in my Sunday best grey suit, with shoes polished on the back of my trouser legs. That could only be done when you grew out of your short trousers in favour of 'longs.' We marched into the hall in pairs and the music filled the area. Suddenly Eddie asked 'Shall we go into my office to look at some photographs?' Having done that we parted, leaving me to take a few more photographs before going on my way to my aunt's house.

I promised to return later and to meet with him again on a future occasion when perhaps I would be able to see the areas which were not available to me at the present time. The old dining room, the library, Shirley Hall itself and all the old classrooms. I would also be able to review again the modern school architecture, which presently leaves me cold I am afraid.

Before leaving to see my aunt, I visited the old Lance Lane playing fields. To my surprise, the school had taken over all the three fields that used to be there - the old Earle F.C. football pitch and the council fields that were between the school field and Church Road, I suppose that made up for the loss of the school's home football pitch, which is now the car park.

Frank Irwin (1950-1957)
Now living on Wirral.

SOME THINGS NEVER CHANGE!

THE SCHOOL FRONTAGE 2007

BLUE COAT CHAMBERS, LIVERPOOL c 1708

CHAPTER 13
BEAUMARIS REVISITED

I read so much about the evacuation to the town of Beaumaris, in Anglesey (on Monday September 4th 1939), that I decided to pay a visit to have a look at the place first hand. I have visited Beaumaris many times before, but now I would look with a different pair of eyes. The evacuation was supposedly to protect the school's pupils against Hitler's bombs which would be dropped on Liverpool; having read the exploits of the Old Blues, it was probably done to protect Hitler from the lads.

I decided that as well as looking into the places discussed in order to enhance the book, my personal interest called for a degree of illustration to supplement it. I therefore decided to call in on the place to see for myself, with my camera batteries fully charged.

Accordingly, Barbara and I made the visit on Tuesday, August 28th 2007, some 68 years after the events did indeed happen. Quite naturally our first port of call was the Menai Bridge itself. Harry Thomas remembered the annual visit to Beaumaris, travelling by sea on the S.S. *St. Tudno* sailing from Liverpool. Albert Blundell also remembers the event, but many years earlier, when the ship used for the annual voyage was the S.S. *La Marguerite*.

Harry recalled that members of the band enjoyed an extra trip each year, but they had to 'earn their corn' by playing music during the voyage between Llandudno and the Menai Bridge, as well as at the start and completion of each trip. The bridge still looks well now and must have been a pretty amazing sight in those far away days.

Next we visited Beaumaris Castle. Stan Evans recalls being led into the castle during air-raid practices. No mention of stray bombs has ever been mentioned in old boys' annals, so it looks like the place was safe from the Germans after all. Looking at the state of the castle though, perhaps it was unwise to unleash Blue Coat boys in there. The damage looks horrendous, or is it the passage of time that is responsible?

Stan also mentions sumptuous meals of sausage and mash in the Beaumaris gaol at 2 o'clock in the morning: his reward for running messages for the Home Guard. He states he wasn't a prisoner! Does he 'protesteth' too much? I hope he wasn't charged the current £3.50 entrance fee for each visit!

An anonymous article mentions that the school's Army Cadet Corps was required to maintain signals and communications for an area of approximately eight miles radius from the headquarters installed in Beaumaris gaol.

Peter Clarke also recalls the evacuation to Beaumaris and mentions Red Hill, as does Arthur Martin. Arthur was very well looked after at Plas Meigan, the home of Mr. and Mrs. Richard Williams-Bulkeley, later to become Sir and Lady Bulkeley.

The population of Beaumaris describes the Bulkeley's as pretty much owning the whole place, including the castle: incidentally they also tend to pronounce his name the way we would say, 'Buckley'.

We found Red Hill; but couldn't discover the whereabouts of Plas Meigan. The large houses to the right hand side as you go up the hill have entrances without names, and the houses themselves are not visible from the road. However we found a place with two circular gate-house type lodges, one each side of entrance drive. The place looked like it was owned by somebody who either was, or used to be, rather affluent, so we walked down the drive. After quite a way, we still couldn't see the residence, but were approached by a rough looking gamekeeper who wanted to know what we were doing on the property. After explaining ourselves, he indicated that the land was called Baron Hill estate and it was still owned by the Bulkeley's. However, he added that the original property is now a heap of rubble, and no, I could not approach it to take a photograph. We seemed to be in the right general area though.

Reading between the lines of his discourse, it became apparent that the current landowner was not a particularly amiable person and it would not be worth the gamekeepers while to tell me the location of the old building, nor to allow me to encroach any further into the estate. Disappointedly, we left. In the town itself there are many references to the Bulkeley's. Hotels and bars etc. are named after him: the reportedly kindly disposition apparent in 1939 does not appear to have been passed down through the family lineage to the present day.

Making further enquiries in the town, his suggested demeanour was borne out by many other residents so I decided to pursue the matter no further. I did however discover that there are plans to rebuild the old building façade as a sort of monument to the family, but not to withstand human habitation.

Arthur also mentioned St Mary's church, in Church Street, 'Church parades were still held every Sunday when we marched through the town, preceded by the school band, along Castle Street and then up Church Street to St. Mary's Parish Church where the whole school would then become the choir!' recalled Arthur.

The church is still there, but there was nobody about to ask about the memories of the old school choir.

I also tried to make enquiries in the Tourist Information Centre. There were plenty of leaflets about but nobody was available to deal with my queries. I walked through a door at the rear and up a set of stairs into a suite of offices, but still nobody was about. It was a good job that my Blue Coat days were behind me, as the whole office suite was uninhabited but well stocked.

One anonymous article mentions Home Farm. My enquiries led me to understand that the place is now a caravan site.

Henllys Lane also mentioned, now leads to Henllys, a hotel close to a golf course: the lane was getting too narrow for me to go all the way down, I believe better access is afforded from the other end.

All in all a pleasant day for both of us, with an enjoyable picnic lunch alongside the harbour wall.

Frank Irwin (1950-1957)
Now living on Wirral.

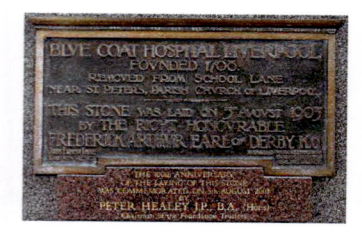

CHAPTER 14
LOOKING BACK

So then, this is a collection of our experiences and our thoughts: what now? Why were we sent to the school, how have our lives been affected by our times of incarceration there, how has the school affected our relationships in after-school life, did it mould us in any particular way in selecting our career paths?

Speaking for myself, my father was killed in WWII and my mother not believing she could look after me properly, gave me up for adoption. I was fortunate enough to be adopted at 9 months of age, but my adoptive parents split up four years later, with my father looking after me until he re-married some 5 years on. The wedding took place during my first year at the Blue Coat School, and I only learned of that event when a fellow pupil showed me one of their wedding photographs which had been reproduced in the *Liverpool Echo!*

So I had been deposited into the school earlier that year and had not been invited to my dad's wedding, a good start. I suppose that shaped my life at the school, although I have no conscious memory of it. The school became my home for the greater part of my formative years. Although my father did his best to ensure that I had a good education, the same cannot be said of my time at home, where I felt I was not really wanted. So there I was; most of the kids around me had either one parent or perhaps none: I on the other hand by the age of 10, had experienced three mothers and two fathers.

Being at the Blue Coat School as a boarder meant that you had to be able to look after yourself, to eat well, to learn well, and to develop an independent spirit in order to survive the experience. If you failed to do that you ran the possible risk of being institutionalised. When we consider the number of school leavers who joined the armed forces, it would appear that on occasions that indeed did happen. It was an easy option for most, but to be fair it was also a good career choice for others.

Having been well grounded in first the Boy Scouts and then in the Army Cadets boys had a good education and grooming for that kind of life: in fact I well remember when I attained my 'crossed-swords' I was asked to sign up and was told I would be made a corporal on completion of my basic training. I replied that I wanted to be an officer, but that was not an easy option, one had to apply quite differently so I declined.

Some of the ex-pupils who signed-up reported that army life was very similar to school life, so I suppose that was what made the career choice easy. My father having informed me that he would no longer support me through university, I joined the Merchant Navy as an apprentice engineer, so I eventually became an officer anyway.

As part of my apprenticeship I was sent to Birkenhead Technical College full time for 2 years and during that time I met the girl who was to become my wife. Whilst I was studying for my Diploma in Mechanical Engineering, Barbara was training to become a shorthand typist, a job not in as much demand nowadays because of the introduction of personal computers.

At the end of my apprenticeship, having sailed on Shell Tankers to various parts of the world, including Japan four times, India, Iran, Iraq, Holland, Borneo, Sarawak, Singapore, Trinidad and many other places I left Shell to come ashore to get married. Incidentally, on my return home on leave after my first voyage which lasted 8 months, I discovered that I no longer had a room or a bed to sleep in. I had to sleep on the floor on a lilo, now that really made me feel wanted!

Barbara and I were married in 1961 and we set up home together initially in a flat in Oxton, Birkenhead. I was told later that my parents gave the marriage 6 months, 46 years later we are still together; all marriages have their ups and downs and ours is no different but we are still going strong.

Two years on we bought our first house in Prenton, (It cost £3,200 an enormous amount at the time) moving some 25 years later to our present home in Thingwall, near to Heswall in Wirral.

My father died in 1978, but despite the problems at home with my parents in my early days, we have maintained a friendly contact with my mother, sister and two brothers and I am happy to say that for the past 25 years we have got on together very well.

Barbara and I had two children, both girls and I struggled with home life as I had never had a satisfactory one myself. Relationships were difficult as I had been used to an independent childhood where I had to look after number 1. It wasn't really until we had grandchildren that I understood how a family unit should feel and how life should be. This is probably one of the downsides of boarding school life.

Food is another example. I never remember whilst at school failing to eat all the food put before me, nor do I remember others leaving anything on their plates either. The food was basic and I suppose for good reason. Providing a diet of curry and chicken Kiev in those days would have resulted in starving schoolboys. To this day I like basic food. I never eat curry or what I call foreign muck, I like my fillet steaks, sirloin steaks and rump steaks (not that we were served steaks at school). I love a good old fashioned roast dinner, whether it is beef, lamb or pork. Egg and chips, only we don't seem to get proper chips, (made from Maris Piper potatoes and fried in beef dripping) anymore; we have to settle for the bland but healthy oven variety now, sausage and mash, braised steak and liver all go down well, perhaps owing to the school diet of those long ago days.

Sports, well the school went a bundle on such activities. The book outlines what we did but if you had an interest or a basic talent, the school gave you the opportunity to develop it and to compete and hopefully shine. I learned to play table tennis whilst at the school, on a table, that as part of a team led by Mr. Hickman, I helped to construct. Having played competitively in the Wirral Table Tennis League for many years I eventually qualified as a National Coach in order to give something back to the sport. The group that I coached with never charged for its services, in order to ensure the coaching was available to all who wished to either learn or to improve.

Similarly, having been introduced to other games like tennis, basketball, football and cricket, I enjoyed a small amount of success as an amateur after leaving school, but sailing off into the wide world with Shell Tankers Ltd. curtailed that severely.

However, my point is the opportunities were there at school to be trained and to develop one's ability to compete, and I am sure many availed themselves of it.

My final thought on the subject, is that of careers and jobs apart from the armed forces. Reading accounts of our contributors' experiences, it is amazing the number of Old Blues who became self-employed in one form or another. I myself after having been made redundant, when the factory in which I worked was shut down, became a self-employed consultant engineer and enjoyed 10 years of success, as well as the freedom to work where and with whom I wished. I treated that horrible experience of redundancy as an opportunity to be grabbed with both hands. I therefore underwent a course with the local Business Link organisation, to learn some of the pitfalls of self-employment, and took it from there. Blue Coat experiences of the entrepreneurial type certainly didn't let me down.

Now retired, I can look back on my school days and my life with some degree of satisfaction and with some small degree of regret, a happy mixture I would add, and one with which I can live. I think the school regime, in making us all learn to be independent and to look after ourselves first (not always an admirable way of life) engendered a spirit of entrepreneurial existence, which helped in later life.

What I like to remember fondly, despite the harsh bullying regime under which we lived, was the school building itself. The wood panelling, the paintings, the high ceilings, the marble corridors and tiles, the chapel and the music. I still love to this day Elgar's *Pomp and Circumstance* marches and Holst's *Jupiter* from *The Planets* suite, the kind of traditional music that engenders patriotism.

Talking about music, although I must confess I do not attend church as much as I would like, on the odd occasions that I do go, I find that I know and can sing most of the words of the hymns without referring to the hymn book, and I still enjoy both the words and the music.

I find that I know all of the words some of the time, and some of the words all the time, but I never know all the words all of the time: now where have I heard that before? The words of hymns were with us all the time at school, attending chapel and Shirley Hall services three times each week and for me, they are still there.

In conclusion it is apparent that for us boarders, the school became a major part of our lives; it is natural therefore that the memories will remain and linger until one day we shuffle off this mortal coil. For that reason it is paramount that our stories are told as they have been here, to remain in print as a historical record. It is also essential in order that the present and future generations are able to understand what life was like, and to be able freely, to compare it to that of a schoolboy at the Liverpool Blue Coat School today.

Note.

The production of this book has also given me the opportunity to follow one of my favourite hobbies, photography. Apart from the photographs that I took on my visit to Anglesey and my return visit to the school, I have managed to clean up and refurbish all the old black & white photographs made available to me, as featured in the illustrations section. In addition I have also enhanced and trimmed to an effective size, the other colour pictures submitted. I hope it makes for good viewing as well as good reading.

Frank Irwin (1950-1957)
Now living on Wirral.

CHAPTER 15
ILLUSTRATIONS

ROGUES GALLERY

Margaret Thompson

Frank Irwin

Ken Hughes

Eric Woodbine

Dave Kennedy

Dave Bolt

Hubert Manwaring-Spencer

Peter Clarke

Ray Livingston

Brenton Williams

John Howarth

Harry Thomas

Billy Bowden

Frank Hulford

Stan Livingston

Albert Blundell

Harry Thomas c 1936

Alan Blundell and his brother Les, c1923

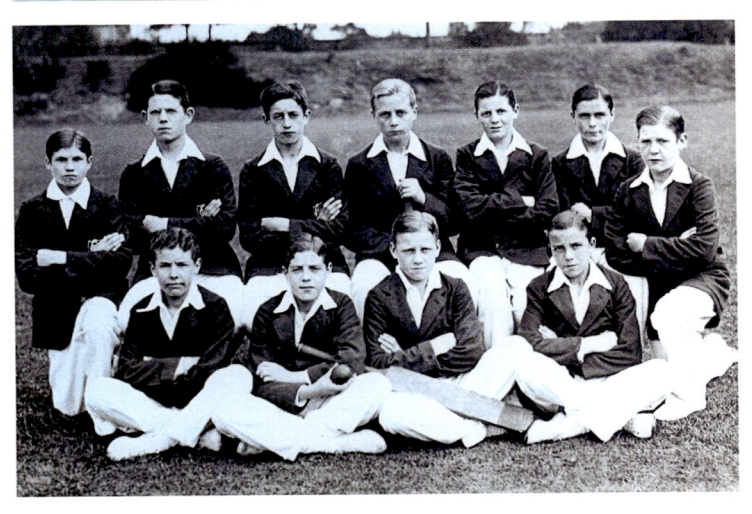

Blue Coat School cricketers 1925.

In the 1920s, the pupils used to be given a 'Triennial Treat' by the Brotherly Society. This photograph, to mark the occasion was taken in 1926.

Ken & Griff Hughes c1947

Ken Hughes, c 1948, in the uniform to be worn when in chapel and Shirley Hall. It was customary at that time, on leaving Shirley Hall, to bow to the trustees, whilst Mr. Watcyn the headmaster, sat behind them keeping an eye on events.

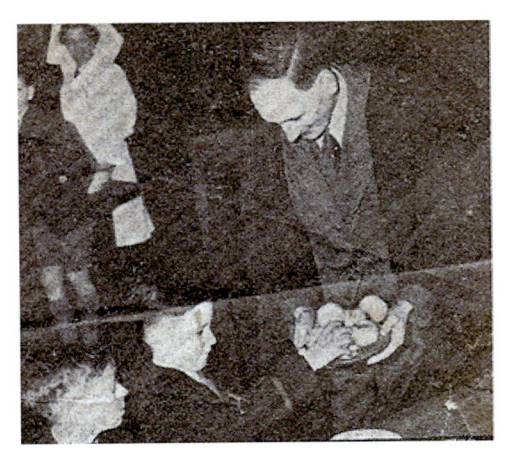

A newspaper cutting from around 1948. Mr. G.G. Watcyn, the headmaster, giving away apples to some schoolboys. The apples had been sent to the school as a gift from somebody in Canada. After the apples had been given out to the boys for the purposes of the news release, they all had to be given back until such time as every boarder could be given one.

A class of 1948.

Rear: L-R: Wilkinson, P. Hornby, L. McDonald, --?-- , --?-- , Clark, P. Staines, --?--,
Front: L-R: L. Bond,--?--, --?--, --?--, --?--, K. Hughes, A. Fagin.

Another class of 1948.

Hubert Manwaring is 5th from the left on the rear row. The boy kneeling on the left end of the front row is Ian Hamilton.

More girls in 1948, off to Wolverhampton.

HISTORIC DAY FOR THE BLUE COAT

Boys and girls of the Liverpool Blue Coat School walking through the grounds to the Commemoration Service held in Shirley Hall on a Sunday afternoon in 1948. The girls are leaving the school (in future for boys only) and their uniforms will not be seen again except for a few ceremonial occasions.

The inset shows Millicent Hughes the first girl to say a prayer at the service since the school opened in 1708, and, of course, the last, with co-education having now ended. (Newspaper article at the time)

END OF AN EPOCH

The picture shows the end of an epoch in the 'two-and-a-half-centuries' history of Liverpool's Blue Coat Hospital, founded in 1708, when Queen Anne reigned, for at the Old Blues' first Commemoration Weekend the scholars wore for the last time, the picturesque uniforms so long familiar about the streets of the city.

Into Shirley Hall they filed, for a service attended by the Lord Mayor and Lady Mayoress, Alderman and Mrs. J.J. Cleary.

The boys wore their long trousers, navy blue cutaway coats with gleaming buttons, and collars, with tails. The girls wore blue frocks topped by large starched white linen collars.

The old Blue Coat tradition will remain, though the girls and the familiar garb have gone, but 50 specimens are to be preserved, some in Liverpool Museum.

The picture shows, left to right: William Hilton (15) of Gorsey Lane, Wallasey and Barbara Morris (14) of Burns Road, Liverpool, wearing the old uniform and Peter Clarke (14) of Elm Vale, Liverpool and Patricia Stages (13) of Willowbank Road, Birkenhead, in modern day uniform. (Newspaper article at the time)

FAREWELL TO THE GIRLS

Boys and girls of Liverpool Blue Coat School wearing the old-style uniforms for the last time at a service in Shirley Hall, which marked its end as a co-educational institution after 241 years. In future only boys will attend the school. (Newspaper article at the time)

Dorothy James, Barbara Murray & Marion Lloyd
'LADIES OF THE LIVERPOOL BLUE COAT SCHOOL'
Painted by Nora Heyson in 1948.

Cadets on parade c 1953. Colin Avery drumming on the right with Tommy Hudson behind him. Central drummer, Noel Harrison

The Blue Coat School Army Cadet Force c1955. Photograph taken where the tennis courts used to be, outside the staff room.

Back row L-R. Egerton, Dave Bolt, Philip Killen, Neil Burgess, Dave Williams, B.A.S. Wooldrage,
Centre row. L-R. Colin Avery, Alan Murray, R. Adkins, Billy Hatton, Tommy Hudson, Noel Harrison.
Front row L-R. Stafford Gunstead, Norman Hudson, Eric Woodbine, Frank Irwin.
The trophies on display are The Moorhead Efficiency Cup and the Bassett Swimming Shield.

Headmaster G.G. Watcyn and the chapel choir, taken in the Shirley Hall c1955
L-R: C.E. Rawlings, --?-- , D.L. Williams, Paul Cox, Wootton, Stan Livingston (head choirboy) Mr. Watcyn, Nigel Parry, Michael Lyon, Jimmy Nunnen, Richard Stimson, Roger Moore, --?--.

The Blue Coat School Army Cadet Force c1956, advanced training camp, on the Yorkshire moors. Here below, some of those pictured.

Frank Irwin, Bill Birch, Philip Killen, Nigel Parry, Arthur Haygarth (Haggis), Noel Harrison, John Hatchard, R.A.C. King, S. Hollis, Colin Avery, D.A. Gadd, M.F. Gaskill, R. Adkins, McPherson, B.A.S. Wooldrage, Roy Forrest, Paul Cox, Rawlings, Brayford, John Howarth, Eric Woodbine, Captain Tait.

Brigadier Toosey inspects the school cadets accompanied by Captain Tait. The bombardier in the front centre is Eric Woodbine. The pictures were taken on the north playground in 1958. Holy Trinity church is evident in the background.

Blue Coat School Scouts, c 1954
Irwin & Connor doing '1st Class
Journey' to complete badge. Both
passed and became First Class Scouts.

Sports Day 1956 at Lance Lane.
Frank Irwin with the 'T' shirt of
Shirley House & mother in support.

School trip on The Royal Iris to Manchester Ship Canal c1955.
L-R: Peter Heatley, Eric Baldwin, Pettersen, Alan Murray, Frank Irwin

In Paris c1955 taken on a school holiday in France.
L-R Parry, Geoff Wilson, Butch Harwood, Frank Irwin.

Swimming Gala c1954

Back Row. -- ? -- Neil Burgess, Anthony Gihon, Dave Bolt, -- ? -- Alan Bonner.
Centre Row: -- ? --, -- ? -- Colin Blakemore, -- ? --, Frank Irwin.
Front Row: --?--, Thompson, D.A. Gadd. --?--.

Annual Camp 1958 which was at Blackshire Moor Camp near Leek in Derbyshire. For the record, it was the year that half the camp (of a number of different A.C.F. units) went down with enteritis!
Rear: E.P. Leggott, --?--, Bill Cocken, Dave Ellis, --?--, --?-- Denis Roby,
3rd row. : K.M. Clement, M.J. Reynolds, Eric Woodbine, Roger Moore, 'Bugs' Rawlings, Bill Birch, --?--, C.W. Benn.
2nd row. Colin Avery, U/O James Lyon, --?--, Capt .John Tate, Lt. Walker, RSM Dave Bolt. --?--.
Front row. : D. Radley, Alex Williams, --?--, --?--, Brenton Williams, Johnson

Eric Woodbine, c1958 adjacent to the north playground and football pitch. Behind Eric, are what used to be flowerbeds.

Swimmers c1954
Left to right: Anthony Gihon, Alan Bonner, Frank Irwin, Colin Blakemore.

Eric Woodbine, ---?---, Mike Hinds.

The Western Command cross country race, held in 1956 during an annual cadet camp at Barnard Castle, was won by Neil Burgess and Frank Irwin was second.

Frank Irwin in Paris c 1955, On top of L'Arc de Triomphe during a school trip.

On the recorders Ikonomides & Leonard and on the piano, Bateson.

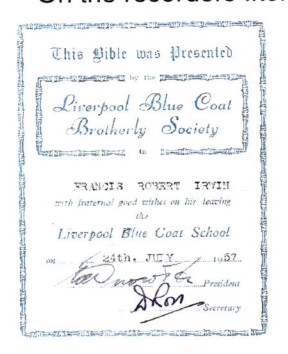

In our day, The Liverpool Blue Coat Brotherly Society gave all school boarders a leather bound bible as a leaving present. Sadly this custom has now ceased, probably because of the costs involved, inflation having taken its toll of such niceties. The picture shows the printed label inside my bible, which despite my lack of regular church attendance, is a treasured memento of my school days. Note, it is signed by Danny Ross.

Royal Iris trip again, to Manchester Ship Canal c1955

Left to Right: Pettersen, Stuart Callaghan, Ernie Foulder, -- ? -- Graham Pollitt.

Mr. Sephton's choir in Shirley Hall.

UNDER 15's CRICKET TEAM
Blakemore, G.J. Wilson, B. May, M.B. Norcott, D. Cass, S. Knowles,
L. Houghton, N. Baker-Bates, S. Vian, R. Roberts.

FOOTBALL TEAM 1958
Rear L-R: Wilson, Ward, B. Knowles, Slater, Townsend, R. Taylor
Centre L-R: --?--. --?--, P. Huish, White, Walker,
Front L-R: J. Adkins & L. Adkins.

UNDER 13's FOOTBALL TEAM
Rear L-R: G. Parry, K. Brassey, J. Blissett,
Front L-R: White, McChrystal, S. Lynch, --?--, P. Devoy
Extreme front L-R: K.J. Bevan & P. Huish.

PREFECTS 1957
Rear L-R: A. Hughes, P. Sharpe, P. Farrell, G. Greaves, A. Price.
Front L-R: W. Hickman, A. Gihon, --?--, K. Gray, T. Hodgins.

SHIRLEY HALL (Pre 1950)

THE DINING ROOM (Pre 1950)

C. Lyon.   H. Smith.   S. Vian.   S. Gunstead.

A.Otton, K.Brassey, M.Duggan.   C.Macpherson, C.Elliott, N.Parry

THE FOURMOST

Brian O'Hara top centre and Billy Hatton extreme right. Brian and Billy were both dayboys at the school and were classmates of Frank Irwin and Ernie Foulder in the grammar stream from 1952 to 1957.

Sadly, Brian died in 1999 at the age of 58.

From 'The Torchbearers'

Rear: Paul Cox, Michale Lyon,--?--,
Roger Moore, --?--,
Front: --?--, --?--, Richard Stimson.

Eric Woodbine (left) as Nelly Fell.

4G Debating Society in the Geography Room c1957. L. Houghton in 'The chair' (Rear centre) and teachers Messrs. Hulford & Perry looking on.

1958. Scene at the dedication of the Ceremonial Gates.

The Dedication and Presentation of the Ceremonial Gates took place on Saturday, 31st May 1958. In the afternoon, a short service in the chapel was followed by the formal presentation ceremony at the gates. The photo shows the choir leading the way to the site. The service had been conducted by the school's Hon. Chaplain, the Rev. John E. Morris, and the Bishop of Liverpool, Dr. Clifford A. Martin was present, as was the Lord Mayor of Liverpool and his Lady Mayoress, Mr. & Mrs. Livermore, and a number of other dignitaries. At the gates, the key was formally handed over to the treasurer Sir Alan Tod by W.A. Snowden, President of the Blue Coat Brotherly Society. Then the gates were officially opened by Major C.V.R. Blundell-Hollinshead Blundell, who was a direct descendant of Bryan Blundell, the school's founder. Also present for the occasion was one particular dignitary of note, the President of the Old Girls' Society, Mrs. A. Harding.

On the photo, the boy on the extreme right is John Holmes. Behind him, right at the end of the line, is Graham Harwood, and in front of Graham Harwood is Parry.

Left to right: Mr. G.G. Watcyn, Treasurer, Sir Alan Tod C.B.E. T.D. D.L., Lady Mayoress Mrs. Harry Livermore, Lord Mayor of Liverpool, Alderman Mr. Harry Livermore and Eric Woodbine (macebearer).

Eric Woodbine (macebearer), Lord Mayor of Liverpool, Alderman Mr. Harry Livermore and Lady Mayoress Mrs. Livermore.

STYTHE HOUSE, SPRING 1959. Mr. PERRY, SECOND ROW, CENTRE.

```
PRAYER DESK
FOUNDED 1708
                    LIVERPOOL BLUE COAT HOSPITAL
Telephone No.:              WAVERTREE,
SEFTON PARK 17.
                    LIVERPOOL, 15................19

        Fourth Sunday after Trinity.

        Hymn 167    O worship the King All-Glorious
                        above

        Prayers

        Hymn 282    Be Thou my Guardian and my
                        Guide

        Catechism
        Chapters

        Hymn 550    Angel Voices, ever singing,
                        round Thy Throne of light

        Prayers

        Hymn 31,    Saviour, again to Thy dear
                        Name we raise with one accord
                        our parting hymn of praise
```

Order of service c 1949.   Keystone adornment.

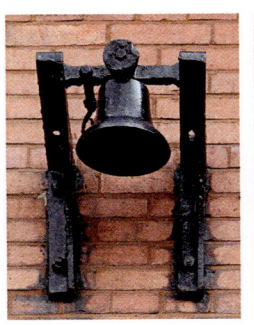

Original 'drain tun' dish with BCH (Blue Coat Hospital) logo, the fire bell and the drinking fountain (dated 1868).

Holy Trinity Church, a landmark familiar to us all.

Inscription above the old library, on the west elevation: translation below.

Consecrated to the promoting of Christian charity and to imbuing in meagre boyhood with the principles of the Anglican Church, founded in the year of salvation 1717, removed from the city and restored in 1905.

The old north toilet block, by the old playground and sports field.

THE SCHOOL AS IT IS IN 2007

The new north elevation.

The old and the new! Which is the better aesthetically?

The western front.

The clock tower, viewed from the south.   The old north west corner.

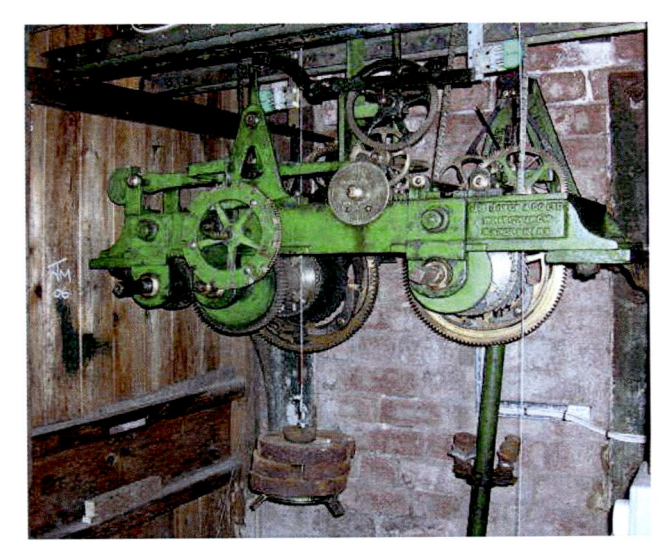

The tower clock works.

The quadrangle, looking north west.

The view looking westward with the Wavertree Playground (Mystery) in the background. The shot was taken from the clock tower and the large roof in the centre is Shirley Hall.

The chapel organ as it is today (2007) following refurbishment.

The old dormitories, now sold off as domestic private property.

The modernised side of the school looking westward.

New private accommodation looking eastward

The school chapel.

In the quadrangle, looking eastward.

New plans for the Lance Lane playing fields.

MISCELLANIA

Frank Irwin's impression of the school frontage c1910. The clock tower having been built in 1914.

Pictured at the 1989 Beaumaris evacuees' reunion.
L-R: Peter Clarke (1943-1951), Charlie Mills (1942-1951), Sam D'Eathe (1942-1949) & the late Teddy Taylor (1942-1950)

BEAUMARIS EVACUEES REUNION 1989. ARTHUR SIDDALL, (President of Old Blues') FRONT CENTRE

CHAPTER 16
SLOW MARCH IN 'D'

Many thanks to Frank Hulford for salvaging what we thought was a lost document, Dr. Dickerson's *Slow March in 'D'*, a piece of music saved purely because Frank some time ago transcribed it for his own use, and finally Roy Bradshaw (not an Old Blue) for producing the finished written musical article.

To be able to appreciate this written piece, it is essential that it is played on an organ. A piano does not do it justice.

Additional thanks must go to Mr. Anthony Hill (not an Old Blue) who computerised the score on to CD as a favour to me.

Frank Irwin (1950-1957)
Now living in Wirral

Regarding the slow march, my mum used to say it brought tears to her eyes to watch us march into Shirley Hall, all of us swaying together in unison. We would put the modern army to shame, including the changing of the guard.

Brenton Williams (1955 – 1959)
Now living in Liverpool

I listened to the CD of the Slow March right to the end and then had an overwhelming desire to find the nearest tall building and jump.

Margaret Thompson (formerly Bond, 1941-1948)
Now living in Cambridgeshire

March in D

F. W. Dickerson

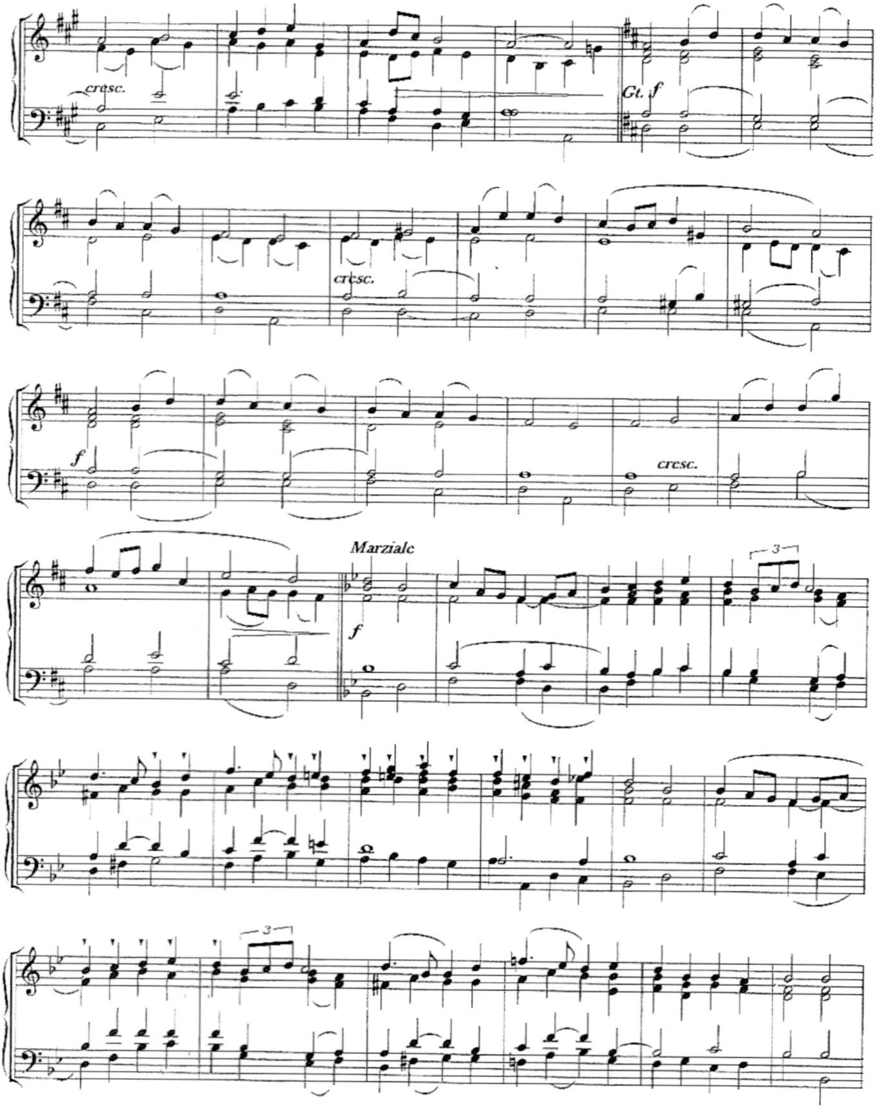
cresc.
Gt. f
cresc.
f
cresc.
Marziale
f

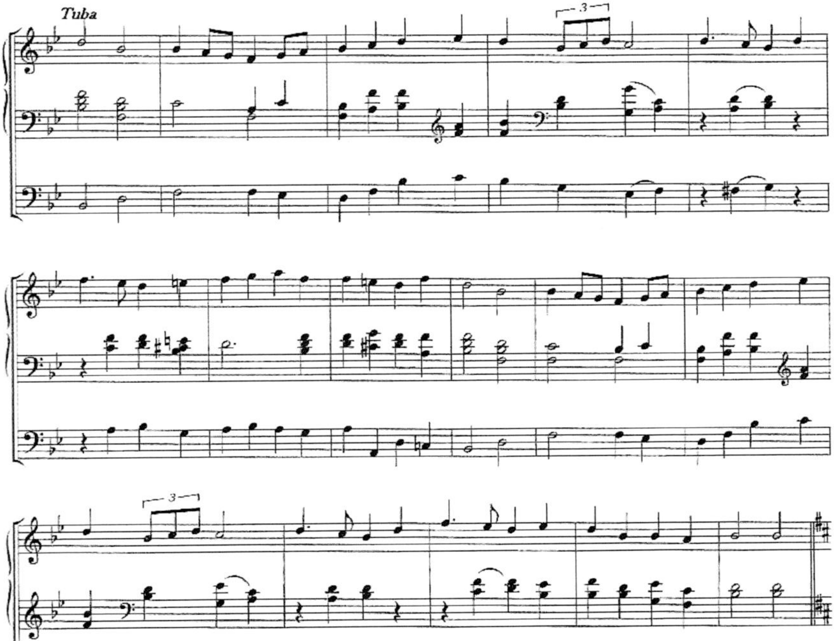
Tuba
3
3
Gt. ff

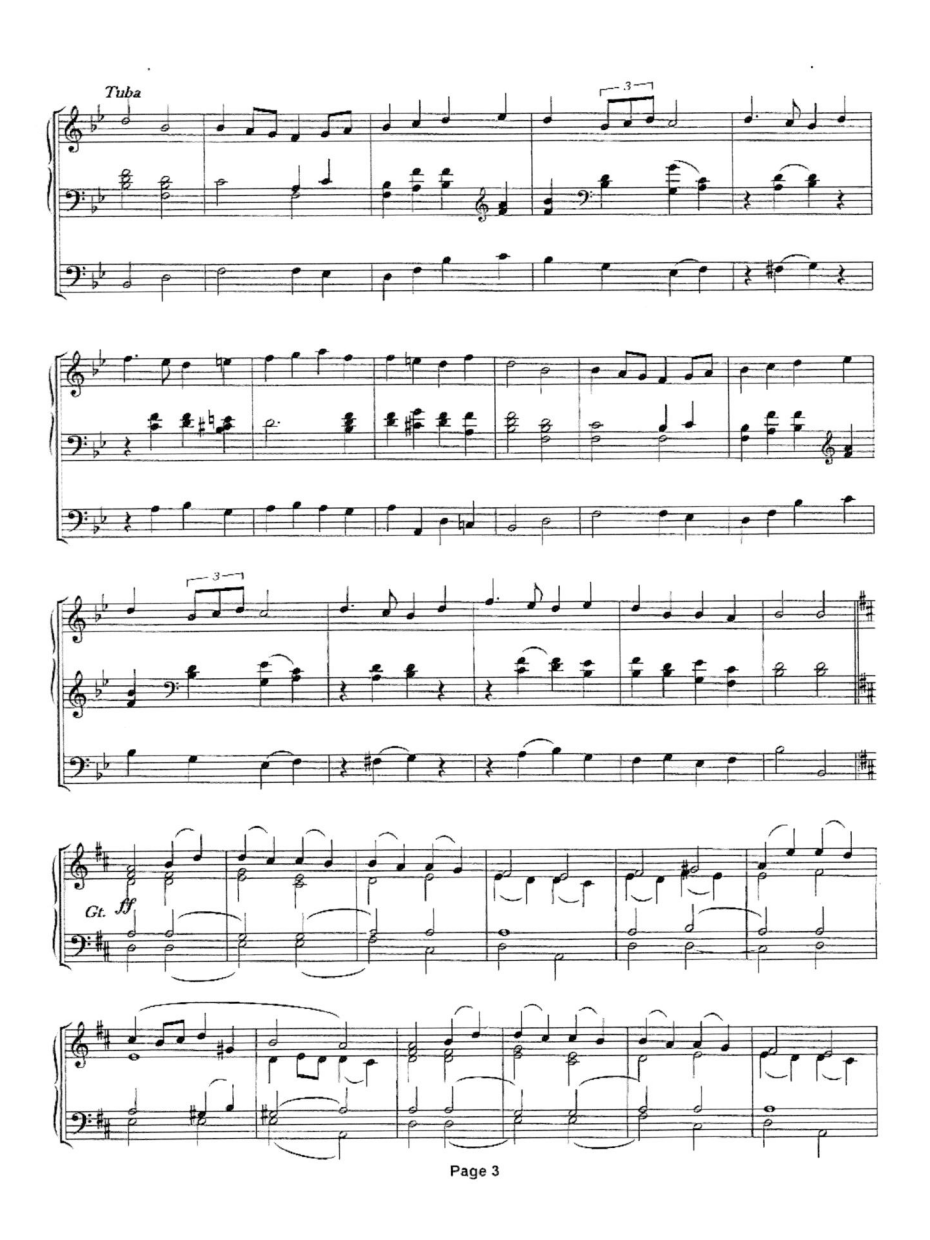

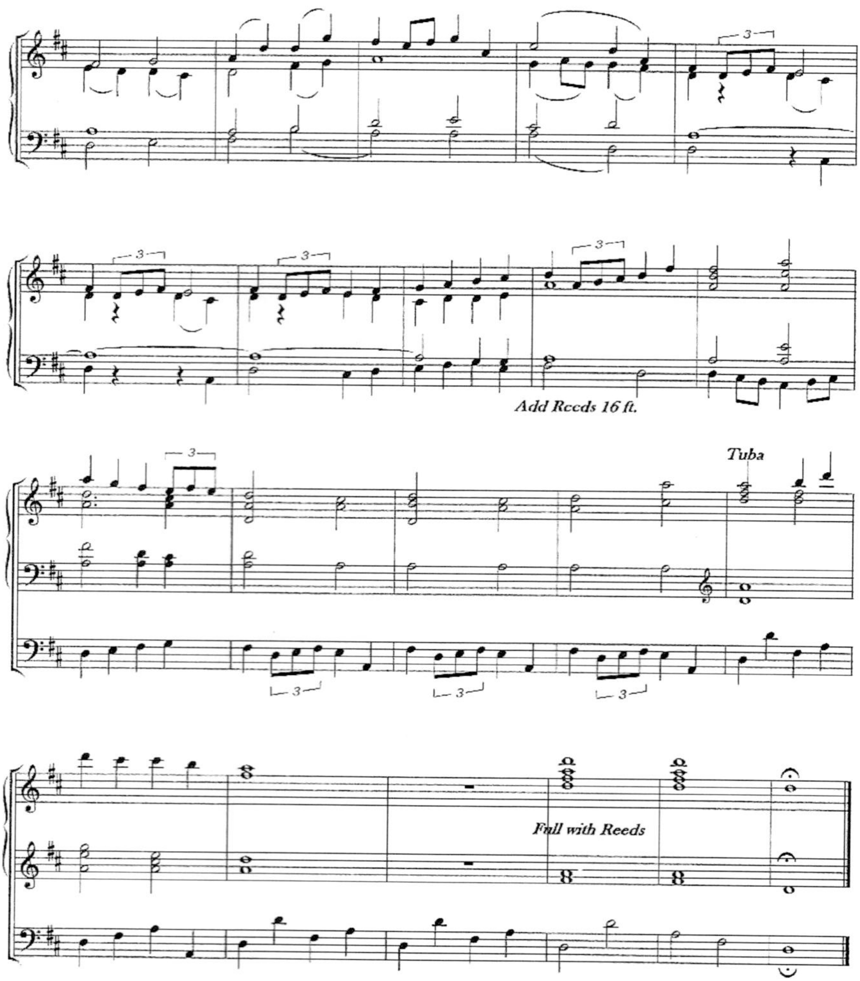
Add Reeds 16 ft.
Tuba
Full with Reeds

CHAPTER 17
SETTING THE RECORD STRAIGHT

BRYAN BLUNDELL (1676-1756)

Ship-owner and founder of the Liverpool Blue Coat School.

Bryan Blundell was born into a wealthy Liverpool family in 1676 and became a shipmaster at the age of 21. Eventually he owned his own ship, had shares in several others and was a very astute maritime merchant. A very religious person, he was Mayor of Liverpool twice and administrator of the Blue Coat School, of which he was one of the founders. In 1715 he initially paid for over 25% (later increased to 50%) of the school buildings.

He has often been accused of trading in slaves or indentured servants and sending pupils at the school to sea in almost slave conditions. The Society for Promoting Christian Knowledge, of which he was a member investigated the accusations at the time and completely cleared him.

He has been linked with slavery even to this day - not as a slave trader, but merely on the supposition that he traded in tobacco and that all tobacco was handled by slaves. However although a major portion of his cargo was tobacco, it came from northern Virginia and there seem to have been very few slaves in the area before 1712 and perhaps none on the eastern shore (Chesapeake Bay).

Members of his family built Ince Blundell Hall at Crosby (north of Liverpool) and later made a collection of statues from ancient Greece and Rome some of which are now in the Walker Art Gallery and the World Museum in Liverpool.

CHAPTER 18

PHOTOGRAPH SUPPLEMENT

1958 Easter, Lake District outside Red Lion, Grasmere. Michael Reynolds, David Gadd, Butler, Anthony Price, Peter Scott, Quellin, Alan Bonner, Arnold, Cantlay, Roger Hardman, David Kewley.

1958 Mystery Mile start. Tom Hudson, David L Williams , French, William Birch, Wise, Hackett, Roger Moore, RC Thompson, Ken Begley, C. Rawlings, Slater, Nigel Baker-Bates, Chris Lyon, Michael Norcott, Robert Roberts, Anthony Gihon.

1958 Mystery Mile spectators. Mr. W.C. Crebbin, Mr. Hugh Gibson, Mr. Ray Slater, Mr. Joe Sephton, Mr. Les Price, Mr. Harry Jamieson, Mr. W.T. Edwards

1958 Sports Day spectators. (Blue for Blundell & Red for Shirley).

1958 Sports Day final score. S. Callaghan (Blundell) with winners' cup, Carl Bowerman, Graham Harwood & Nigel Baker-Bates.

1958 School Trip Caernarvon Castle. Philip Hedges, Bruce Mair, Graham Coldrick, Ronald Foulk.

1958 School Trip to Rhyl. Mr. Harry Jamieson & Mr. Ron Scarland.

1958 Bellinzona, Switzerland. Michael Lyon, Mr. Ray Slater & Mr. W.T. Edwards.

1958 On The Channel. Wise, Tipper, John Hothersall, Chris Lyon.

1959 School Trip Chester Zoo. Relph & Anthony Davies.

1959 School Trip Chester Zoo. P Ludlam, Orriel & Scally.

1959 School Trip Chester Zoo. Mr. Mervyn Clarke, Mr. Joe Sephton.

1959 School Trip Chester Zoo. Robin Edwardes & Collinson.

1959 School Trip, Chester Zoo. Fisher, Cantlay, Roger Hardman, Shaw, Hastings, Smith, Cox, Lea, Mellor, Butler, Booker, Wash, ?, Arnold, Dolan.

1959 School Trip, Chester Zoo. Swash, Peter Rowley, Lockwood, Faulkner, Roy Biggs, John David Molyneaux.

1959 School Trip Chester Zoo.
Mr. Jeff Holiday

1960 Easter, Yorkshire Dales. Adrian Kershaw, Ian Roberts & Paul Carlton.

1960 Easter, Yorkshire Dales. Leatherbarrow, Stephen 'Marmalade' Hall, Adrian Kershaw, Robin Edwardes, Coleman.

1960 School Trip, Chatsworth. Mr. Ron Scarland, Mr. Peter Vere, Jeff Holiday & Mr. J.L. Davies.

1960 School Trip, Chatsworth. Mr. J.L. Davies, Mr. Jeff Holiday, Charles Maxwell & Orriel.

1960 Home field. Keith Caulkin, Naylor & Lockwood.

1960 School Trip, Chatsworth. Robin Edwardes, Andsell, Cocken, David Tucker, Betney, Fricker.

1960 Home field. Judge, P. Ludlam, Elliott, Chatfield, McCracken, Jones, Richard Clough, Caulkin, ?, John Blissett, Hodgson, Stanley Lynch, Geraint Parry, ?, Keith Brassey, White, Peter Huish.

1960 Home field. John Blissett, Peter Huish, Geraint Parry, John & Lawrence Adkins, Leatherbarrow.

1960, Prefects. Alan Bonner, David Kewley,, Keith Clement, Robert Roberts, Richard Stimson, Len Houghton, Slater.

1960 Tennis. Mr. Fred Unwin partnering Mr. J.L. Davies.

1960 Malham weekend. Mr. Frank Hulford and five boys.

1961 School Trip, Bowness. Bateson, Brown, Cule, Hirst & Brian Knowles.

1962 Aintree. Mr. Fred Unwin, Anthony Davies, P. Ludlam, Relph & Hirst.

1962 School Trip, Caernarvon. Boys in the castle.

1962 School Trip, Rhyl. Mr. Henry Thomas & Mr. John Williams.

1963 School Trip, Harewood House. Mr. Jim Henderson, Mlle. Annie Boulanguier, Mr. Mike Tearney, Mr. Peter Vere, Mr. John Barry-Peters, Mr. Henry Thomas, Mr. John Williams, Mr. Alec Pattison, Mr. Mervyn Clarke.

1963 Snowdonia Crib Goch. Adrian Kershaw & Gordon McDonald.

1963 Snowdonia Crib Goch. Gordon McDonald, John Whitehead, Adrian Kershaw & Hutchings.

1963 Snowdonia Tryfan. David Aspinall.

1964 South Wales. Mr. Henry Thomas & Mr. John Barry-Peters.

1963 Snowdonia Tryfan.
Christopher Keating

1963 Snowdonia Crib Goch. John Whitehead, Hutchings, Roy Biggs & Adrian Kershaw.

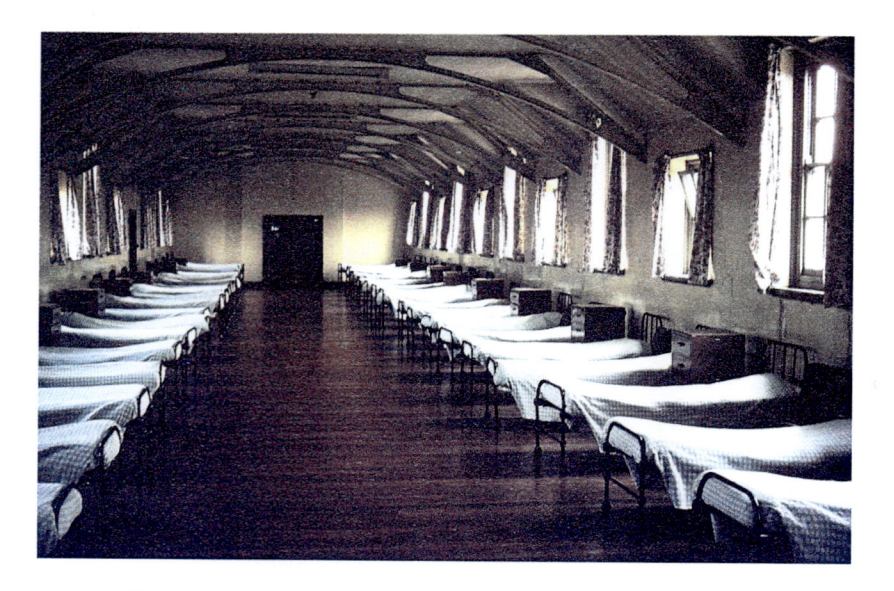

Bingham dormitory, subsequently renamed Macaulay.

Ray Livingston's impression of the south corridor.

WE ARE SURVIVORS

(For those born in and before 1940)

We were born before television, before penicillin, polio shots, frozen foods, Xerox, contact lenses, videos and the pill.

We were born before radar, credit cards, split atoms, laser beams and ball point pens, before dish washers, tumble driers, electric blankets, air conditioners, drip dry clothes and before man walked on the moon.

We got married first and then lived together. (How quaint can you be?) We thought fast food was what you had to eat in Lent.

A 'Big Mac' was an oversized raincoat and 'crumpet' we had for tea. We existed before house husbands and computer dating.

'Sheltered accommodation' was where you waited for a bus. We were before day care centres, group homes and disposable nappies.

We never heard of F.M. radio, tape decks, artificial hearts, pacemakers, word processors or young men wearing earrings.

For us 'time share' meant togetherness, a 'chip' was a piece of wood or fried potato. 'Hardware' meant nuts and bolts and 'software' wasn't even a word.

Before 1940 'Made in Japan' meant 'junk', the term 'making out' referred to how you did in your exams, 'stud' was something that fastened a collar to a shirt and 'going all the way' meant staying on a double-decker bus to the terminus.

In our day, cigarette smoking was fashionable, grass was mown, 'coke' was kept in the coal house, a 'joint' was a piece of meat you ate on Sundays and 'pot' was something that you cooked in. 'Rock Music' was a fond mother's lullaby, 'Eldorado' was an ice cream.

A 'gay' person was the life and soul of the party, whilst 'Aids' just meant beauty treatment or help for somebody in trouble.

We did not have Playstations, Nintendos, or any video games at all. There weren't 150 channels on T.V., no video movies, D.V.D. or surround sound, no cell phones, personal computers or chat rooms. We had friends and went outside and found them.

We fell out of trees and off walls, we broke bones and teeth, and there were no lawsuits arising from these accidents,

We who were born in and before 1940 must be a hardy bunch when you think of the way in which the world has changed and the adjustments that we have had to make. **But despite everything, we have survived.**

NON SIBI SED OMNIBUS

1708 - 2008

Editor's final note. All you Liverpool Blue Coat School teachers out there take note. Be nice to your pupils and fellow teachers, because nothing is more certain than there will be another book produced, perhaps in 50 years time, and you may well feature in it.

Frank Irwin

THE END

INDEX

Abbey Cinema 97.
A Blue Coat Boy of the 1920s (book) 10, 24.
Adkins, John M. 281, 318.
Adkins, Lawrence W. 281, 318.
Adkins, R. 272, 273.
Affray H.M. Submarine 101-102.
Air-raid shelters 76, 92, 104, 181, 243, 245.
A-Level, General Cert. of Ed. 222, 225.
Allen, Miss 147, 230.
Allerton Road, army barracks 161.
Altcar shooting ranges near Hightown 161, 183, 187-189.
And when did you last see your father? (painting) 62, 162-163.
Amicus trade union 35.
Anfield Stadium 159.
Andsdell, A.E. 317.
Archer, Peter 34.
Archer twins 99.
Ardren, Eddie, Blue Coat Foundation 241-242, 248, 250, 251.
Armistice Sunday 14.
Army Cadet Corps 15, 30, 36, 64, 118, 129, 151, 156-157, 161, 181-194, 245, 254, 258, 272-274, 277, 278.
Arnold, R. 307, 313.
Arnold-Craft, Mr. H.P., headmaster 1968-1989 173.
Art room 19.
Aspinall, David 324.
'Aunt Batch', (see Mrs. Lewis)
Avery, Colin 272, 273, 277.
Baggus 220.
Baker-Bates, Nigel 79-80, 142, 171-172, 281, 307, 309.
Baldwin, Eric 275.
Balmer, Herbert, Chief Inspector 57.
Band boy v. worker 16.
Band Room 19.
Band, school 18, 24, 27, 30.
Bangor, Nth.Wales 28, 29, 38, 42, 45.
Banks, David 288.
Banks, Ian 288.
Banks, Robin 156.
Bannen, Thelma 42.
Baptism before confirmation 164.
Barnhill Road 140-141.
Baron Hill estate, Beaumaris 28, 255.
Barr, Peter 153.
Barry-Peters, Mr. John 322, 324.
Bassett Swimming Shield 272.
Bateson, L.R. 279, 320.
Bath night 113-114, 147, 231.

Bathroom 132, 165, 326.
Battersbee, Iris, senior prefect 39, 42.
Beatles, the 68, 144.
Beaumaris Castle 31, 254, 255.
Beaumaris Gaol 30, 36, 254.
Beaumaris period 10, 27-38, 253-256, 299.
Beaumaris, school trip 127.
Bedtime 16, 108, 114, 134, 137-138, 231.
Bed-warming device, Mr. Perry's 202.
Bedwetters' dormitory 19, 26, 292.
Beeching, Dr. 121.
Bee Hive, pub 56.
Beer 172, 221.
Begley, Ken 307.
Bell 230, 231.
Bemrose, Eric, Ltd., Aintree 150.
Benefactors, school 235-236.
Benn, C.W. 277.
Bentham, Geoff 120-121.
Bentham, Ian 120.
Betney, George 288, 308, 317.
Betting 23, 54. 80-81, 161, 177-178, 214-215.
Bevan, K.J. 282.
Bible College 171.
Bible, leaving gift 21, 26, 279.
Bi-centenary gates, dedication of 168, 286, 287.
Biggs, Roy C. 314, 325.
Bingham dormitory 85, 90, 91, 112, 139, 143, 145, 179, 227-228, 326.
Bingham House 215.
Bioletti, Mr., school barber 17, 25, 68.
Birch, Bill 273, 277, 307.
Birkenhead Technical College 132, 258.
Birthday treat tradition 144.
Bisley 183.
'Bisley 100' status 183, 189-190.
Blackpool 11, 26.
Blackpool Art School 126.
Blakemore, Colin 276, 278, 281.
Blank rounds (bullets) 192, 193.
Blanco 182.
Blissett, M. John 282, 318.
Bluebell Lane, Huyton 182.
Blue Boy (painting) 62.
Bluecoat Chambers, School Lane, Liverpool 17.
Blundell dormitory 18, 19, 91, 101, 148, 227-228.
Blundell, Alan 21, 241.
Blundell, Albert (1923-28) 11, 21-27, 241-242, 253, 264, 265.
Blundell, Capt. Bryan 6, 9, 22, 250, 286, 305.
Blundell-Hollinshead Blundell, Major C.V.R. 286.
Blundell House 215.

Blundell, Jonathon 6, 250.
Blundell, Kenneth 22, 241.
Blundell, Leslie 22, 241, 265.
Blundell, Muriel 22, 241.
Blundell, Shelley 22, 241-242.
Boarders 83, 160, 210, 219, 229, 230, 233, 238, 257, 259.
Boardroom 7, 112, 234, 241.
'Bob-a-Job' 197-198.
Boiler house 90, 246.
Bolt, Dave (1951-57) 4, 56-58, 79-80, 87, 155-157, 216-217, 235-236, 263, 272, 276, 277.
Bolton Wanderers F.C. 160, 207.
Bond, Douglas 44-45, 46.
Bond, L. 268.
Bond, Malcolm 38, 39-40, 42, 44, 47.
Bond, Margaret (1941-48), (now Thompson) 4, 38-48, 206, 263.
Bonner, F. Alan 276, 278, 307, 319.
Booker 313.
Booker Avenue 175.
Boot polishing 19, 145, 186, 230.
Boots 20, 33, 158.
Boulanguier, Mlle. Annie 322.
Bowcock, Mrs. 147.
Bowden, Florence 110.
Bowden, Mrs. Carol 121.
Bowden, William T. ('Billy') (1949-56) 4, 110-124, 143, 180, 264.
Bowden, William Thomas, R.N. 110.
Bowerman, Carl W. 288, 309.
Boxing 144, 184.
Brabazon, airliner 131.
Braithwaite, Jean 42.
Brassey, Keith 282, 284, 288, 318.
Brayford P.R. 273.
Breakouts from school 140-141, 162, 178-179.
Breck Road 158.
Bren gun 190-191, 193.
Brilliantine 165.
Bristol-Myers Squibb Pharmaceuticals Ltd. 132.
British Army 169, 257-258.
British Columbia, Canada 157.
British Rail, Telecomms. Section 138.
Broadgreen School 158.
Broadhurst, Peter 34.
Brotchie, Mike B. 288.
Brotherly Society, Liverpool Blue Coat 1, 2, 3, 21, 160, 279, 350, 351.
Brown, Ian 139, 288.
Brown, Kenneth Maxwell, solicitor 101.
Brown, Murray 139.
Brylcreem 135, 249.
Bryn-Bac 197.

Bryn School, Beaumaris 30, 39, 41.
Buckle, Charles 99.
Buckle, George 99.
Buffers, The 121.
Bulkeley Arms Hotel, Beaumaris 41.
Bulkeley Monument, Beaumaris 36, 37.
Bulkeley, Sir & Lady (see Williams-Bulkeley).
Bullen, Billy 110.
Bulleted blank 190-191, 193.
Bull's Head pub, Beaumaris 40.
Bullying 96, 114, 132, 143, 147, 167, 207, 260.
Bumper (see Dummy)
Burgess, Miss 113-114.
Burgess, Neil 272, 276, 278.
Burstall, F.H., F.R.C.O. 9.
Burtonwood U.S.A.A.F. base 181-182.
Butler, J.M. 307, 313.
'Butter, a' 54.
Butts, the 187-188.
Byers, Miss Mary 23, 44, 77, 164, 240.
Cabot H.M.S. 110.
Cadets (see Army Cadet Corps)
Calderstones Park 70, 115, 133.
Callaghan Stuart W. 160, 246, 280, 309.
Cameo Cinema Murders (1949) 56-58.
Cammell Laird, shipyard 34.
Canadian Pacific Steamship Co. 157.
Cantlay, P. 307, 313.
Cap, uniform 14, 25, 155.
Carbolic soap 132, 165.
Caretaker 126.
Carlton, Paul 315.
Carrington Viyella Ltd. 155.
Carr, Major, Liverpool Scottish Regt. 157, 183-184, 188, 189-190, 194.
Carson, Violet (actress) 200.
Cass, D. 281.
Castle Rushen School, Isle of Man 118.
Castle Street, Beaumaris 29, 255.
Catapult, homemade 130.
Cathedral Sunday 55, 60, 243.
Catterall, John Bernard 56.
Caulkin, Keith G. 317, 318.
'Cease to Maintain' threat (1984) 7.
Cemetery Hill, Beaumaris 29.
Central heating 52, 150, 223, 229.
Chandler, Chingo 130, 131.
Chapel 23, 58-59, 107, 129, 142, 147, 163, 165, 169, 180, 223, 241, 246, 248-250, 261, 267, 294, 296.
Chapter readers 15-16, 169.
'Charter Royal' radio programme (1957) 200.

Chatfield 318.
Chemistry laboratory 126.
Chess 149, 225.
Chester College 161.
Childwall 136-137, 155.
Childwall Fiveways 113, 142.
Chipping, Rev., (visiting minister) 23.
'Chips, Mr.' (see Mr. J.L. Davies)
Choir, chapel 150, 154, 200, 273.
Christmas 20, 25, 41, 47, 97.
Church of England 135, 169.
Church Road 17, 25, 85, 97, 103, 115, 128, 153, 217, 224, 246, 251.
Church Street, Beaumaris 29, 255.
Chynoweth, Mr. 11, 21, 23.
Clark 268.
Clarke, Mr. Mervyn 312, 322.
Clarke, Peter (1943-51) 4, 32-35, 254, 263, 270, 298.
Classics Illustrated (comic) 75-76.
Class size 16, 219-220.
Cleaning staff ('skivvies') 25.
Clement, Keith M. 277, 319.
Clock tower 15, 25, 82, 143, 234, 262, 292, 293, 294, 297, 298.
'Clocky' 15.
Clough, Richard 318.
Clynderwen, Pembrokeshire 207.
Cobbler 20, 90, 126, 158.
Cocken, Bill 277, 317.
Coinage in 1950s 238-239.
Coldrick, E. Graham 309.
Coleman, R. 315.
Collar (starched) 129, 168.
Collinson, M.P. 313.
Comet, airliner 102-103.
Commerce, Liverpool College of 155, 156.
Common rooms 19, 90, 91, 92, 113, 210, 228.
Communion service 163-164.
Condensed milk 109.
Confirmation 16, 135.
Connolly, Charles 56, 57.
Connor 275.
Conservative Club, Church Road 140-141.
Coronation (1953) 152, 159.
Countess of Sefton's Own Regiment, Royal Artillery 181.
Cowan, Mrs., geography teacher 218.
Cowley, Les 30.
Cox, Paul 273, 285, 313.
Crebbin, Mr. Walter C., English teacher 33, 59, 78, 112, 117-118, 142, 162, 171, 219, 221, 223, 224-225, 228, 229, 308.
'Crispies' 136.
Crookham family (Eddie, Margaret & Elizabeth) 32.

Crossed Swords badge (P.E. Instructor's) 182, 184, 258.
Crossville Ltd. 142.
Crouch, David 308.
Crypt, chapel 107-109, 126, 142.
Crystal sets 16, 23, 101, 128, 133.
'Cubbo' 186.
Cubby-hole (remote common room for seniors) 92, 93, 94.
Cuckoo patrol 197.
Cule, L. 320.
Cumberland Street 107.
'Currant bango' 14,
Curry, Edwina 7.
Dale Street 15, 98, 147.
Dance training 192.
Dating of girls 22, 34, 163.
Davidson, B. Stuart 130-131, 308.
Davies, Anthony 311, 321.
Davies, Mr. Brian 172.
Davies, Mr. J.L. ('Dai'/'Taffy'), physics teacher 116, 144, 153, 164-165, 167-168, 171-172, 207-208, 220, 223, 224, 228, 235, 246, 316, 319.
Davy Crockett (song) 137.
Davy, Ian 113.
Dawson, Betty, deputy head girl 39, 41, 42, 46, 206.
Dayboys 160, 163, 217, 221, 230.
D-Day 223-224.
Deaf and Dumb School 131.
D'Eathe, Sammy 33, 298.
Debating Society 285.
'Delvanté' (see Mr. Derek Jones)
Denderfield, R.F. 63.
Dentist 17, 151.
Devoy, P. 282.
'Dewdrop' (see caretaker)
Dickerson, Dr. F.W. 4, 11, 15, 32, 45-46, 58, 59-60, 62, 106, 126, 163, 169, 200, 205-206, 244, 248, 250, 251, 300, 301-304.
Diekirch, Luxembourg (tragedy-struck school trip) 50.
Dig for Victory 30.
Dingle, Liverpool 160.
Dining room 11–12, 63, 79-80, 85, 195, 230, 242, 251, 283.
Diphtheria 20.
Dodd, Mr. 130.
Dolan 313.
Donegan, Lonnie 78, 143, 164.
Dormitory, cleaning of 135-136.
Dormitory, locations of 18.
Dormitory toilets ('offeys') 71. 75, 114, 242.
Dotheboys Hall 219.
'Douse!' (warning) 15, 214-215.
Drummer in the school band 24.
Ducts, under-floor 52-53, 171.

Duggan, M. 284.
Dummy, floor-polishing 19, 21, 122, 135-136, 143.
Dunkirk evacuation 31.
Dunlop Rubber Co., Water Street 160.
Eade, Mr., French teacher 34, 105, 130, 159.
Earle dormitory (formerly Blundell) 89, 148, 227-228, 245-247.
Earle F.C. 113, 251.
East corridor 22, 77, 103, 136, 172, 178, 242.
Economy, Board of 218-219.
Edge Hill railway sidings 57.
Edge Lane 100, 170.
Edwards, Mr. W.T. history teacher 95, 131, 133, 156, 177, 308, 310.
Edwardes, Robin. 313, 315, 317.
Egerton D. 272.
Electric Power Installations Ltd. 119.
Elliott, B. 318.
Elliott, C. 284.
Ellis, Dave 277.
Ellis, Ruth 168.
Ellison, R. 308.
Elmsford Plant laboratory 120.
Empress of Canada (ship) 157.
End of term excitement 170.
Epstein, Brian 144.
Evans, Stan (1936-44) 30-31, 254.
Everton F.C. 16, 207.
Ewan, Mr., art teacher 11.
Examinations 26, 34.
Excursion, annual 16, 18, 25, 253.
Exhibitionist neighbour 179.
Export Practice, degree course 155, 156.
Extension, new 291, 292.
F.A. Cup Final 134.
Fagging 167.
Fagin, A. 268.
Fallowfield Road 10.
Farrell, Mr. Brian, woodwork teacher 219, 226-227, 228, 235.
Farrell, Peter, head boy 200, 282.
Farrell, Mr. Ted 158.
Fascists (rise of in 1930s) 16.
Faulkner, I.G. 314.
F.I.E.S. 132.
Film shows 17, 86, 87, 115, 129, 149, 208.
Finney, Mr. 23.
Fire incident 217.
Fireworks, homemade 69.
Fisher, R. 313.
'Flora' 44-45, 46.
Flynn, Mr., maintenance man 71, 158.
Food parcels 24.

Football pools 54, 80-81.
Football team 24.
Ford Motor Company 120, 157.
Forrest, Ian 288.
Forrest, Roy M.T. 273.
Foulder, Ernie (1952-57) 4, 160, 251, 280, 284.
Foulk, Ronald A. 309.
Fourmost, the 144, 284.
Fowler, Mr. 33.
France 157, 161, 166, 177, 225.
French, J. 307.
Fricker, C. 317.
Friends Reunited website 8.
Frodsham crag 148.
Fulneck School, West Yorks. 202-203, 226.
Fusco's, Spellow Lane 110.
Gadd, David A. 273, 276, 307.
Games – All Aboard 212.
Games – Athletics 215-216. - Basketball 216. – Beaches On 212. – British Bulldogs 210-211. – chariot racing 137-138. – Cigarette cards 214. – Conkers 210. - Crab football 145. – Cricket 215, 216, 225. – Football 215, 225. - Indoor football 212. – Marbles 215. – Raffles 177-178. – Realio 212. – Rugby 27. – Table Tennis 213. – Tennis 213-214, 220. – Three-Card Brag 214-215. – Two-Ton Tessie On 211-212.
Gardens for pupils 165-166, 170, 277.
Gardner Merchant Ltd. 157.
Garrett, Mr., French teacher 11.
Gaskill, M.F. 273.
Garvey 58-59, 249.
Gavel in dining room 12, 23.
Gibson, Mr. Hugh A., history and geog. teacher 141, 195-196, 232, 308.
Gihon, Anthony V.C., head boy 167, 276, 278, 282, 307.
Girls' transfer to a Wolverhampton school 34, 47, 269, 271.
Glamorgan Cricket Team 207.
Glasshouse 192-193.
Gleave Mr. A. 350.
Goodbye Mr. Chips (film) 208.
Goodison Park 208.
Governors, School 21, 107, 111, 240.
Grace, mealtime 12, 66, 230.
Graham, Billy, American evangelist 169.
Graham dormitory 18, 19, 90, 91, 139, 227-228, 241-242.
Graham House 24, 215.
Grammar school classrooms 245.
Grammar Schools Cup, football competition 159.
Grammar v. Secondary Modern education 149.
Grand, The (cinema) 158.
Grand, Peter 83-84.
Grant Avenue 88-89, 221, 244, 294.
Gray, K.W. 282.

Gravesend Sea School 157.
Greaves, G.S. 282.
Greenbank Park 50.
Green Lane 26.
Greig, Peter 103-104.
Grey suits 84, 168, 169, 251.
Gunstead, Stafford 272, 284.
Gymnasium 220.
Hackett, D.C. 307.
Hackett, Miss 11.
Hall, Bob 26.
Hall, Ivy 22.
Hall, Rodney 50.
Hall, Stephen ('Marmalade') 315.
Halverson, Hilding, religious singer 147, 169.
Hamilton, Ian 268.
Hamilton, 'Mousey' 127.
Hanson, Colin 288.
'Hard-boiled egg' incident 116, 143, 164-165.
Harding 24.
Harding, Mrs. A., president of Old Girls Soc. 286.
Hardman, Roger 307, 313.
Harling, Mr. 11, 23.
Harrison 94.
Harrison, Alan 171.
Harrison, Noel 272.
Harvest Festival 180, 249.
Harwood, David 288.
Harwood, P.J.G. ('Butch') 276.
Harwood, Graham W. 286, 288, 309.
Hastings, M.J. 313.
Hatchard, John W. 273.
Hatton, Billy 144, 160, 272, 284.
Haygarth, Arthur 160, 273.
Hays brothers 99.
Healey, P., former chairman of the governors 308.
Hedges, Mike 288.
Helsby crag 148.
Head-lice 165.
Headmaster's house 84, 104, 153, 246, 317, 318.
Health 17. 20.
Heatley, Peter W. 160, 275.
Henderson, Mr. Jim 322.
Hedges, Philip 309.
Henllys Lane, Beaumaris 36, 256.
Hickman, Mr. J. Mark W., woodwk and metalwk teacher 33-34, 259.
Hickman, W.S. 282.
Heyson, Nora (artist) 271.
Hicks, John, school's baker 14.
Hilton, William 270.

Hinds, Mike 278.
Hipkiss, Miss 11, 23, 39, 46-47.
Hirst, P.A. 320, 321.
Hodgins, T.M. 282.
Hodgson, G. 318.
Hoist 91.
Holiday, Mr. Jeff, woodwork teacher 103-104, 142, 314, 316.
Hollis, Mr., science teacher 11, 17.
Hollis, S. 273.
Holly, Buddy 92, 143.
Holmes, John 286, 288.
Holy Trinity Church 88, 171, 217, 274, 290.
Home Farm, Beaumaris 36, 256.
Home field 246, 251, 277.
Home Guard, Beaumaris 30, 36.
Homer, Miss, matron 45.
Homesickness 39, 49, 84-85, 123, 132, 146, 148.
Hornby, Peter E., head boy 117-118, 268.
Horne Bros., Whitechapel, tailors 34, 111-112, 119. 122.
Hothersall, John R. 311.
Houghton, Lennie E. 160, 281, 285, 319.
Howarth, John (1952-57) 4, 171-172, 264, 273.
Hudson, Tommy R. 51, 65-66, 133, 183, 272, 307.
Hughes, A. 282.
Hughes, Arthur 99.
Hughes, Eric 99.
Hughes, Griff 99, 266.
Hughes, Mr. Harry C., headmaster 1920-26 22, 23.
Hughes, John 99.
Hughes, K. 288.
Hughes, Kenneth (1945-53) 4, 98-99, 157-158, 181-182, 197, 263, 266, 267, 268.
Hughes, Lennie 32-33, 35.
Hughes, Millicent, 269.
Huish, Peter D.M. 281, 282, 318.
Hulford, Mr. Frank S. geography teacher 4, 81, 95, 148, 166, 202-203, 218-233, 264, 277, 285, 300, 320.
Humphreys, Bill 33.
Hutchings 323, 325.
Hydrogen sulphide 168.
Ikonomides, P. 279.
Initiation rites 162.
I.R.A. 187, 193.
Irwin, Frank (1950-57) 1, 3, 4, 49-68, 71-75, 76-77, 80-81, 84, 87-89, 92-95, 96-97, 100, 101-102, 105-106, 132-138, 165, 169, 178, 180, 182-186, 187-193, 195-196, 197-198, 199, 205, 207-208, 210-216, 238-239, 243-261, 263, 272, 273, 275, 276, 278, 279 284, 300, 328.
Italian P.o.W. camp, Anglesey 44.
Jackson, Mr. 99.
James, Dorothy 271.
Jamieson, Mr. Harry, crafts teacher 149, 308, 310.

Jansen, Hank (author) 129.
W.T. & R.T. training 182.
Japanese officer's sword 167.
Jetex engine (for model aircraft) 131.
Johnson 277.
Johnson, Reginald D. 108-109, 288.
Jones, Mr. Derek (a.k.a. 'Delvanté') English teacher 55, 151, 152, 204-205, 226-227.
Jones, Mr. & Mrs. J.O. 29.
Jones, Peter E. 288.
Jones, Willy 165.
Judge, C.J.S. 318.
Keating, Christopher 325.
Kelly, Bob 126, 129, 142-143, 234-235.
Kelly, Edna 42.
Kelly, George 56-58.
Kennedy, Dave (1948-55) 4, 76, 82-83, 83-84, 158-160, 176, 186-187, 195, 202, 209, 263.
Kenny, Mr. 116, 119.
Kershaw, Adrian C. 315, 323, 325.
Kewley, David 307, 319.
Kiel-Kraft aircraft models 131-132.
Killen, Philip 272, 273.
Kimber, Anthony 288.
King, R.A.C. 273.
King's Regiment, 5th 24.
Knowles, Brian 281, 320.
Knowles, Stanley 281, 288.
Lairig Ghru, Cairngorm Mts. 148.
La Marguerite, S.S. 25, 253.
Lancashire Amateur Football League 160.
Lancaster, bomber 200.
Lance Lane sports field 17, 24, 65, 113, 153, 251, 297.
Latin 167, 202-203.
Laughton, Bill 34.
Laundry room 90, 112.
Lavatory block – north 70, 138, 158, 178, 291.
Lavatory block – south 70.
Lea 313.
Lead weights in trousers 186.
Lea Enfield .303 rifle 181, 183.
Leatherbarrow 315, 318.
Leaving clothes 21, 119.
Lee, Jeffery 308.
Leggott, E.P. 277.
Lennon & McCartney 144.
Leonard, R. 279.
Leslie, Frank J. 9.
Leverhulme, Lord 236.
Lewis, Mr., boiler man 223.
Lewis, Mrs. ('Aunt Batch') 39, 40, 42, 43, 47.

Lewis, Sylvia 42.
Libby, 'Doc' 206.
Library, Old Blues' Memorial 245, 251, 290.
Liddell, Billy 159.
Life-saving classes 71-72.
'Lights Out' 231.
Lime Street 157.
Lime Street Station 24, 27, 45.
Lindsay, David 288.
Ling, Mr. Peter 4, 233.
Lion Patrol 196.
Litherland Theatre Club 57.
Little Richard 147.
Livermore, Harry, lord mayor and solicitor 147, 286, 287.
Liverpool Anglican Cathedral 60, 243.
Liverpool, Bishop of 249, 286.
Liverpool, bombing of 32.
Liverpool & Bootle Constabulary 57.
Liverpool Education Committee 221.
Liverpool & North Wales Steamship Co. Ltd. 18, 25.
Liverpool City Council 7,
Liverpool F.C. 16, 120, 159, 207.
Liverpool Magic Circle 204.
Liverpool Polytechnic 160.
Livingston, Ray (1955-59) 4, 60-61, 63, 68, 69-71, 75-76, 83, 84-86, 89-92, 97-98, 99-100, 100-101, 102-104, 106-107, 138-149, 164, 169, 175, 184, 196-197, 200, 201, 206, 208-209, 234-235, 236-238, 264.
Liverpool Scottish Regiment (T.A.) 183, 191, 192, 194.
Liverpool Show, the 69-70, 87.
Livingston, Stan (1952-57) 4, 56-58, 60-61, 63, 84-85, 95-96, 97, 99, 106, 107, 115, 147, 149, 150-154, 180, 237, 264, 273, 326.
Liverpool University 24.
Llanddonna, Beaumaris 36.
Llandfaes Church 30.
Llandudno 18, 253.
Llanfairfechan, Nth. Wales 195-196.
Llorett de Mar, Costa Brava 120-121.
Lloyd, Marion 271.
Lockers 14, 20, 210.
Lock-picking 108.
Lockwood, B. 314, 317.
Lofthouse, Nat 159.
Lookout on north shore 188.
Lord Mayor of Liverpool 83, 131, 147, 152, 270, 286, 287.
Lovatt, Mr. Philip, history teacher 232-233.
Lower Castle Street 101.
Loyal Regiment, The 161.
Ludlam, P. 312, 318, 321.
Luger pistol 183-184.
Lynch, Stanley 282, 318.

Lyon, Chris 98, 284, 307, 311.
Lyon, James, under officer 191, 277.
Lyon, J.S. Ltd 98.
Lyon, Michael 98, 273, 285, 288, 310.
Lyon, Peter 98, 288.
Lyons, Mr., engineer and factotum 20.
Macauley dormitory (formerly Bingham) 89, 227-228, 245-247, 326.
MacChrystal, W. 282.
MacCracken, R. 318.
MacDonald, Gordon 323.
MacDonald, L. 268.
Mace, Mr., geography teacher 166, 218.
Mace, ceremonial 55, 205, 243, 287.
MacLaughlin, Keith 34.
MacPherson Colin 273, 284, 288.
Maes Hyfryd, Beaumaris 42.
Magic Circle, The 204.
Mair, Bruce G. 309.
Manchester University 161.
Manwaring-Spencer, Hubert (1948-55) 4, 56-58, 66-68, 126-132, 184, 263, 268.
March in D (see Slow March)
Margaret Street, Beaumaris 29.
Marsden, Harry 9.
Martin, Arthur (1934-41) 29, 254, 255.
Martin, Philip W. 308.
Maryport 240.
Mason, John 288, 308.
Mather Avenue 175.
Matron 113-114, 117-118.
Maxwell, Charles H. 316.
May, B. 281.
Mellor 313.
Menai Bridge 16, 18, 25, 27, 45, 253.
Menai Straits 31.
Menlove Avenue 175.
Merchant Navy 132, 138, 157, 258.
Merchant Taylors' School, Crosby, Liverpool 101, 218.
Mercury (traces in laboratory benches) 168.
Merseybeat phenomenon 144.
Mersey, River 148, 159, 175.
Metalwork lessons 113, 297.
Midnight feasts 103-104.
Military Police 119.
Mills, Charlie 32-33, 34, 298.
Molyneux, John David 314.
Monitors 13, 23.
Montreal, Canada 155.
Moody Bible Institute, U.S.A. 87.
Moore, Mr., maths teacher 74, 176, 229.
Moore, Mr. & Mrs. 170.

Morath Brothers 15.
Moore, Roger G.A. 163-164, 273, 277, 285, 307.
Moorhead Efficiency Cup 272.
Morris, Barbara 270.
Morris, John E., (hon. chaplain) 286.
Morris, Josephine 42.
Morris, Miss 230.
Morse code 182.
Mosspits Lane Primary School 7, 113, 127, 155.
Mount Field, Beaumaris 42.
Mount Pleasant 56.
Mugglestone, Mr., crafts teacher 115, 208-209.
Murray, Alan 272, 275.
Murray, Barbara 271.
Murray, W.H. 238.
Music room 248.
Mystery, The (see Wavertree Playground)
Mystery Mile (annual race) 17, 87-88, 244, 307, 308.
National service 183, 224.
Naylor, A.H. 317.
Nellie, Aunt 110.
Newmark watches 93.
Norcott, Michael B. 281, 307.
North corridor 19.
North playground 27, 216, 245, 277.
North quadrangle 61, 136, 293, 295, 297.
Numbering of pupils 13.
Nunnen, Jimmy 273.
O'Hara, Brian 144, 160, 284.
O-Level, General Cert. of Ed. 100, 160, 161, 167, 222.
Old Blues' Sunday 14.
Old Boys' Football Club 160.
'Old Lady' (ghost) 245, 247.
Olive Mount Children's Hospital 21.
Olive Mount School for Girls 145.
Orriel, S.M. 312, 316.
Oswestry army camp 184.
Otton, Alan 284.
Ouija boards 92-95, 151-152.
Over-14s dormitory 19.
Owning up to misdemeanours (need for) 49-50, 55, 165, 176.
Parachutes, handkerchief 129-130, 247.
Parry 276.
Parry, G. 282, 286.
Parry, Geraint 288, 318.
Parry, Nigel 156, 273, 284.
'Parsimony, Board of' 134, 218.
Pattison, Mr. Alec 322.
Peanut butter 139-140.
Peewit Patrol 196.

Pea soup ('pea-wack') 14. 23.
Pearce, Alec 96, 114, 180.
Pearson, Mr., woodwork and metalwork teacher 11, 23.
'Peg Leg' (ghost) 76-77, 82, 245, 247, 250.
Penmon Radio Station (BBC) 30.
Penny Lane 25, 115, 163, 179.
Penny Lane (song) 68.
Pensions, Ministry of, Orleans Hse, Edmund Street 111-112, 116, 119.
Perry, Mr. J. Brian, Latin teacher 89, 97, 138-139, 146, 152, 170, 177, 179, 201, 202-203, 219, 223-224, 226-227, 228, 245, 285, 288.
Petite, Miss 17.
Pettersen, R. 73, 275, 280.
Phelps, Ernie J. 308.
Pickford, Cyril 288.
Picton Clock 134.
Picton Library, Wm. Brown Street 152.
Picton Road 56
Picton Road Baths 20, 25, 72, 113, 145.
Picton Road Library 145.
Pierrepoint, Albert, hangman 57, 67.
Pillow-fights 170.
Piperno, Mrs., wardrobe-mistress 84, 112, 119, 168, 186.
'Plas Meigan', Beaumaris 28, 254, 255.
Play, annual 89.
Playroom (see Common room)
'Plumduff' (see Kennedy, Dave)
Pollitt, Graham J. 280.
Pornographer 153.
Porridge 128.
Porter, Sergeant/Sgt. Major 15, 24, 26.
Potosi silver cutlery 166.
Prefects 23, 48, 163, 165, 167, 173, 179, 228, 229, 319.
Presley, Elvis 143.
Preston Art School 126.
Price, Anthony D. 282, 307.
Price, Mr. Les S., maths teacher 97-98, 219, 223, 226-227, 308.
Prince Alfred Road 87-89.
Prince, Derek 128.
Privacy, lack of 139, 236-237.
Prize Day (see also Speech Day) 13, 15, 19, 161, 236.
Providence Store, The 196.
Puckey, Charlie 128.
Pugh, Margaret 42.
Punishment – caning 23, 33, 44, 49-50, 67, 82, 95, 103, 115, 116-118, 145-146, 156, 158, 163, 171, 248. – cold baths 95, 199. – cruelty 127, 129. – detention 96, 115. – expelling 129. – 'gating' 115. 163. – hitting 11, 67-68, 74, 78, 96, 130, 139, 143, 176, 177, 209. – hurling of objects 177, 245. – lines 96-97, 139. – loss of privileges 115. – slippering 66, 95, 99, 115, 145, 161, 171, 176. – standing motionless 200.
Radio Luxembourg 133, 143.

Purchasing & Supply, Institute of 160.
Queen's Lancashire Regiment, The 161.
Quellin, M.A. 307.
Radio Officer, Merchant Navy 138.
Radio sets 16, 23, 47, 128, 143, 226.
Radley, David 277, 28.
Raffles 177-178.
Raps (see rhymes)
Rawes, Godfrey 177.
Rawlings C.E. ('Bugs') 273, 277, 307.
Real Love (video) 68.
Record Cards, pupils' 221.
Red Cross 26.
Red Hill, Beaumaris 28, 32, 36, 37, 254, 255.
Red Hill House, Beaumaris 42, 43, 46., 47.
Redman, Don 9.
Red Wharf Bay 29, 197.
Rees, Mr., school secretary 112, 117, 235.
Reid, Jimmy 34.
Relph, J. 311, 321.
Remembrance Sunday 59, 61-62, 64, 169, 251.
Reynolds, Michael J. 277, 307.
Rhymes (raps) 70, 80,
Rice pudding 24.
Ridgway 288.
Rix, Lord Justice 57.
Roberts, Ian K. 315.
Roberts, Owen 30.
Roberts, Robert E. (Bobby) 160, 281, 307, 319.
Roberts, Vera, head girl 39, 41, 42, 46, 47, 206.
Roby, Denis 277.
Rockets, homemade 69.
Rock Ferry High School 226.
Rock Island Line (song) 143.
Rock 'n' roll, arrival of 144, 147.
Rodney Hall Chess Trophy 50.
Romans, the 156.
'Ronuk' polish 19, 122, 135, 138.
Ross, Danny 10, 15, 22, 24, 26, 160, 161, 279, 350.
Rourke, Danny 288.
Rowland, J.H.J. (Jimmy) 308.
Rowlands, Mr., French teacher (a.k.a 'Tan Tan') 78, 95-96, 105-106, 140, 176-177, 199.
Rowley, Peter 314.
Royal Army Medical Corps 182.
Royal Artillery 119, 183.
Royal Electrical & Mechanical Engineers 182.
Royal Engineers 171.
Royal Insurance offices 107.
Running away 44-45, 158.

Royal Sailors' Rests.. 171.
Royal Street 110.
Royal Welsh Fusiliers 30,
Rupert Road Secondary Modern School, Huyton 204.
St. John's R.C. School, Fountains Road 110.
St. Lawrence's Church, Barlows Lane 110.
St. Lawrence C.of E. Primary School 110.
St. Mary's Parish Church Hall, Beaumaris 29, 255-256.
St. Tudno, S.S. 18, 253.
Salmon, Tony (1971-77) 4, 21, 172-174, 350.
Sanatorium (see also sick bay) 45, 103, 118, 127, 165, 222.
Sargent, Sir Malcolm 59.
Saunders Roe 'Catalina' factory, Anglesey 30, 42.
Scally, R. 312.
Scarland, Mr. D. Ron, art teacher 89, 95, 115, 130, 150-151, 177, 179, 310, 316.
Scarlet fever 16. 20.
School office 11, 20, 23, 24, 112, 224, 234, 251.
Scotland Road 162.
Scott, Peter 307.
Scouse (stew) 24, 77.
Scout Troop, 31st Wavertree 181, 182, 195-198, 258, 275.
Secondary modern school classrooms 143, 245.
Second World War 169.
Sefton General Hospital 175, 240.
Sefton Park 70, 115, 133, 163.
Senior girls 13.
Senior Wing, created 1957 222-223.
Sephton, Mr. Joe E., music teacher 154, 161, 200, 223, 226-227, 280, 308, 312.
Sex education 99-100.
Sharpe, P.W. 282.
Shaw, B.W. 313.
'Shed, the' 90, 245, 247, 295.
Shell-shock 139, 141.
Ship, model 158-159.
Shirley dormitory 19, 91, 162, 227-228.
Shirley Hall, the 6, 14, 15, 17, 25, 35, 59, 61-62, 83, 112, 117-118, 129, 130, 163, 169, 206, 224, 229, 235, 241-242, 251, 261, 267, 269, 270, 271, 280, 283, 294, 300.
Shirley House 215, 275.
Shirley, W.H. 6.
Showers, communal 145.
Sick Bay (see also sanatorium) 222.
Siddall, Rev. Arthur, president of brotherly soc. 299.
Simpson, Richard 171.
Skerry's College, Rodney Street 152, 204.
Skiffle, arrival of 143-144.
Slater 281.
Slater, J.R. 307, 309, 319.
Slater, Mr. Ray, scripture teacher 60-61.73, 100, 130, 141, 169, 177, 308, 310.
Slow March 11, 23, 58, 59, 129, 165, 244, 248, 251, 300, 301-304.
Smith, Mrs. Dorothy, headmistress 33, 38-39, 40, 43, 46, 47.

Slump, the 14.
Smith, Harry A. 284, 309.
Smith, Mr. Kenneth I., English teacher 209, 223, 225-227.
Smithdown Road 68. 75, 99, 131, 140-141, 158, 244.
Smoking 151, 166-167, 170, 214-215, 217.
'Sneaking' (see owning up)
Snowden, W.A., president of brotherly soc. 286.
South corridor 89-90.
Southport F.C. 159.
Southport gardens 25.
South quadrangle 90.
Sparrow Hall Isolation Hospital 21.
Spectacles 17.
Speech Day (see also Prize Day) 55, 59, 131, 235.
Spellow Lane 110, 115.
Spiritualism (see Ouija boards)
Sports Day 215-216, 275.
'Spud corridor, the' (see east corridor)
'Squares' (see 'currant bangos')
Staff dining room 13, 46, 49, 52-53, 136, 171.
Staff room (south) 91.
Staff trips to Stratford-upon-Avon, etc. 226-227.
Stafford Street 24.
Stages, Patricia 270.
Staines, P. 268.
Staircase, main (to dormitories) 91.
Stanley Street 100.
Star Stores, Menai Bridge 25.
Stimson, Richard 273, 285, 319.
Styth, Rev. Robert 6.
Stythe dormitory (formerly Graham) 89, 141, 201, 227-228, 245-247, 288.
Suez Crisis (1956) 146.
Sunday School 26.
Sunday Walk, the 99, 104, 114-115, 133, 142-143, 163.
Swash, S.R. 314.
Sweets (weekly ration) 47, 78.
Swimming pool 20, 24.
Tait, Mr. John M. (Captain) 117-118, 144, 145, 151, 159, 179, 190, 194, 226, 246, 273, 274, 277.
Tank Regiment 26.
'Tan Tan' (see Mr. Rowlands)
Tape recorder, demonstration of early model 154.
Tawd Vale, Ormskirk 196.
Taylor, Arthur 24.
Taylor, Mr. (Mayor of Beaumaris) 35.
Taylor, R. 281.
Taylor, Teddy 33, 298.
Tearney, Mr. Mike 322.
Telephones 224-225.
The Squirrel, school's magazine 17, 47, 150, 201, 209.

Tennis courts 26, 90, 245, 246-247, 295.
Territorial Army 181, 191.
Thamos, Sister 99.
Thetis H.M. submarine 29.
Thomas, Harry (1931-37) 10-21, 253, 264.
Thomas, Mr. Henry 322, 324.
Thomas, Leonard 56.
Thomas, Sister 45.
Thompson 276.
Thompson, Margaret (see Bond)
Thompson, R.C. 307.
Thornton, Stuart 288.
Those Greylands Girls (book) 46.
Tinne dormitory (formerly Shirley) 89, 201, 227-228, 245-247.
Tintern Street 110.
Tipper 311.
Tippets 41.
Tittershill, Sandy, headmaster 2001-present. 27.
Tod, Sir Alan, school governor 169, 286, 287.
Tom Dooley (song) 164.
Toosey, Brigadier 274.
Toothpaste 17, 26.
'Toppers' (crusts) 14, 54.
The Torchbearers, (play) 89, 285.
Torches 108.
Towels 134.
Towel fighting 90, 152.
Tower of London 127.
Town Hall 10, 27, 131, 147.
Townsend 281.
Trafalgar Day 13.
Trams 128,
Treacle 23.
Tri-centenary celebrations (2008) 8.
Triennial treat (brotherly soc. gift) 266.
Trouser-pressing 134.
Trustees, school 15, 17, 21, 26, 169, 267.
Tucker, David 317.
Tudor, Barry 199.
TV room (introduced 1958) 148.
Tweedale, Beryl 42.
Uniform 13, 14, 84, 115, 119, 169, 173, 243, 270.
Union of Lancashire & Cheshire Institute (examinations) 100.
Unwin, Mr. Fred R., deputy headmaster 34, 79, 81, 82, 116-118, 127-128, 129, 146, 168, 223, 245, 317, 319, 321.
Vancouver, Canada 155.
Vere, Mr. Peter 316, 322.
Vian, Stanley 281, 284.
Vyner-Brooks, R.H., solicitor 101.
Wash 313.

Walker 281.
Walker, Frank 29.
Walker, Lt. 194, 277.
Walton Hospital, Rice Street 110.
Walton Prison 57.
Warcop tank range 191-192.
Ward 281.
Wardrobe room 19, 112, 168, 240, 292.
Warren, Charles L., trustee and builder 26.
Warren, Miss 40, 83-84, 218, 224.
Warrington, Bishop of 16.
Washroom 19, 91, 230.
Watch-mending 146, 201.
Watcyn, G.G., master 1926-45, headmaster 1945-68. 11, 21, 23, 27, 33, 34, 35, 36, 48, 49, 58-59, 69, 79-80, 82, 83, 99, 100, 105, 106-107, 116-118, 123-124, 126, 127-128, 130-131, 134, 146, 148, 149, 153-154, 155, 156, 157, 158, 162-163, 164, 169, 172, 175, 181, 195, 200, 204, 205, 212, 217, 218, 219, 222, 224, 248, 250, 267, 273, 287.
Watcyn, Miss Daphne 175, 246.
Water Street 160.
Wavertree Playground (The Mystery) 20, 25, 69-70, 87-88, 99, 294.
Weedall, Mr. J.N.D., P.E. teacher. 144, 183.
Wellington bomber, crashed 42.
Wellington Road Barracks 15.
Welsh Guards 31.
West Derby, Liverpool 136.
West front (a.k.a. 'western front') 11, 26, 76, 92, 173, 181, 243, 245, 292.
Western front' (see west front)
West, Roger 288.
Wexham Street, Beaumaris 30.
White D.J. 281, 282, 318.
Whitehead, John 226, 323, 325.
Wilkinson 268.
Williams, Alex 277, 288.
Williams, Brenton, (1955-59) 4, 107-109, 160-161, 264, 277, 288, 300.
Williams, David L. 149, 272, 273, 307.
Williams, Mr. John 322.
Williams, Mrs. 111-112, 116.
Williams-Bulkeley, Mr. & Mrs. Richard 28, 29, 254-255.
Wilson, Andy 85.
Wilson, G.J. 281, 288.
Wilson, Geoff 276.
Wilson, Rev. R. Bruce, headmaster 1927-1944 11, 15, 21, 23, 29, 32, 38.
Winterbottom, Eric 140-142, 201, 288.
Wise, C. 307, 311.
Woodbine, Eric (1953-59) 4, 68-69, 77-78, 82, 89, 161-170, 171, 176-177, 178-179, 205-206, 262, 272, 273, 274, 277, 278, 285, 287.
Woodgarth, Beaumaris 32, 42.
Woodhead, John 33, 35.
Wootton, W.D. 273.

Woodside Station, Birkenhead 32.
Woodwork room 219.
Wooldrage, B.A.S. 272, 273.
W.T. & R.T. training 182.
Yangtse Incident (1949) 223.
York 120, 121, 122.
Youth Employment Office, Edge Lane 100.

OTHER BOOKS IN THIS SERIES

The Tricentenary Series is published by the Liverpool Blue Coat Brotherly Society

A BLUE COAT BOY IN THE 1920s
By Danny Ross

In 1996 Danny Ross published this book describing his time at the school. Sadly, Danny passed away in 2005 but his family has been very supportive and has allowed us to re-publish this unique book.
ISBN 978-0-9557484-1-7

RETURN TO THE BLUE COAT
By Tony Salmon and Alan Gleave

Tony was a day boy at the Blue Coat School from 1971 until 1977. This book tells the story of his time at the school, and his nostalgic return in 2004.

Alan was a teacher of English at the school from 1975 until 2005. He looks at the Blue Coat School in the 1970s from a different perspective..... or does he?
ISBN 978-0-9557484-0-0

THE BLUE COAT BROTHERLY SOCIETY
Motto: And may all its proceedings be characterised by brotherly love.

The Blue Coat Brotherly Society was founded on 12th February 1838, with the principle objective of assisting, advising and promoting the well-being of the boys who attended the school. Members of the society would 'look after' Blue Coat boys for at least two years after they left the school, visiting them at home or work, and providing financial assistance where necessary and appropriate. This was of great benefit to the boys, and the care thus shown had a tremendous influence on their lives and careers.

Since the school's return to Liverpool after the Second World War, there has been less need for this sort of assistance, so the society has turned its efforts towards objects that would benefit the school in general.

Evidence of the generosity of the society over the years can be found throughout the school. In 1938, to celebrate its centenary, the society provided the oak pews in the chapel. In 1963 (the society's 125th anniversary) it provided the stained glass south window of the chapel. The Old Blues' Memorial Library was presented in 1952 in remembrance of the Old Blues who gave their lives in the two World Wars. The splendid gates in front of the old main entrance were provided in 1958, when the school celebrated its 250th anniversary.

The predominant item on the society's agenda at the moment is the Tri-centenary celebration weekend in 2008, when past pupils will be travelling from many parts of the world to visit the school that served them so well in their formative years. A tremendous amount of work is being done by the society to make this a most memorable occasion.

The Liverpool Blue Coat Brotherly Society is a registered charity (No. 1072458)

Website: www.bluecoatbrotherlysociety.webeden.co.uk